34

D0055739

DISCARD

The
Power
Beyond

IN SEARCH OF
MIRACULOUS
HEALING

The Power Beyond

Jack Grazier

Macmillan Publishing Company

New York

*To my wife, Debbie, my best friend
and the best reader of my work and me;
and to my children (in alphabetical order),
Ian and Stacey.*

Copyright © 1989 by Jack Grazier

All rights reserved. No part of this book may be reproduced or
transmitted in any form or by any means, electronic or mechanical,
including photocopying, recording or by any information storage and
retrieval system, without permission in writing from the Publisher.

Macmillan Publishing Company
866 Third Avenue, New York, NY 10022
Collier Macmillan Canada, Inc.

Library of Congress Cataloging-in-Publication Data
Grazier, Jack.
   The power beyond.
   Includes index.
   1. Spiritual healing—United States—History—
20th century.   2. Grazier, Jack.   I. Title.
BR732.5.G73   1989   234'.13   88-27348
ISBN 0-02-545180-4

Macmillan books are available at special discounts for bulk purchases
for sales promotions, premiums, fund-raising, or educational use.
For details, contact:

Special Sales Director
Macmillan Publishing Company
866 Third Avenue
New York, NY 10022

10 9 8 7 6 5 4 3 2 1

Designed by Jack Meserole

PRINTED IN THE UNITED STATES OF AMERICA

CONTENTS

315552

PREFACE

From the cowardice that dare not face new truths,
From the laziness that is contented with half truth,
From the arrogance that thinks it knows all truth,
Good Lord, deliver me.

—Kenyan prayer, *The Oxford
Book of Prayer*

"WHADDAYA think about the Singing Nun killing herself?" I asked my co-workers in the *Erie Daily Times* newsroom.

"I think it shows that nuns shouldn't sing," one reporter grumbled, staring into the screen of his computer terminal.

A few days later I asked a deskman whatever had become of his anorexic friend, that strange, quiet ex-weight lifter who used to come in and hang around the city desk.

"Why? Wanna take him out to lunch?" he asked. "Wouldn't cost much."

We eastern, liberal, pseudointellectual reporters can be a bunch of crass, crude, coarse, tasteless, hardened, cynical, sarcastic, sneering, foul, disagreeable, ill-tempered, mean-spirited, unrefined clods. (Just imagine how our mothers felt, cuddling their infant, beady-eyed Sam Donaldsons to their breasts: *What do you mean, your milk hasn't come in yet?*)

We Annoying Observers are trained to deal with facts and empirical data, things that can be seen, heard, touched, documented, and waved under somebody's nose.

So you'd think a reporter would be about the last person to put much stock in "faith healing." But it was an experience with supernatural healing that renewed my belief in The Infinite Unseen.

Sometimes God seems to have gone as far away from the newsroom as the newsroom has from Him. We're constantly bombarded by wire stories that blink onto our computer screens telling us things like how the Soviets jokingly told a group of Afghan women that their husbands, whom they had just slaughtered, would make good fertilizer for the potato crop. Or about how a bereaved parent came to found a group called "Parents of Murdered Children."

News is by definition bad news. Harmony doesn't make headlines. Strong sword-arm of justice! Bright sunbeam of truth! That endless book the newspaper—our national glory!

It's unfortunately part of our job to chronicle the spiritual malaise of our times; to get the smell of warm blood into our copy.

In our office there's a black antique typewriter stand at the front of the city room where we're supposed to put the Wirephotos from Associated Press after they come out of the fax machine. When you see head-and-shoulders photos of beautiful little children sitting atop that stand, you know the kids have probably been murdered.

Our profession, somehow, doesn't provide fertile ground for an abiding faith or a strong belief in the supernatural.

But it does prompt many of us, especially the aging baby boomers, to ask, after a grisly day at the office:

"My God! Is this all there is? Is all the world so cruel? Is God holed up in a flat in Cleveland?"

This book tells the story of my search for something to believe in and my encounters along the way with as disparate a group of people as you'll ever find—two happy faith healers: Erie mayor Louis J. Tullio and Pittsburgh mayor Richard S. Caliguiri; Washington Redskins' Super Bowl star Dexter Manley and his wonderful wife, Glinda; presidential press secretary James Brady and Melissa Gilbert of *Little House on the Prairie*; Robbie Snyder, a little boy left in the land of Oz by a tornado; a doe-eyed, jaundiced "miracle" baby named Eric Danowski; and many others.

Through this journey and as a reporter of twenty years' experience, I've found that at our best and worst moments—when we are most truly ourselves—the door between our own reality and a supernatural one seems to open a crack. During moments of stress or fear or courage or faith, the door budges a little so we can almost peek through the crack to glimpse the Truth and thus understand how much we don't know.

"*There are more things in heaven and earth, Horatio, than are dreamt of in your philosophy,*" as Shakespeare wrote.

When I was younger and working on the wire desk, I'd sometimes trash the gruesome stories and search for good news to fill my section. I figured a mother in Erie didn't need directions on how to microwave a baby from a mother in Topeka, Kansas. But evil is in the world and can't be explained away. As ugly and repulsive as it is, evil must be revealed. And faced.

It doesn't have to be accepted, however. If divine healing does exist, if

God is not just a historical event but still grants individuals wondrous cures and makes them whole so they can enter into healthy relationships —then we can still hold out hope for the renewal of our society and the healing of evil.

This is a book for the bemused, the barren, the bereaved, and the hard-of-healing who want to know if God still works miracles.

*   *   *

After I flunked my draft physical because of allergies and was told I wouldn't see battle until Lady Bird Johnson did, I met a woman named Claire at a party in a Walnut Street brownstone across from Rittenhouse Square in Philadelphia. That was in 1968. I was twenty. She was forty. She told me what she thought of writer Henry Miller's friend, diarist Anaïs Nin:

"I think she's a little schizophrenic."

"Schizophrenic?"

"She's concerned with herself too much. With her own importance. She can't see the world except in relation to herself. She was separated from reality by her own consciousness. She never forgets herself. She watches herself *see*, she watches in order to see herself watch. If she should look at a tree, for example, it's always her own consciousness of the tree she contemplates, never the tree itself. She sees the world distorted through her self-awareness. She uses her diary like Narcissus used his pond."

(I'd tell Claire now that Anaïs Nin's writing created and developed her spirit much as this book, I think, has created and developed mine. I do have to agree that a writer's constant observations can be annoying to those observed and even to the writer as well.)

I told Claire I'd written a letter to Anaïs Nin, a fan letter of sorts, and she just laughed and said I reminded her of Saul Bellow's Herzog, who wrote letters to everybody, including the president, and never got answers.

"I bet she'll answer my letter."

"We'll see."

Then she told me a story about Bishop Fulton J. Sheen.

She had met him at LaSalle College or someplace and was really taken by him. "Very persuasive, with keen eyes. Strangely enough, he invited me to have breakfast with him the next day. It was wonderful, he's such a dynamic man." She smiled. "And after we talked for a while, he pulled a rosary out of his pocket and gave it to me."

Her eyes sparkled when she talked, and each time she got excited about what she was saying, she leaned closer. "I liked him so much I wrote him a letter afterward. You know what he did? He sent me a trunkful of his books! No answer, no letter, just a trunkful of his books.

Why, that was just awful! Anybody can send books, but they're not an answer to a letter. Right up to my attic they went and the bishop never got a letter from me again.

"But I had an Italian friend whose mother was flying to Italy. She had arthritis and she was scared to death of flying. Do you know what I did? I gave her the rosary. She prayed with it all the way over and back. The bishop's rosary! She was very excited. And best of all, her arthritis was healed on the flight!"

I thought of that story when I sat down to write my own book—on healing—twenty-one years later. I'd always wondered what really cured that woman's arthritis.

I had a story called "A Faith Healer Gave Us Our Child" published in the October 1987 issue of *McCall's*.

For months after publication of the piece, my wife, Debbie, and I received from three to seven phone calls a day as well as three or four letters daily from all over the country. Had faith healers really helped us to conceive? people asked. I received many letters from women desperately seeking to have their own babies, and others from people with everything from arthritis and unbearable head and neck pain to cancer and AIDS and hearing disorders. I also received letters from parents of autistic children.

The questions the letters asked:

"Does faith healing really work?"

"Do you really believe in this sort of thing?"

"How did it change your life?"

"Are you more religious now?"

This book is my attempt to answer those questions for myself as well as for those who thought to ask.

Looking back, I see nothing wrong with Bishop Fulton J. Sheen's response to Claire's letter. I like his answer and don't think it was any less personal because it was published for everyone to read.

I think Anaïs Nin would have liked it, too. She answered my letter with a stack of *her* books, as it turned out.

All them were signed. The inscription I like best is this one:

For Jack Grazier

write your letters to

the world — as a

writer must — a letter

to all of us.

Studs

ACKNOWLEDGMENTS

THIS BOOK would not have been possible without the help of many people. I particularly want to acknowledge my debt to my wife, Debbie, and to Ted Benson, Jr., who were in this with me from beginning to end, providing limitless support and encouragment.

Special thanks also to my parents; to Charles and Frances Hunter; to Lou and Grace Tullio; and to Dick and Jeanne Caliguiri.

Thanks also to Tony Zona and Nancy Benson for their help and participation and to Ray and Joan Fels for their support and the turkey dinner.

I'd also like to acknowledge John Donovan, Karen and Dave Zimmerman, Pat Benson, Margot Gilman, Len Kholos, Michele Ridge, Chris Dubbs, Paul Gibbens and the Reverend James Peterson. These kind souls all provided time, knowledge, assistance, and motivation.

Thanks also to Glinda Manley for keeping her faith and sharing it with strangers; to Barbara Schneider and Amy Welsh for their limitless patience; to Bob Barker for the Archko volume; to Dee Perry for her faithful transcriptions; and to Rick Kern and Paul Jenkins for trying to get me out of the house.

Finally, thanks to my patient and kind editor, Stephen S. Wilburn, for giving me the freedom to do *my* book; to my agent, Jonathon Lazear of Minneapolis, for his sense of humor and guidance through the maze; and to the Times Publishing Company for the use of certain material which appears herein.

In addition, I would like to thank the following for the use of copyrighted material in their control:

For portions of news stories on Erie Mayor Louis Tullio and Richard Caliguiri by Associated Press Writer Tara Bradley Steck. Reprinted by permission of Associated Press (New York, N.Y.).

For various works of Charles and Frances Hunter. Reprinted by permission of Charles and Frances Hunter and Hunter Books (Kingwood, Tex.).

For excerpts from "I Believe in Miracles," by Kathryn Kuhlman. Copyright © 1962 by Prentice-Hall, Inc. (Englewood Cliffs, N.J.).

Reprinted by permission of the Kathryn Kuhlman Foundation (Pittsburgh, Pa.).

For items published in the *Erie Daily Times* and the (Erie) *Times-News*. Reprinted by permission of the Times Publishing Co. (Erie, Pa.).

For portions of the article entitled "Faith Is Blind, But It's Not Stupid," by Cal LeMon. Copyright © 1988 USA Today. Excerpted with permission of USA Today (Washington, D.C.) and Cal LeMon.

<table>
<tr><td>CHAPTER

I</td><td># Where Did You Come From, Baby Dear?</td></tr>
</table>

> Where did you come from, baby dear?
> Out of the everywhere, into the here.
> —George McDonald, *At the*
> *Back of the North Wind*

THE YEAR WAS 1985.

We tried for six years, after we had our first child, to have another. And we tried everything—fertility specialists, superaccurate basal thermometers to indicate ovulation, and a box of loose, baggy underwear my wife, Debbie, bought for me under the flashing blue light at K mart.

"They'll keep you cooler than the other kind so you'll produce more sperm," Debbie explained.

"Wear them!"

A fertility specialist finally found that Debbie wasn't ovulating, and prescribed a fertility drug. But even after a year, that treatment bore no fruit. Finally, we signed up for nine weeks of classes on coping with handicapped children in preparation for adopting one.

A week before we were to commit ourselves to the adoption process, a friend told us about the "Happy Hunters," a *world-famous healing couple,* coming to Jamestown, New York, that Sunday.

"Maybe we should go," my wife said. "We've tried everything else."

"Well, if the weather's okay, maybe we can," I hedged, certain that the snow-covered and slippery roads we'd had all winter would continue to be snow covered and slippery on Sunday. The last thing I wanted to do was to drive *into* a Great Lakes snowbelt on a Sunday afternoon to see the Ozzie and Harriet of faith healing.

But Sunday dawned bright and warm, with steam rising from the sunny, bare roadways. I had no excuse.

The theater in Jamestown was a seedy little example of neo-Egyptian architecture. It was cold and dark inside, and the hundred or so people who had come to see the Hunters were huddled in the darkness, clutching their coat collars around their necks.

Four shiny chrome-plated microphone stands stood at attention at the center of the stage, flanked on both sides by large, pink, Depression-era vases filled with plastic flowers. A baby grand piano hulked on one side, an organ hunkered on the other. And extending out over the orchestra pit like a big bat was a plywood eight-by-eight-foot platform, painted black.

"If you think I'm going to stand up on that thing and be healed in front of this audience like something out of *Elmer Gantry*, you're crazy," I said to my wife. "No way."

Debbie just shook her head. She sympathized with me.

"What are we *doing* here?" I asked.

She just shook her head again.

When Frances Hunter and her husband, Charles, finally sallied onto the stage, they didn't look at all the way I thought faith healers should look. She was about seventy, a large, plump woman wearing bright red lipstick and large glasses with pink-graduating-to-yellow lenses and cuta-way temples. She wore a garish organdy gown, and her lacquered hair was piled high atop her head.

Charles had the withered, overly staid look of an aging Republican.

Much of what Frances Hunter said, in her loud, brassy voice, sounded strange.

She had once had diabetes, she said, but was cured when her husband laid hands on her. I could accept that, maybe, but she kept referring to how Charles had "operated on" her and, through the power of Jesus Christ working in him, gave her a *brand . . . new . . . pancreas!*

And then there was the business about warrior angels.

On February 4, 1978, Frances said, she and Charles were at the Civic Center in Abilene, Texas, and while they were ministering, at the very beginning of the service, "God stationed a huge warrior angel with us and spoke words which are burned into my heart. As I looked at this huge angel, in complete astonishment and amazement because I had never before seen an angel, God said, "That's a special warrior angel I have sent to protect you and Charles from the fiery darts of the devil until Jesus Christ comes back again."

A *warrior angel* at the Abilene Civic Center?

Indeed.

Alarm bells really rang, though, when the Hunters began asking for money.

They said they were planning the "largest healing team service" ever held. They told us that 240 "real believers" empowered by the Holy Spirit to heal would lay hands on every person in the Pittsburgh Civic Arena, curing their physical, spiritual, and mental ills.

But they needed money to bring it off. The arena cost a fortune to rent. And didn't we, sitting in the audience, want to be part of it?

Of course we did, Frances assured us.

She told us just to sit there quietly, close our eyes, and *listen to God,* who would tell each of us how much to contribute to this healing extravaganza.

"*I don't care how much God tells you to give,*" I hissed to my wife. "*I'm telling you not to give more than two dollars.*"

The Hunters apologized for having to ask for money, but reminded the audience that without money, they couldn't continue their ministry.

Apparently they hadn't heard of bingo.

Finally, Frances said, "Okay, now we'll do the healing. Anyone with a physical or spiritual need, or a desire of the heart, can come right up on the stage."

Virtually everyone, except Debbie and me, stood up and shuffled slowly down the sloped floor of the theater in two long lines.

The lines went up the steps to center stage. Charles Hunter ministered to the line that had formed on the left, and Frances to the one on the right.

As we watched, the strangest thing happened. One by one, the Hunters spoke quietly to the people in line and placed a hand on each chest. And then:

Plop. Plop. Plop.

Right down the line, the people fell over.

Flat onto their backs. To lie, apparently unconscious, on the floor.

As each person fell, he or she was caught under the arms by one of two young men fastidiously dressed in gray suits, every hair on their heads in place. There were two of these fellows onstage, and they moved down each line, catching each person as he fell and lowering him gently onto the floor and his back. Then they'd cover him with a blanket.

Those on the floor remained motionless for from two to ten minutes.

"*Just what is going on?*" I whispered to Debbie.

"What's going on?" she whispered in turn to Karen Zimmerman, sitting at her other side. Karen was the friend who had urged us to visit Jamestown. She had come along for the ride.

"They're being slain in the Spirit," Karen said. "When the power of the Holy Spirit is great enough in a healer, it can literally knock you over. Just like the Roman soldiers were knocked off their horses when they wanted to take Jesus to Jerusalem, but he wasn't ready. He didn't even touch them, and they fell from their horses."

"It's probably just some form of mass hypnosis," I said. "These people *want* to fall over."

Debbie just sighed as we watched the people continue to drop. "Aren't you two going up?" our friend leaned over to ask us.

"No way," I said.

"You've come all this way, you might as well," she said. "What harm can it do?"

What harm could it do? There's a strange old fat lady up there sucking peoples' immortal souls out of their bodies and she's asking me what harm it could do?

But anyone who's ever tried unsuccessfully to have a child knows how obsessive the need to conceive can become. After regulating our lives by basal thermometers . . . scheduling sex when it would be productive rather than enjoyable . . . handing jelly jars containing sperm samples over office counters to pretty young nurses . . . having bright young golfers with stethoscopes around their necks involved in the most intimate psychological and physiological aspects of our sex lives . . . and hearing our baby-breeder friends constantly complain about their children . . . going up on that stage was just another humiliation to endure in the hopes of producing a child.

"She's right," Debbie said. "What harm can it do? We've tried everything else."

As Frances Hunter moved down the line toward us, I was sure we'd be the only ones left standing. Debbie, at my left, was shaking. Her eyes were tearing. This wasn't like her. She said afterward that she felt extremely emotional until Frances gently but firmly grabbed both of her upper arms and held her. At that moment, she said, a sense of warmth and peace suffused her, and she became calm.

"And what is the desire of your heart, honey?" Frances asked.

"We'd like to have another baby," my wife said, smiling and looking toward the floor.

Frances Hunter's face lit up and she clapped her hands.

"Oh, that's wonderful! Babies are my specialty! The Lord and I have made black babies in Africa, yellow babies in China, red babies out West . . . ,"

Just get the color right, lady, I thought.

"Now, I want you to be happy, because you're going to conceive a baby within a year. And when you have this baby, remember what the Bible says—all good and perfect gifts come from Jesus." Smiling, she placed the index and middle fingers of one hand on my wife's sternum.

Plop. Over Debbie went.

Oh, no, not you, too . . .

I was dismayed that Debbie had suggested herself, like all the others, into falling over. Now, here they were, covering her with a blanket, too.

Her knees had just buckled. And over she went.

Self-hypnotized.

Well, it wasn't going to happen to *me*.

I scrolled my mind quickly to be sure no part of me wanted to go along with this thing. So as Frances Hunter approached me, I spread my feet apart and leaned toward her, to place my center of gravity forward so she would have a hard time shoving me back.

That must have been it. She gave everyone a shove, and then they fell over because they thought that was expected of them. Well, *not me, lady!*

"And what do you need, young man?" she asked brusquely. She seemed to sense my attitude.

"Well, I have fibrositis," I stammered. "It's sort of an arthritic condition in my chest that—"

She cut me short by placing a hand on my chest.

"Fibrositis be gone!" she commanded.

The last thing I remember is flying backward, my feet lifting from the floor.

I was aware that I was falling and that I had absolutely no control over what was happening to me. It was like being punched on the jaw—a tingling sensation but no pain. It was like being shocked by a cattle prod. (No, she didn't have one up her sleeve.) It was like being blown off my feet by an exploding gas main. I had never felt anything like it before in my life.

My wife said later that I flew up and back and landed like a ton of bricks. For some reason, catchers were someplace else and there was no one there to catch me. "You made such a thud, I thought you landed on your head. I expected you to have a concussion," Debbie said. "The whole stage shook when you hit."

We lay there for a few minutes, and then Debbie helped me to my feet. As we wandered, dazed, off the stage, Debbie, holding on to my coat sleeve, simply said, "There are a lot of things in this universe that we don't understand."

I just shook my head.

"Now, *push me*," I told Debbie. We were standing in our living room, in front of the sofa.

She gave me a light push, with one hand, square in the chest. Nothing happened. I didn't feel the least inclination to fall backward.

"Harder," I said.

Still nothing.

"Use two hands."

She pushed with both hands, and we found it takes quite a shove to push somebody backward off their feet. We agreed that the light touch of Frances Hunter wouldn't have been enough to nudge either of us, let alone knock us off our feet and into the air and onto our backs.

Besides, my fibrositis was gone. It had plagued me every winter for years, making my chest feel like the wrestler Hulk Hogan had jumped on it all night. But after Frances Hunter touched me, the pain disappeared.

Did we make it up? Since our stories matched, it was unlikely that the experience was a dual hallucination. And it wasn't as though we had been caught up in the group psychology—both of us had tried very hard not to fall.

The unavoidable truth was that something had happened for which we had no explanation. It was not an intellectual experience, but apparently a spiritual one.

It was a revelation that forced me to examine the religious bric-a-brac that had been gathering dust in my head for years. Because I was a semiretired Catholic, my adult religious experience had consisted of visiting church one or two Sundays a year to daydream about working on the boat. Now I was beginning to appreciate the fact that if we are to believe in an infinite being while we ourselves float in infinity, perhaps there is more to religion than sitting grimly on a hard pew, trying not to look at anyone.

A few months later, Debbie and I were sitting on the stairs, calling our daughter over to us. Debbie looked radiant, her dark brown eyes shining, her long brown silken hair framing her smiling face. "Something wonderful is going to happen to our family, something we've been waiting for, for a very long time," my wife told our little girl.

"What is it, Mommy?" Stacey asked, wide-eyed.

"We're going to have a new addition to our family. Can you guess what it is?"

Stacey didn't hesitate a second.

"Oh, Mommy . . . Daddy! We're getting a horse!"

"No, honey. We're having a baby. The doctor just told us Mommy is pregnant."

When I tell the story of how my wife got pregnant, people gape and say, "If anyone else but you had told me this, I'd never believe it. But you've always been such a"—here they grope for a kind word—"skeptic."

"It's all true."

Then they fidget. "Do you really believe that . . . faith healing . . . caused the pregnancy?"

Then I fidget. I know coincidences can happen. I know the mind can do strange things. I know there's a lot to be said for the power of suggestion. But even after we went to the Hunters, my wife still cried at night because she didn't think she'd ever get pregnant. We never had faith that faith healing would work.

The bottom line was that after trying to have a baby for years, we couldn't. And didn't. Not until we were touched by the Hunters and slain in the Spirit.

So when people ask me if a faith healer caused the pregnancy, I fidget, but I answer yes, I do believe that Frances Hunter and an external, divine power channeled through her did it.

On April 22, 1986, the baby that Frances Hunter said we would have, arrived, after more than six years of trying to have a child, after we had given up hope. Ian Christian Grazier was born a perfect little boy with all ten fingers and all ten toes, and dimples to boot.

As I held him for the first time in the birthing room at Saint Vincent Health Center, my wife's eyes widened as she stared in my direction.

"What's the matter?" I asked.

"Look at that," she said, pointing to a picture of a mother and baby on the wall behind me.

And as I looked, I recalled what Mrs. Hunter had said: *"When you have this baby, remember . . . all good and perfect gifts come from Jesus."*

"GOD'S GIFT," read the inscription under the picture.

Dark Night of the Soul

For every child, rich or poor, there is a time of running in a dark place . . . God save the little children . . . they abide and they endure.
—James Agee, *Night of the Hunter*

When Ian was about eight months old, he was startled awake one evening by the ringing of the telephone.

"It never fails. Every time I get him down, the phone rings," Debbie said with a sigh. "Get that, will you?"

"This is Ian Christian's grandmother," the woman on the phone said. She laughed a deep, hearty laugh.

It wasn't our baby's real grandmother. There was no mistaking that loud, cheerful voice, even over the telephone. It was Frances Hunter.

I had written about our faith healing experience for the *Erie Times-News*, and someone had sent her a copy of the story. "Anointed," she called it. She said she called to tell me how much she had liked the story: "It captured the skeptical attitude of many people exactly like you and it showed how God will do anything to get a person's attention."

"Charles and I have often laughed about how our meetings at that moldy old theater in Jamestown were among the most miserable we ever had," she said. "It just goes to show you that God takes a mess and makes a miracle out of it."

As she talked, I couldn't help but remember how she'd touched me and I'd fallen over. I was hoping she wouldn't try it over the telephone.

After our visit to the Hunters, I had done some checking into the "slain in the Spirit" phenomenon. I was surprised to find that Christians of every denomination, charismatic and otherwise, were falling onto their keisters all over the country in churches, gymnasiums, auditoriums, and even in their own living rooms.

They were wilting not just under the hands of evangelists like the Hunters with healing ministries, but also at the hands of priests, pastors, and laymen in a pervasive healing renewal that far surpassed, at least at a grass-roots level, anything ever experienced in American society.

One of the more famous healers, Vicki Jamison-Peterson, even tells of how, when she was new to healing and hadn't learned to control her power, she walked out of an elevator and everyone she passed fell to the floor.

The falling over isn't an end in itself, Frances explained to me, but just a manifestation of the power of the Holy Spirit, evidence for skeptics like me that the Spirit has touched a soul. Medical science, mental attitudes, or other natural forces may indeed have caused my wife's pregnancy, she said. But what, Frances asked, was the impetus that finally pushed those natural forces to work, after six years?

She said it could be like the driver who, when his windshield was spattered by a truck and he couldn't see, prayed for rain to clear the windshield after he found his car was out of wiper fluid. "Rain" then miraculously fell from the sky. The driver found later the rain was the overspray from the wiper fluid of the car ahead of his.

"God is certainly smart enough to follow his own laws of physics in making miracles," she said.

"What do you tell people who don't believe in what you do?" I asked Frances.

"We tell them that if they don't believe in miracles, then none will ever happen to them."

I asked her why I had reacted to her touch in such a pronounced manner.

"You were hungry for everything God had, even though you might not have admitted it," she said. "You just sucked the power right out of me and that's why it bowled you over like that."

*   *   *

When it comes to religion, I've always been pretty much of an Anythingarian, secretly agreeing with Joseph Conrad's notion that God is for men, religion for women, especially on Sundays in the summertime, when I'd rather be sailing.

Well, not always. As a patient in a hospital for crippled children, I can remember wanting religion in the worst way. It was the night and the loneliness of the boys' ward that made me want to find God and the stability of religion to help me through that time, to help me believe I'd be healed.

I was six years old when the doctors told my parents I had Perthe's Hip, a bone disease that had caused my hipbone to degenerate, eroding much of the ball that fit into the socket. In the 1950s, they treated

Perthe's disease with complete bedrest. The doctor took my parents aside and told them that I'd have to be hospitalized where I would have the supervision I needed. One day I was at home playing with my toys in my bedroom, and the next I was in the car on the way to the hospital, where my parents were forced to leave me for two years.

They turned me over to the nurses and walked quickly to the door, holding on to each other, both in tears.

I sometimes think the terror I felt during those first days in the hospital—it was more than just being separated from my parents—was from some type of archetypal memory, passed down to my generation from, say, some place in the 1800s, where the wards smelled of fatal diseases and where the main concern of the nurses was that their young charges, wrapped in crusty bandages, said their prayers and died in a state of grace.

Deep inside, there was a part of me that knew all about the stinking death that came to hospitals in the night to carry off small children. For the first few weeks, I was afraid of falling asleep for fear I would never wake up.

For two years, until I was eight years old, I had to stay in bed. For most of the first year, I was forced to lie flat on my back, tied down to the bed by a "restrainer," a wide cotton belt like a cummerbund with laces at the ends.

This was in 1952, during the worst part of the polio scare. Mom and Dad and all the rest of the parents were allowed only short weekly visiting periods, to minimize the risk of bringing the virus into the hospital and infecting us all. Once a week, for one hour, from 3:00 P.M. to 4:00 P.M. on Sundays, was all the time allotted.

Even then, when my parents could come to see me, they weren't allowed to touch me.

On Sunday, after the lunch trays were put back onto the food cart and wheeled away, Wayne, the janitor, would come striding into the ward, dressed in his blue jeans and red checkered flannel shirt, two big loops of rope hanging over his shoulder. He'd start at the end of the room near the door, fastening one end of rope to a cleat on the wall, and walk down the ward, past the ends of our beds, winking at us and telling jokes, uncoiling the rope. Then he'd cleat the other end to the far wall.

First one side of the ward, then the other. He'd rope off the beds so that when our parents came, they'd have to stand behind the ropes so they couldn't come to our bedsides to touch us or hold us or breathe on us. The hospital staff had found that unless the ropes were there, the parents couldn't resist the impulse to hold their children.

At the end of the visiting hour, Wayne would come back into the ward to unhook the ropes from the wall and coil them up over his shoulder again. He wouldn't look at any of us.

* * *

Nights were the worst. Night coming through the windows would stain everything a deep blue-black, including the sleeping forms of the children curled into fetal position on their beds.

Many nights I spent staring through the window closest to my bed, my chin propped up on a fist. White and red, white and red, white and red—white headlights, red taillights—as the cars cruised silently by on the street so far from the window.

Maybe Mom and Dad are in that car. No, not that one. Here comes another. It's going slower. Yes, they're in this one. They're going slow, so they can look in the window to see me.

My arm would erupt through the cold iron bed rail with a clang, and I'd wave to whoever it was sitting behind the headlights, wanting to believe it was my parents. The car would pass. Then I'd let the edge of the mattress that jutted into my arm make that limb throb. I'd feel my hand grow turgid with blood, feel it pulse and move with each heartbeat like a pendulum, as it hung over the side of the bed.

At night, with the other children sleeping, I could hear my blood. They wouldn't let us have pillows, and with my head on the mattress, with my ear pressed to the bed, I could hear the blood spurt through my ear, or my head, or wherever the noise came from, with each heartbeat. I hated that, hearing my heart beat—whoosh . . . whoosh . . . whoosh— all night. I always imagined the sound stopping, and then I always waited for it to stop, and then it would be too bad, because I'd be dead.

I'd turn my head to the other ear, but the heart would still be there, so I'd turn it back to the first ear again and start to drum on the mattress with my fingertips. I'd listen to the drumming echo and pound through the springs, the noise masking the beating of my heart. I'd tap my index finger on the mattress in a one-two rhythm until sleepiness would make me forget to keep tapping. And then I'd be almost asleep, and able to forget my heart. It was an old hospital trick of mine.

I remember one night, I was playing my radio, very softly. but the night nurse had ears that extended well beyond the sides of her cap. In she came into the boys' ward, and out I went, clattering bed wheels and all, into the hallway connecting the boys' ward and the girls' ward. She parked my bed underneath a bright hall light, making it impossible to sleep.

The next time she appeared in the hall, about an hour later, I stopped her. I asked her to bend down so I could tell her something very important. She dubiously leaned over the railing. I sat up to kiss her warmly, and wetly, on the cheek. "I love you," I said. Her cheek was cool.

"Hmmph," she said.

I thought it would move her. And move me back to the boys' ward.

But she was unmoved, and so was I. I spent much of that night chipping the paint from my bedrail with a fingernail. The paint came off and fell to the floor in large flakes that were gray on one side and white on the other.

When I was six, I looked for God in the flashlight in the block at the foot of my hospital bed. The "block" was a hollow wooden rectangle, underneath the covers, that pushed the bedclothes up into a little tent to keep them from pushing down on my feet.

Covered with a pillowcase that was neatly wrapped and pinned around it, the block was a great place to hide plastic spacemen, horses, cowboys, airplanes, marbles, feathers, and the flashlight.

At night, after the nurse had made her rounds, you could crawl down to your block, where the covers were cool, and take out your things, being careful not to stick yourself on the pins.

You could sit up straight and prop up the covers with your head, and look into the bulb of the little fountain-pen flashlight.

At first I'd see nothing but shiny stars and whiteness, but soon my eyes would become accustomed to the brightness and I would see things in the flashlight. I could see bright places. And angels. And great dark places, where the witches were.

I'd turn the light round and round, letting my eye become unfocused, staring into the light. I could see myself safe at home if I stared long enough.

"Hey, Jack!" the boy in the bed next to me would whisper loudly.

"Shut up, Lee!"

Sometimes I thought I saw Jesus Christ, who had long brown hair and a beard. And when I did, I prayed to him. I'd stay under the covers a long time, and turn the light round and round.

"Jack!"

"What?"

"Here she comes!"

I'd turn off the light and silently my head would emerge from the covers, but the nurse wouldn't be there.

I'd wait, but she wouldn't come.

"Well, I *thought* I heard her," Lee would say. He was just lonely. He hadn't heard her at all.

"Baker's crying again, Jack."

"I know. I've been listening to him."

Sometimes I'd cry, too, and bury my face in the mattress so Lee wouldn't hear me. There would be a wet spot on the sheets under my mouth, and while I prayed I'd touch the wet spot with the fingers of one hand, the other hand still holding the flashlight.

"Please, dear Lord, make my leg get better," I'd pray.

But God didn't heal me when I asked Him to. It took two more years of bed rest before my hip bone regenerated. Now, all these years later, it's stronger than it was before, and I have no limp, no problems.

*   *   *

Sometimes I think about God when I'm in the bathtub, drinking a beer.

For instance, If God is an infinite being, unfettered by time. He must exist always in the "Eternal Now" as the Being who says, "I am Who am."

If God always exists in *now*, then time means nothing to Him. So He can answer our prayers years before we pray them—like an author who reworks what happens to a character in chapter 1, because that change must lead to character development in chapter 20, which has also already been written.

I've wanted to be a writer for as long as I can remember, and when I was twenty years old, I asked God to do whatever it took to make me one. "If I have to suffer to become a writer, then let me suffer," I wrote in my journal, with romantic visions of growing a beard like Rainer Maria Rilke's Mr. Kappus and starving in a garret somewhere. "If it takes pain to make me introspective, to force me to achieve my potential, then give me pain."

"Like a fine violin, a writer must undergo a sort of curing process through the years if he is to make music," I wrote in my private journal, which I showed to every girl who came to my apartment. But I truly believed that.

I hadn't realized when I was twenty that God had already answered my suffering prayer when I was six.

I don't believe that a loving God would make us ill for any reason, but there could be a purpose for withholding a cure. Who knows? If I hadn't spent two years in the children's hospital, I could have grown up to be a jock, changed my name, and ended up as a left winger with no teeth, playing for the Montreal Canadiens hockey team.

In October 1987, *McCall's* published a story I'd submitted about our baby and the Hunters. They called it "A Faith Healer Gave Us Our Child." The piece seemed to jolt a public nerve. It drew scores of letters and phone calls to the magazine. One editor said it prompted one of the largest reader responses the magazine had ever had.

Charles and Frances Hunter's ministry in Texas received from 6 to 12 phone calls a day for over three months after the story ran, as well as over 175 letters. I was receiving many calls and letters myself.

"That story showed a lot of people had a Jesus-shaped vacuum inside they needed to fill," Charles said.

A short time later, the contract to do this book was signed. I told my wife that the story seemed to have taken on a life and momentum of its own. I got the feeling it was picking up speed and taking us right along with it.

Maybe our lives are like Möbius circles.

The Möbius circle was named for the German mathematician who studied it over a century ago. To make it, take a long strip of paper and glue it into a ring, after twisting one end 180 degrees before joining the ends together.

The surface has many strange characteristics. While the Möbius circle appears to be a two-sided figure, if you run your finger all the way along its surface, you'll find it has only one.

But if you stare at it for any length of time, it seems that although you know it has only one side, it really must have two.

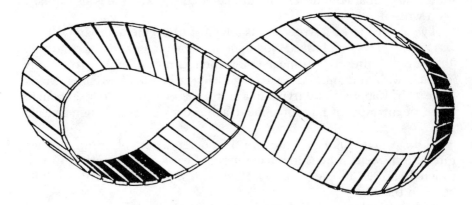

Cut the strip with a scissors down the center, parallel to the edges. You'd think that you would get two separate rings, but instead you end up with only one, twice as large as the original. Cut this ring again and you end up with two rings, but interlocked.

Thus, what appears to be two surfaces is really one, and what is really one surface appears to be two; if you follow one side long enough it becomes the other side; by cutting the surface in half you double its size; by cutting the circle apart you link two identical circles together.

Turn the Möbius ring on its side, with the twist on the side farther from you, and you have a sideways figure eight, the symbol of infinity.

" 'I am Alpha and Omega, the beginning and the end, the first and the last,' saith the Lord."

Some believe that the universe, and time itself, may be a closed circle, and twisted in the Möbius way.

In the physics of relative space, space is finite but unbounded. You can set off today and travel in a straight line and go on traveling, and while you will never come to the end of the universe, you *will* one day come back to where you started. Space itself is curved; straight lines lead in circles. The same may be true of time; although time must be finite, it need not be bounded or have a beginning.

When Salvador Dali, the famous Spanish surrealist painter, was eighty-three, he was described by editor Louis Pauwels in *Le Figaro* newspaper as sitting in an armchair in a huge white robe, his eyes "like two drops of cloudy black water."

"If space-time is curved, why does one not remember the future?" Dali asked. "This would be immensely important."

Take it one step farther. In the past, we don't just remember our future, we begin living it. Did those two miserable years in the hospital make me the kind of person who'd be curious enough about healing to write this book, after a trip to the Hunters and a healing experience with them? Was there a purpose in having to wait six years for our baby? Is it all interconnected, one and the same, with straight lines leading in circles?

25908001142996

New York, New York

> You know those ducks in that lagoon right near Central Park South? That little lake? By any chance, do you happen to know where they go, the ducks, when it gets all frozen over?
>
> —J. D. Salinger, *The Catcher in the Rye*

It was a crisp November day, and I was sitting in the brightly lit makeup room of WABC-TV, New York City, watching a tall, thin man with glasses apply powder to my wife's face.

What in the world are *we* doing here? I thought.

Of course I knew the answer. The Story had brought us here, The Story with the life of its own.

When *McCall's* published "A Faith Healer Gave Us Our Child," our lives changed. People from all over the country kept calling to ask us about faith healers Charles and Frances Hunter. They asked about healing and tried to pick our brains about the Infinite One following our Close Encounter with Him-Her-It.

Then we got the call from a producer of WABC-TV's *The Morning Show*, asking us to appear with hosts Regis Philbin and Kathie Lee Gifford, along with Charles and Frances Hunter. The producer said they'd fly our whole family there and back and pay for an overnight stay in a splendid hotel.

It was as if I had created a story in which I described our experiences —and now the story was looping back, Möbius-like, starting to create me by redefining who I was to other people, changing my life-style, and leading me into new experiences. Both Debbie and I had the distinct impression of being swept up by Something bigger than ourselves.

* * *

A young woman wearing a dark blue suit breezed into the room. She said "Excuse, please" as she passed in front of me, then set a stack of cue cards next to my chair and breezed out. While the makeup man was asking my wife what we would be talking about on Philbin's show, I flipped through the big white cardboard cards.

"Today's guests include actress Melissa Gilbert, White House press secretary James Brady, and faith healers Charles and Frances Hunter," I read to Debbie from the top card. "Oh, that's just great," she said, and sighed. We hadn't anticipated appearing with anyone famous, although I had hoped that actress Jane Seymour, with her coffee-colored hair and her huge exotic eyes—one green, one brown with green and blue flecks—would be lurking under the stairwell.

The cue cards made it sink in: My family and I were going to be on a live TV talk show, trying to convince a sophisticated New York-New Jersey-Philadelphia-Connecticut audience of thirteen million that although we believed a husband-and-wife faith healing team called "The Happy Hunters" had helped us to have a baby after they had zapped our souls with a spiritual stun gun, we really were playing with a full deck, and our children should be allowed to go back to Erie and continue living with us.

A few minutes later I found myself in the men's room, my face powdered and rouged, wondering what plans my autonomic nervous system had for my body once the show started. Would it direct my body to hyperventilate, or would it simply choose to place it twitching, face down with its nose on the floor? I had never liked speaking in public.

I looked up to the men's room ceiling. "You got me into this. Now get me out," I prayed, out of the side of my mouth. A photoelectric eye on the commode made it flush automatically as I backed away. It was not the sort of answer I would have expected, but it would have to do.

My daughter, Stacey, then nine, was standing in the hallway next to her mother and looking unfazed. To Stacey, this TV thing was no more intimidating than getting a class photo taken at school. She looked innocent enough, with her perky blond hair, yellow corduroy skirt, and a pair of red plastic lips with a rhinestone in them pinned to her sweater. We were afraid of what her real lips would do if Philbin should start to ask her questions on the show.

I could still remember the scene in her bedroom the night before we left. I had just told her it was time for another rehearsal:

"I'm Regis Philbin," I said. "Here we are, onstage. And I'm turning to you and saying, 'And Stacey, *what do you think of all this?*' "

"I think it's just a coincidence and my parents are making a big deal out of nothing." She had a twisted smile on her face.

"Are you really going to say that?"

"No, Dad, I won't say that." She patted my arm.

"What will you say?"

"I'm going to say, 'This person's not my brother. My parents really adopted him. They just wanted a free trip to New York.'"

I chuckled, then told my daughter a bedtime story about a little girl who had ruined *her* father's career while on a trip to New York. I told her about all the adventures the little girl had trying to make it home, all alone, on a darkened New York subway train.

But when we finally found ourselves in the "green room," Stacey was on her best behavior. I think she was awed by the balding, heavyset man in the wheelchair with the scar going across the top of his head from one ear to the other. We told her about Jim Brady and how John W. Hinckley, Jr., had pumped one .22 caliber bullet through Brady's brain and another through President Ronald Reagan's lung.

I could remember the mood in the newsroom that day. It was one of those days when it was exciting to work in a newsroom but when you felt like Nero fiddling while Rome burned and kept asking yourself, Why do we hurt ourselves this way? If there is a God, why does he let these things happen?

"Jack's asking himself, 'Why is there air?' again," somebody said.

It's quiet. There are about twenty people in the green room, and almost all eyes are fixed on the monitor, watching Philbin and co-host Kathie Lee Gifford act out their introductory chitchat. We all seem to be using the monitor as an excuse to keep our eyes averted from Jim Brady, not quite knowing what to say to him.

In one corner of the room sits actress Melissa Gilbert, legs crossed, wearing a gray sweater and a very unprairielike black miniskirt and black stockings, her head down with a phone to her ear, probably talking to her agent or some agentlike person. And just a few feet away from her is Brady, a larger-than-life man our baby will be reading about in school someday.

Of course, at eighteen months, Ian's not impressed. While the others in the room are hanging back, not quite knowing what to say to this quiet, tragic figure, Ian teeters up to him, puts his hand on his knee, smiles, and says, "Dada," which means "What's happenin'?" in his language, as well as "Father" and "Daddy's glasses."

"Hi there, little guy," Brady says. "How are you?"

Brady's wearing a dark suit, white shirt, and tie. Ian's wearing blue Oshkosh overalls with mice on the legs, and a white turtleneck shirt with doggies on the sleeves and collar. Doggies knock him out.

The baby squats down to look up at Brady's bottom from underneath the wheelchair. Then his eyes light up as he notices the chair has two of his favorite things: wheels. He bites one of the white rubber tires, thus proving the adage "Give a baby a wheelchair, and he'll eat it."

Then, on tiptoe, murmuring happily to himself, Ian grabs the handles of Jim Brady's chair. It looks like he's going to roll him, feet first, toward the TV tube while this vulnerable, gentle man watches the Happy Hunters cure Regis Philbin's degenerated disk.

Brady chuckles as people lunge for him. But Ian's broken the ice, and the room becomes noisier. People chatter. I tell Brady that I've always admired him, for the way he's shown the rest of us how to live, and how it's a pleasure for me to meet him.

"Thank you . . . very much," he says slowly. He may have lost a third of his brain to Hinckley's bullet, but none of his intelligence or wit. Not only is he lucid—the slow speech, caused by the bullet, calls attention to his intellect so that you get the impression that there sits a mind-at-large, like a vulnerable eye, that is chauffeured from place to place in a wheelchair.

I tell Brady I'm a reporter for the *Erie Daily Times*, figuring, as the president's press secretary, he can relate to a newspaperperson. Then I tell him my wife and I are on the show because we had our baby after going to faith healers, and figure that he will slowly roll away from me. But he doesn't.

He simply shakes his head in understanding and then tells us how he and his wife had been trying to have a child for six years, too, and how a friend of theirs from some tribe in Africa—I think it was the "Beluga tribe"—gave them a "Beluga horn" filled with pele leaves. The friend told Jim and Sarah Brady to put the charm at the head of their bed every night and they would have a baby.

"We put it . . . at the head of our bed. And . . . we had our baby," Brady tells me.

I nod my head at him and press my lips together in a way that's meant to suggest, God Works In Mysterious Ways.

Charles and Frances come back into the green room, having been called out to promo their spot in the show. My family and I end up at the end of the room with the Hunters.

"Got a cure to keep the baby from messing his pants?" I ask Frances. I'm only half joking. The baby had done that in church a week or two before, during Stacey's First Holy Communion, while I was holding his bottom with my two hands.

Frances laughs and takes the question in stride. "Of course I do," she says. She pats the baby on the head and admonishes him with her cure for dirty diapers:

"Jesus says don't mess your pants."

Charles comes up to me and gives me a big hug.

"How are you feeling?"

"Nervous."

He smiles. "Stand up. Give me your two arms. Stretch them out in front of you. More. More. Good. Now keep them real stiff. Good. Now take a deep breath and let it out slowly. Now watch the hands come together as I pray."

He prays, soliciting peace of nerves and neurons for me from Jesus Christ, while slowly pushing my hands together.

"Do you speak in tongues?" Frances asks us.

Glossolalia. The gift of tongues, one of the gifts of the Holy Spirit. The ability to speak a foreign language without having studied it, or to make sounds prompted by the Spirit.

Debbie and I admit we don't.

"You don't? My goodness, that's hard to believe. Your *McCall's* article was so anointed." She looks at us with her head cocked, like a doctor assessing the needs of her patients. "You know, you say you've been having these spiritual ups and downs. To get away from that, you need the Baptism of the Holy Ghost. It's the thing that brings you back to the light." Charles nods. "Now, just put your hands up. All the way up in the air. That's good," she says.

Debbie, myself, Stacey, and baby Ian stand there in a huddle with the Hunters, putting our hands in the air. The baby looks happily from face to face, surprised at how many adults suddenly want to play "Sooo . . . big!" with him.

"Now, just take a deep breath . . . and say, 'Jesus, I love you with all of my heart,'" orders Frances.

Debbie and I repeat the words while Charles prays, "Fill Debbie and Jack with the Holy Spirit."

All this is making me more nervous, not less.

Meanwhile, Melissa Gilbert, "Half Pint" on the old *Little House on the Prairie* TV show, is watching the whole thing. She's all grown up now, very sweet, unaffected, and because she'd said repeatedly we had "such a beautiful baby," obviously a person of great discernment.

But Laura Ingels Wilder had never seen anything like the Hunters back in Walnut Grove. She's standing there, mouth agape.

"Now, to speak in tongues you just start making a series of little sounds and say whatever comes into your mind without thinking about it," Frances says. "Like this: Ah . . . de . . . me . . . kah la me dah sa labahlakawremedo. Kahlahahalremasoalidorume. Demekelakedoha-sotalemekado."

We all still have our hands in the air. Frances is getting louder and picking up speed. "Dolomekalatoredomala. Say it, say it," she commands. Debbie and I mumble squeaking sounds together, sounding like two hissing tea kettles. "Louder. Keep going, keep going!"

I am not comfortable with this. My hands get lower and lower. But every time I shift my body weight and try to detach myself from the group, Mrs. Hunter pushes my head back down. This is not at all how I had envisioned my first meeting with a movie star.

"Just say whatever comes into your head," Frances commands. "Keep going, keep going, keep going!"

"Rice Krispies, Rice Krispies, Rice Krispies!" my daughter whispers.

Later, after Brady and his wife have done their stint before the cameras, the Hunters make their way over to them and introduce themselves. Charles asks Jim Brady if he still has pain. "The Bear" says he has pain in his paws. His feet. Brady refers to himself as a bear. He calls his wife a raccoon.

The Hunters ask if they can lay hands on him and pray for him.

"By all means," Brady says.

The "Happy Hunters" put their hands on Brady's bald, scarred head.

"I command every brain cell, every nerve, every connecting tissue and every part of your brain to heal, in Jesus' name," Charles says softly, with assurance.

"Let there be new brain cells and all connecting tissue and blood vessels," Charles says. He goes on with his prayers, then stops, and asks Brady if he can straighten his legs, pointing out that one leg is a little thicker than the other.

Charles grabs Brady's legs by the ankles and rebukes the pain to leave his body while Frances keeps her hands on Brady's head, praying, gently rubbing her fingers back and forth on his scalp.

There are maybe twenty people in the room: One or two technicians from the show. A man getting permissions slips signed. My family. Another woman, whose injured back was cured by the Hunters years ago. Melissa Gilbert and Brady and Sarah Brady. Brady's publicist. Melissa's publicist and traveling companion. Other people we don't know. All are silent. Not a person there isn't hoping and praying that Jim Brady can be helped—by faith healing, of all things.

It suddenly strikes me that at this moment, a circle has been closed: The Hunters lay hands on us, we have a baby. The baby goes to New York, bringing his parents and the Hunters with him. Frances Hunter pats Ian Christian on the head and says a little prayer, asking the angels to enfold him in their wings. And while he's tugging at Jim Brady's pant leg, the Hunters lay hands on Brady to heal him.

It's all connected. Continuous. All one. All strange.

The love in the room is tangible. We poor, finite creatures seem to have transcended ourselves a bit by the Willing of One Thing for Jim Brady.

Later, Charles Hunter asks Brady if his pain has gone.

"It has," Brady says.

"Say, 'Thank you, Jesus,'" says Charles.

"Thank you, Jesus," affirms Brady, nodding his head as he speaks.

Finally, a stage attendant grabs Debbie and me by our shoulders and shouts, "Get a move on! Go! Go! It's your turn!"

The baby, however, has just threaded my wife's gold chain necklace through her bought-for-the-Philbin-show hoop earring. He's wrapped one end of the chain around his own head so the two are bound together at the neck like Siamese twins.

Debbie has a stage attendant hurriedly unhook the baby, but she still has to run to the brightly lit stage, before the live studio audience, with a chain cutting slantways across her nose.

We got out there and told our story, though.

After the show, our chauffeur, provided by WABC-TV, drove us back to the fancy hotel where the TV station had put us up, a place where the maid puts mints on your pillow at night. Where the sparkling diamond earrings of women with foreign accents and mink and white fox fur coats reflect the twinkling lights of the huge crystal chandeliers in the lobby. Where writer Andy Rooney and the guests from *Saturday Night Live* stay. Dark wood-paneled walls. Polished brass all over the place. Where toast costs three dollars a slice.

As we passed Central Park, the ducks on the pond made me think of *Catcher in the Rye*, and suddenly I felt like a forty-one-year-old Holden Caulfield making a spiritual journey through Midtown Midlife. Holden's voice was sounding in my head:

I mean, if God did have a hand in all this, he must be collaborating with that witty writer, the long-lost J. D. Salinger.

So I asked myself, Just who *is* the author of all this? *What does he want* from me?

Then I imagined myself in a conversation with Tony Zona, my city editor, a man just big enough to wear a dumb-looking cowboy hat in public without getting punched in the face.

Hey, Tony, I had the strangest dream last night, I imagined myself saying to old Tony. It would be 7:00 A.M., and he'd be sitting at the city desk drinking his coffee, pulling at his eyebrow, scanning the morning paper for stories to follow, grumbling because someone had stolen his armchair again and he'd had to search the whole city room to find it.

Get away from me, he'd say.

But I'd go on: *I dreamed that my wife and I tried to have a baby for six years . . . then we went to see some old faith healers, a husband-and-wife team, in Jamestown, and they got us pregnant . . . then I wrote about it* for McCall's, *and they published it under an "occult" headline, and then my wife and I got asked onto the Regis Philbin show in New York City to tell the story. The producers flew the whole family to New York and put us up in a big hotel where pop costs $2.75 a can, but I found out from a maid I could get it for 55 cents a can from the employees' pop machine in the hotel basement. Then Melissa Gilbert, from* Little House on the Prairie, *baby-sat for Stacey in the green room while Kathie Lee Gifford, the girl from the Caribbean cruise commercials who looks so fantastic in that bathing suit, interviewed us with the Hunters on live TV before millions of people. The Hunters had tried to teach us glossolalia just before that so we wouldn't be nervous. That was right after they healed Jim Brady, because he said he had pain in his paws. He called his wife a raccoon.*

Zona would sigh and finally look up at me. *And what did Jim Brady say?*

When the Hunters asked him, for the second time, if his pain was still gone after they healed him, he just smiled, then said—very slowly— "What Jesus gives, Jesus doesn't take away." *What do you think it all means?*

Zona would look back down at his paper. *It means you're goofy. You and your nocturnal admissions.*

<table>
<tr><td>CHAPTER

4</td><td>Whither Goeth
the King?</td></tr>
</table>

> What must the king do now? Must he submit?
> . . . Must he be deposed?
> . . . Must he lose the name of king?
> —Shakespeare, *Richard II*

THE YEAR WAS 1978.

The big cardboard box was like an upright coffin with me inside, standing up, swigging beer to ward off impending claustrophobia. It was a refrigerator container that my friend John Horan, the director of Erie's Housing Authority, had scrounged up from one of his high-rise apartments for the elderly. Wrinkle farms.

Outside the box, in the ballroom of the Hilton Hotel, glasses clinked, ice tinkled, and silverware on plates made convivial sounds. Horan had punched three penny-size air holes in the box at eye level, and looking out, I could see the guests at the mayor's birthday party pause every now and then, forks poised in midair, to stare at the box and wonder what was inside. I envied these unboxed humans for the abundant air they so blithely breathed.

Wrapped in blue wrapping paper and tied up with a big red bow, I was a surprise birthday present for Erie mayor Louis J. Tullio. The mayor had sixty gifts to be opened that night. He wanted to wait until after dinner to open his gifts, and he wanted to save my package for last.

"Great idea, Mayor," my good friend John said. I could hear Horan thump the mayor on the back. When Tullio had gone off, Horan opened the lid just enough to toss another can of Miller's at me. "You're gonna be in there for hours, buddy," he whispered, laughing as he closed the lid.

The mayor and I had had something of a feud going, and Horan wanted to end it. This joke, giving me to the mayor as a present, was designed to break the ice.

24

"You guys can't go on being enemies forever," Horan had told me. "He's the mayor and you report on what goes on in this city. You need each other."

Almost ten years later, Tullio was sitting with me and my wife in a hotel suite in Coraopolis, Pennsylvania, just outside Pittsburgh, telling Charles and Frances Hunter the rest of the story. His good friend Pittsburgh mayor Richard Caliguiri, and Caliguiri's wife, Jeanne, were sitting around a white Formica-topped table with us.

"See, Jack had written this terrible article about me where he called me an emperor, and John Horan was trying to get him on my good side," Tullio said.

I told the Hunters that what had *really* happened was that Tullio's administration had gotten caught flat-footed by the winter of 1976–77.

"The snow on the streets was a foot deep, and the city plows hadn't been out at all," I said. "But the mayor wouldn't believe that. He believed his public works director and his two streets department heads when they told him the streets had been cleared."

I told the Hunters about the column I wrote the next day that compared Tullio to the emperor in the emperor's new clothes fable. It compared his three administrators to the three tailors who told the emperor he was clothed, although he was really naked.

The mayor wouldn't talk to me for almost a year after that—even though we'd been friends for a good ten years previously.

"That article was *terrible*, just terrible, terrible," Tullio fussed to the Hunters.

"Naked. Jack called me naked!"

Everybody laughed.

"So there I am at my birthday party, and, I'm down to my last present. I go to open the box, not knowing what to expect. Out pops Jack! He shoves a snow shovel in my face and says, 'Here, if you want the job done right, do it yourself!'" Everybody laughed again.

The mayor reached across the table in my direction. "I love 'im anyway. We've been friends ever since."

But an illness the doctors had defined as "terminal" had taken its toll on the seventy-one-year-old man, who had been mayor of Erie for twenty-three years, the second-longest term in office for a big city mayor anywhere in the United States. As I grasped his thin and uncharacteristically limp hand, I didn't want to let go. I thought of the "Wall of Fame" in his city hall office, where there's a photo of President Ronald Reagan with his arm around Lou, and a photo of President Carter with his arm around Lou, and a photo of President Nixon with his arm around Lou, and a photo of President Johnson with his arm around Lou. There was even a photo of Ted Koppel, the Grand Inquisitor of midnight TV news, with his arm around Lou.

I wanted to put my arm around him myself. Doctors estimated he had about eighteen months to live.

As Tullio told his story to the Hunters, I watched him closely. He just didn't look like a man with a fatal illness.

But that wasn't what the page one headline from the October 15, 1987, edition of the *Erie Daily Times* had shouted. "MAYOR TULLIO HAS INCURABLE DISEASE," the headline read.

"Mayor Louis J. Tullio disclosed this morning that he has amyloidosis, a rare, incurable disease that may limit his life expectancy to eighteen months, but he said he hopes to remain in office," the article said. It described amyloidosis as a noncontagious disease in which the body deposits excess amounts of a fibrous protein called amyloid in vital organs, interfering with their function. Tullio's doctors had said at a press conference that morning that the disease was affecting the mayor's heart, causing a stiffening of the muscles and a decrease in the pumping effectiveness of that organ.

Tullio had two years to go to finish his sixth term in office. "I want to finish my term," he told reporters. "I'd rather be carried out of City Hall than carried out of my home."

When I'd watched Mayor Tullio announce that he had a fatal disease on the seven-o'clock local TV news, I couldn't help but think of the Hunters. It certainly seemed that they had helped us have a child. They were credited with hundreds of miraculous healings by other reputable people who knew them, like the publisher of the Christian magazine *Charisma*. How could it hurt to remind the mayor about them?

The mayor used to hate it when I'd tell the Jack-in-the-box story to other people. He'd pull me aside and say, "Hey, gee, Jack . . . that column was bad enough. . . ."

But at some point he'd decided the tale was funny and that maybe it even made him look good somehow, so he adopted it as his own.

While the mayor was telling the story, I noticed Frances Hunter holding his hand on the tabletop.

She picked up on my gaze and then looked at the mayor's wife, Grace.

"I hope you don't think I'm getting fresh with your husband," Frances said, leaning toward Grace. "I'm not really holding hands with him. I'm just letting the power of God in there."

She looked at Tullio, then Caliguiri, and spoke to both:

"If you had to choose a time in history to get sick, this is the time to get sick. Because never has God's power been poured out as much as it is today. Never have there been healings like there are today."

"Let me tell you the story of Joppa Wiese's miracle," Frances said to both mayors. "It's the story of a man who had a heart problem, just like you."

Caliguiri, dressed in a gray suit and tie, with his hands folded together on the table top in front of him, was the picture of composure as he stared across at Frances. His lips were pressed tightly together, suggesting that hearing some faith healing story—about a man named *Joppa*—was definitely not about to give the mayor of Pennsylvania's second-largest city a great deal of confidence.

It was a strange story I'd heard Frances tell before, and Joppa and his wife, Nancy, had told it to me, too. It was like something out of Dickens, a summer, southern *Christmas Carol.*

I had interviewed Joppa and Nancy at length, hoping to find details in their experience which might give hope to the mayors, or at least make me feel more confident that bringing the mayors together with Charles and Frances might really do some good. The story was so odd, though, I hadn't told anybody about it.

Joppa. The name sounded Iranian or Middle Eastern, but Joppa Wiese was born and raised an American of German descent. His strange name, I'd discovered, was significant.

Frances began her narrative, and as she spoke, the low southern drawl of Joppa's voice sounded again in my ears, and my mind played back his story for me like a videotape. Joppa's strange story is a singular example of the workings of the supernatural world— a world at odds with the 1980s, a world hauntingly out of context in the suite of the Royce Hotel in Coraopolis:

It was June 10, 1987, a glorious sunny summer day in Chattanooga, Tennessee, where Joppa Wiese and his wife Nancy lived in a little frame ranch house on the outskirts of town. But the curtains in the bedroom were drawn, as they had been for weeks. Joppa, sixty years old, would have nothing to do with summer because his time for dying had come. He knew he would be dead within the next two hours and that when Nancy arived home from work at the church, she would find there on the queen-size bed, propped up on two pillows, only the shell of his six-foot, one-inch body, all three hundred pounds of it.

It was almost as if he could feel the cells in his body dying one by one, like lights winking off in a big city after midnight. It was an odd smell that his body had today; it was a stench that seemed to permeate the room. He knew death was in the house.

"Your husband's dying" was what the doctor had told his wife just a few weeks ago, and Joppa had welcomed what he'd heard.

The doctor had shown them the X-rays, which revealed a heart so enlarged that it seemed to fill the whole chest cavity, leaving very little room for his lungs. "Congestive heart failure," the doctor had said. "Your heart is completely worn out."

Joppa remembered the doctor looking first at him, then at Nancy, and saying, "I'll be praying for you both. But Joppa, I'm not even going to put you in the hospital. As bad as you are, there's no point in taking your money. I can tell your wife the same thing I'd tell the nurses, as far as giving you your medication goes, and if she needs to call me, she can."

Joppa didn't care one way or the other. *So what? I'm gonna die.*

He was pretty sure his wife hated him, and he was pretty sure he hated her, and if this bad heart of his meant he could leave the whole mess behind, so much the better. He was tired of the marriage; tired of her; tired of being sick; tired of not being able to get a decent breath into his body. He was tired of being tired.

"Hell, Joppa, I am tired of foolin' with you."

Joppa looked around the room.

Maybe this is what happens when you die—you start hearing things. Voices.

The TV was off; Joppa had been busy dying and didn't have time for game shows.

How strange it was, that voice. Maybe it came from someone outside the house.

Naw, the closest house was a quarter mile away.

Right near the nightstand was where it seemed to come from. Not the voice but a soft, gentle breeze that seemed to touch his right arm and linger.

There it was again, this little breeze, like somebody was standing there by the nightstand fanning on his arm with his hand.

The room had no fan and the air conditioner was off. He could see that the window was cracked a bit, but the curtains weren't moving, even though he could feel a breeze on his arm clear across the room. If he was going to get a brush of air across his arm from the window, how could it settle on just his right arm in a corner of the room?

He recalled a phrase from Scripture: *"The wind bloweth were it listeth, and thou hearest the sound thereof, but canst not tell whence it cometh, and whither it goeth; so is everyone that is born of the Spirit."*

No, this wasn't a normal wind. It wasn't your typical breeze. Because now there was a Presence in the room. There was *Glory* in the room. There was an *anointing* in the room.

God is in this room.

"Nah, I'm dreamin'."

"Or dyin'."

"One or t'other."

Then he heard it again. The voice:

"I'm SO TIRED of foolin' with you. For eight years now, as long as you've been married, you could have had a good life. I've had something for you to do for the past eight years and you haven't obeyed Me. You haven't done anything."

This voice, it was coming from all over the inside of the room, filling his spirit and his mind and his heart and his ears. The voice was quiet yet firm; it spoke with authority and listed his sins and called him out for the mean-spirited man he was, a nasty, gluttonous, jealous old sinner who hit his wife and called her vile names.

And yet he wasn't being judged, he was being loved. The room seemed to glow, but it wasn't the light that Moses saw or the light that blinded the apostle Paul. It was just a gentle, peaceful glow that seemed to come from nowhere and everywhere and was reflected from all four walls of the pale blue room.

Joppa sniffed again. The stench of his dying was gone. It had been replaced by a sweet smell, a sweet odor he'd never smelled before. Sight, sound, smell, touch, even a taste like honey in his mouth—all his senses were being assailed.

"Eight years and you haven't obeyed Me. You haven't done anything." And then the God-as-Voice said, *"My number one complaint with you is this—it's your wife, the way you treat her. you complain to your pastor about your wife, you complain to your family about your wife, you complain to your friends about your wife. But Joppa, it's not your wife, it's YOU."*

For some reason, Joppa glanced at the doorway. Standing there, silhouetted by the light behind it, was a shadow, a dark shadow in the doorway, just looking at Joppa from a no-eyes face. The thing had no features, no discernible arms or legs, but it did have a hooded, shrouded appearance.

The first thing that entered Joppa's mind was, *"Nancy didn't lock that damn door, and now here's someone comin' to my room fixin' to kill me."*

Then the voice spoke again. *"I have kept you alive because when you were stricken, you prayed to Me. But I can't do a complete healing in you until you obey Me and do what I want you to do, and if you won't . . . then I will allow Satan to have his way."*

God didn't say he was going to kill Joppa. He said he would let the devil take him. And when Joppa looked at the dark figure in the doorway, he could see it for what it was. The complete absence of light. A figure of incandescent darkness. A nothingness. A black hole in the rough shape of a man.

The chill coming from the shadow moved inside him and congealed his blood and gave him gooseflesh.

A black corona seemed to emanate from the shadow, hiding its head, its face, and its form. The very air in which the shadow stood seemed to reflect a dark light of doom and anguish. Its intrusive presence filled him with a grave dread. He felt the hidden, dusky eyes looking at him keenly. He knew that death was the shadow's dominion.

He knew that Satan was ready for him.

The Healed Heart

. . . it was yet dark, and no appearance of day or moonshine, and as I opened mine eyes I saw a light in my chamber, at the apparent distance of five feet, about nine inches in diameter, of a clear, easy brightness, and near its center the most radiant. As I lay still, looking upon it without any surprise, words were spoken to my inward ear, which filled my whole inward man. They were . . . the language of the Holy One spoken in my mind. The words were, CERTAIN EVIDENCE OF DIVINE TRUTH.

—John Woolman, *The Journal of John Woolman*, *1757*

FRANCES leaned forward in her chair as she told her story, and as she spoke, I could recall Joppa telling me he had no doubt it was Satan standing at death's doorway in his own house, waiting to take him once he'd sucked his last breath.

He'd told me how—when he had stopped caring to live anymore, when he had started hating everyone, including himself—he had simply started eating and applied fat to his form like links of thick, heavy chains. He ballooned from 185 pounds to 325.

A *Christmas Carol:* "I wear the chain I forged in life. . . . I made it link by link and yard by yard; I girded it on of my own free will, and of my own free will I wore it."

But Joppa knew God was telling him the game wasn't over yet. God was giving him one last chance. Joppa could *break* the chains of ill health. He could either choose to follow the Lord, or the Lord would let the shadow standing in the doorway take him on down.

"Well, I'll tell you what," Joppa had recalled to me in his deep, mellow voice. "You know what purgin' is? It's when God purifies your spirit—it's like gold, you heat the gold up and you melt it to purify it. Well, God will purify you if your heart's right. He'll give you a cleansing of the spirit and of the body, and what happened to me was, my heart just opened up to God and I got to cryin' and a-weeping', and I mean *deep, deep weepin'*, because . . . *I can't explain to you exactly what it does* . . . it made me feel so ashamed of myself that the tears that was comin' down my face was actually burnin' my cheeks, and I got to the point to where I really didn't know as to whether I'd been saved or not. So I just went right back to the cross, and that's where we all have to go—back to the bottom of that cross where Jesus died.

"I just asked Him to come back into my heart. I told Him that I was sorry and I repented for everything and I wanted to be born again, and I wanted to be part of His family.

"I wasn't being judged. I felt like I was being loved. I was being given an opportunity to serve God again. You know, He sits over there in the corner, He never tells us what we have to do, He just waits on us, that's all."

When Joppa asked God to come back into his heart, it all left. The light, the smell, the taste, the breeze, the voice, and the black apparition in the doorway. Vanished. And the hatred—it left too. Joppa felt alive again.

Later, Joppa told Nancy about the visitations.

"Did you know Charles and Frances Hunter are coming to our church Saturday night?" she asked. "Do you think that maybe you ought to go?"

"I don't think I can stand in that prayer line," Joppa said in the car. "I'm just too sick."

"God brought you from your deathbed to this car," Nancy said. "He'll get you through the prayer line too."

Nancy was about forty-five, a pretty woman, about five feet, five inches tall, a little on the plump side with curly blond hair. She was a spirit-filled Christian and had been walking "in the supernatural" with God for years. She'd seen many miracles in her life, not the least of which was God giving her the strength to stay with this man beside her.

Nancy couldn't really blame Joppa. So much had happened to bring him to this point. He and his first wife, Mary, had been married for thirty-one years and had raised two boys and a daughter to adulthood. They'd had a good home and he had a good job and he had Mary. And then she got cancer of the brain and died.

After thirty-one years of marriage, there was no way he could have prepared himself for Mary's death. Nancy should have seen the signs that he was trying to escape it all. His buying binges, for example. Travel-trailers. Cars. Boats. Stereos.

Even her.

He'd finally admitted he had married her, three months after Mary died, as an escape too.

He abused Nancy both physically and verbally. He was jealous of her for no reason whatsoever and would accuse her of all sorts of awful things.

He picked at her daily. He'd swear and say, "You don't clean the house right, Nancy. . . . You don't cook right. . . . You don't fix your hair right." She couldn't do anything right as far as her husband was concerned. The problem was, she didn't do things like Mary would have done them.

Sometimes Nancy wanted to leave her husband, but she knew that was not God's will. She had to make the decision to love him as a Christian would, and keep making that decision every day.

It was a nighttime service. As they walked into the church, Nancy could see her husband pick himself up and stand a little straighter as he met the friends and ushers who hadn't seen him in church for seven months. People kept coming up to him and hugging him, telling him how good it was to see him back.

"Let's go sit down, quick," Joppa said, pulling at Nancy's elbow. They walked past Charles and Frances Hunter, sitting at a table and signing their books at the front of the church, and Nancy was surprised at how happy the Happy Hunters really did look. Frances was sitting there talking and laughing in her big booming voice, and Charles was smiling and hugging people. Just to look at them, she felt sure something good would happen tonight, whether Joppa wanted it to or not.

They made their way to the front, and Joppa sat down heavily in an outside chair on an aisle about midway to the altar. Nancy guessed there were probably four hundred or five hundred people there. She heard a groan next to her and looked at Joppa, who looked as if he were going to pass out. And then, all of a sudden, the pastor stood up at the microphone, looked right at Joppa, and said, "Joppa Wiese, I want you to come down forward right now!"

By this time, the Hunters were up there with the pastor. When they saw Joppa headed their way, they both started down off the altar area, almost running toward Joppa, who was walking slowly down the aisle to them.

The Hunters were coming at him with their hands outstretched, as if to hug him.

Joppa wasn't going to have to wait till the end of the service after all.

"God wanted to heal me right then and there—the devil had been showing me all the things that weren't going to happen," he recalled afterward.

The Hunters hadn't even touched Joppa when suddenly he crumpled to the floor, slain in the Spirit. It was the power of the Lord. He'd gone down like he was hit on the back of the head with a two-by-four. The Hunters had been a good twenty feet away when he fell.

A few minutes later, Joppa was back in his seat. He watched the pastor call the Hunters over, and again the pastor stood at the microphone and spoke to Joppa.

"Joppa, I want you to come down forward again," he said.

Joppa turned to Nancy and said, "What's going on here?"

"There's more wrong with you than just your heart," she whispered. "I guess they know the job's not done."

As Joppa walked forward again, the pastor turned to the Hunters and said, "I want him to have a double portion."

"And what happened then," Joppa said later, "was just a quiet healing. There wasn't any of that screamin' and hollerin' and yellin' for the devil to come out of me. Frances just layed her hands on my chest, and Charles laid his hands on top of hers. Frances looked into my eyes, and to this day I can't describe to you what I saw in her eyes. But the sweetest words came out of her mouth as she prayed for me.

"And I went out that time again. I mean, I went down. And when I got up, I knew that God had done something in my body. My chest felt like all kinds of funny things were going on inside.

"I started back to my seat and sat down. My chest felt warm inside. It was like warm water. Air bubbles. I'd put my hand up there to my chest and then jerk it down because I'd think, 'If I touch my chest, the congregation will think I haven't been healed.' But I knew something was going on inside there."

That was on a Saturday night. The next Monday afternoon, Joppa had an appointment with his doctor for his regular X-rays and blood tests.

"What in the world has happened to you?" the office nurse said. Joppa was a changed man. He was smiling, and his face was a healthy pink, not the color of old gray dirt, as it had been for months.

"Dr. Jesus got ahold of me Saturday night," said Joppa.

When the doctor listened to his heart, he said, "I don't understand. Your heart is just as strong as any heart I've ever heard. Let's go back and get a picture of it."

"When that doctor came out of the X-ray room, he was as white as a ghost," Joppa recalls. "He says to me, 'You know what? Not only do you have a new heart, but look at these lungs—Your emphysema is apparently gone as well."

Later, when Joppa Wiese told his story to *Charisma* magazine, *Charisma* quoted a letter from Joppa's doctor:

"When he [Joppa] was initially seen by me, his congestive heart failure was as severe as any patient that I have seen in 20 years and nothing short of a heart transplant would have kept him alive. . . . Mr. Wiese will return to work on the 20th of July (1987) and without a doubt could never have survived his heart failure without the Lord's intervention. It was indeed an act of God."

Acts, chapter 9, tells the story of Tabitha, a believer who was always doing things for the poor. The woman became ill and died, but the apostle Peter prayed for her and raised her from the dead.

This healing miracle occurred near the town of Lydda, in a city named . . . *Joppa*.

Joppa Wiese was not raised in a religious family, but his father did belong to the Masonic Lodge. The lodge brothers picked out the name Joppa for the Wiese baby. They named him for that biblical city on the Mediterranean Sea where Tabitha's healing occurred, where that old woman was raised up from the dead. The name would stand him in good stead, maybe, the brothers thought.

The Masons had given Joppa a name that went back to the eighth century before Christ, when the Lord taught Jonah the same lesson of obedience he taught Joppa:

God said to Jonah, "Go to the great city of Nineveh, and tell them I will destroy them for all their wickedness. But Jonah was afraid to go and he ran away from the Lord."

He went to the city of *Joppa* instead.

"'*Joppa*,' that's me, all right," Joppa told me. "I ran away and hid from the Lord for years, and I didn't obey him all that time. "You know, there's a lot in a name, Jack. You got to wonder how much your name will do for you in your life."

Just like his father, Joppa didn't have much faith in preachers and healers. He'd watch those religious shows on TV with preachers like R. W. Shambach and Norvell Hayes, and "all those dudes being pushed to the front in their doggone wheelchairs," and then the preachers would lay hands on those fools and up they'd jump to run around the auditorium shouting, "Hallelujah!" But they couldn't fool Joppa. "They're payin' those 'sick' people to travel with 'em from town to town," he'd say. "They travel with that preacher everywhere he goes."

If somebody had told Joppa that one day God would talk to him and heal him through people like the Hunters, he would have spit.

But now, Joppa and Nancy have seminars on healing in their home every Thursday night. They tell their story and show the fourteen hours of videotapes called *How to Heal the Sick* made by Charles and Frances Hunter.

The Hunters believe, and they say so in their tapes, that anyone, not just the big-name healers, can heal the sick and work miracles. All you have to do is believe, they say.

"We've done healings ourselves," Joppa says. "Any believer can do it. Anyone can pray, can't he? You can't just sit on a pew being taught all your lives. Sometimes you gotta stand up and use what you've learned."

"I'm not gonna tell you I feel like a million dollars. But I'll tell you what—I feel good," Joppa says today. "I haven't had to go back to the doctor once since I was healed. I don't take any medication anymore. My blood pressure's normal, and it used to be up to 250 over 114.

The Wieses say their marriage has been healed also. Joppa no longer abuses Nancy, either physically or verbally.

"We love each other," Nancy told me. "I can't really say that God has restored our love, because there was no love there to begin with. But He is building a love that is founded on Him."

When Frances finished Joppa's story, it was hard to gauge the mayors' reactions. Caliguiri looked a little nervous, but thoughtful. Tullio was fidgeting impatiently in his seat, chomping at the bit to get healed himself.

I could imagine how they felt. Joppa's story, especially in this day and age, is a strange one. I had a hard time myself, with God and the devil in Joppa's room, imagining God speaking in a southern drawl.

But there are all kinds of incidents in the Bible in which an infinite God somehow circumscribes his being in space and time and speaks to finite man, which must be like trying to have a conversation with a subatomic particle that has a life span of a millionth of a nanosecond.

In Acts 9, for example, God talked to Paul, who, hating everybody, "still breathing threats of slaughter against the disciples of the Lord," was on his way to Damascus to persecute the Christians. He was going to round up any believers, men or women, he could find there to bring them in chains to Jerusalem.

As he was nearing Damascus, "A light from heaven shone all around him," and Paul fell to the ground. He heard a voice say, "Saul, Saul, why dost thou persecute me?"

"Who art thou?" Paul asked.

"I am Jesus, whom thou art persecuting," the voice said.

Like Joppa Wiese, Paul, who had been filled with hate, had seen the light and heard the voice.

A Cautionary Note

> God offers to every mind its choice between truth and
> repose. Take which you please—you can never have
> both.
>
> —Ralph Waldo Emerson,
> *Intellect*

WHEN I tried to contact Joppa Wiese's doctor to verify Joppa's cure, he declined to talk to me, despite the fact that he had gone on record for *Charisma* magazine as saying Wiese "without a doubt could never have survived his heart failure without God's intervention. It was indeed an act of God."

Charisma's Steve Lawson wasn't at all surprised.

"Doctors don't like to go on the record with things like this," said Lawson, an associate editor at *Charisma*, which regularly publishes articles on healing.

Even if doctors *can* be persuaded to comment, they're almost always vague, Lawson told me. "They give us that thing about, 'Well, there's always that element of science that we don't understand, I've never seen anything like it and it *could* have been God, *but* . . .' There's always that qualifier, that '*but.*'"

One of Lawson's jobs is to verify healing stories before publication. "The approach we take here is that maybe God *did* do what people claimed He did in a particular case, but if it can't be documented we're not going to write about it."

Healing testimonies are checked at *Charisma* before they're assigned to writers. "We get lists and lists of healings from people, but trying to document them well enough to write about them is another thing," he says. "You obviously start with a person who claims to have been healed. Then you get their testimony. A lot of times, the story breaks down right at that point. We looked into one case where a woman had risen from the dead in a service, at least judging by all the reports that we had. We asked her to explain exactly what happened, and she said, 'Yes, *I came back from the dead.*' We asked her how long she was dead. She said, '*Oh, about a minute.*' How can a person be dead for about a minute? Then she referred us to the doctor who confirmed that she was dead. The 'doctor' turned out to be a dentist."

Because such things happen so often, the magazine must look carefully into reported healings. "The ones we like are where there are X-rays before and after a healing. That makes verification real easy," says Lawson.

In Joppa Wiese's case, the X-ray taken before the Hunter healing service shows a greatly enlarged heart. The X-ray taken afterward shows a heart that appears to have shrunk by 20 percent.

A friend of mine, a Cornell-educated cardiothoracic surgeon with an impressive array of board certifications, examined Wiese's X-rays and told me, "The heart definitely appears a great deal smaller on the film taken after the service. If you knew both these films were done the same way, you'd have to say there was a dramatic improvement."

But what could that mean in terms of verifying a divine healing? It all depends on the treatment Wiese was receiving. If he'd been given a diuretic, that drug would have reduced the size of his heart along with expelling fluid from his chest cavity.

Thus, to be sure a divine healing had taken place, anyone trying to verify the healing would have to know that no drugs were administered, a fact that wouldn't show up on any X-ray.

"You simply have to know what interventions, if any, were done," my doctor friend said. "If the guy didn't drink any water for a long time, for instance, it's possible he could have even dried out that way. But if his heart got smaller a day or two after the healing service, without any medical intervention, you'd be hard pressed to say it wasn't related to the service."

Wiese's doctor did certify the healing in writing, but that letter did not list the treatments Wiese had been given. "It didn't tell us what drugs Mr. Wiese was on or anything like that," my friend said. "Some drugs are very powerful, and if he was taking a lot of drugs at one time, it's possible that one of them was even *causing* the heart failure—and if he stopped taking the drug after the service, his heart would indeed have gotten better.

"Even if all the evidence appears to hold in a case, you have to remember one thing," my friend said. "It took about 20,000 case studies to make sure a procedure as orthodox as coronary bypass worked. So trying to draw a conclusion for a case even as dramatic as Mr. Wiese's appears to be is almost impossible."

My friend made me realize that it was far beyond my ability to verify, even with the help or opinions of the doctors involved, the healings described in this book. If it took 20,000 case studies to verify the efficacy of bypass surgery, if it took 174 doctors examining the records of Serge Perrin in Lourdes to verify his miraculous recovery from stroke, then presenting unassailable evidence would be far beyond the capacity of one reporter. I would have to accept the fact that there are few things beyond some degree of ambiguity, especially in the world of medicine.

But that's okay. Because although I started out to write a book about divine healing, I ended up writing about God and my search for Him, and God can be incandescently ambiguous, at least in terms of our ability to apprehend Him in all his sovereignty.

Lawson told me about another case in which a wrestler claimed to have been cured of a muscle problem after being prayed for. "In this case, when we checked with an independent doctor, he said the wrestler's condition could have reversed itself naturally, that to be sure a healing had occurred, we'd have to wait for ten or fifteen years to make sure his illness didn't recur. So we didn't write about that one. It probably was a healing, but we decided to back off because a spontaneous remission could have occurred."

I asked Lawson if, having handled these stories at the desk, he believes divine healing through God's intervention exists.

"Definitely," he said. "I think God does heal, and I have no problem with that. I do think we all can get excited about many things that aren't necessarily healings, though. I may believe one thing as a Christian, I may feel in a certain case that a healing did indeed happen; but as a journalist, I am not going to write about it if it isn't verifiable. Maybe God did raise that lady from the dead, or maybe He somehow touched her life. A lot of times God will do things that are meant to be personal, individual experiences, and to think that we can measure these and weigh the evidence—it just doesn't work that way. I don't think God is all that interested in our media. I don't think He heals so we can write about it.

"When we do write about a healing, we word it very carefully," Lawson told me, because it is risky to declare anyone healed. "For example, there is one case where a Christian broadcaster prayed for an old man on his show and declared he was healed on national television. Two days later, the man died."

For as long as there have been healers, there have been those trying, like Lawson, to document their successes. One of these is Louis Rose, a British clinical psychologist and the author of *Faith Healing*, published in

1968. Realizing it is extremely difficult to verify healings, Rose narrowed his quest to a handful of cases, looking for just one example "in which the intervention of a faith healer led to an irrefutable case."

He examined ninety-five purported cures. In fifty-eight of those he was denied access to medical records that would have helped confirm the cures. In twenty-two cases, medical records contradicted testimonies. In the rest of the cases, there was temporary improvement followed by a relapse, or the improvement occurred while orthodox medical treatment was being administered.

He was unable to verify to his satisfaction even one cure by a faith healer.

Typical of many cases he examined was that of a nine-year-old boy with muscular dystrophy who visited the British faith healer Harry Edwards, seeking a cure. Edwards told the boy he would get better, but two years later the boy's physician reported the child had gotten "very definitely worse."

Another case involves a boy said to have been unable to speak and who also was supposed to have a distended abdomen and paralysis in both legs. A faith healing experience supposedly left him cured of all ailments. But when Rose contacted the hospital that treated him, he was told the boy never had any of the ailments that had been cited.

William Nolen, a surgeon from Minnesota and author of *Healing: A Doctor in Search of a Miracle* (1974), reported in his study similar incidents in cases involving alleged cures by Kathryn Kuhlman, a healer reputed to have healed thousands at her "miracle services" in the 1960s and 1970s.

One woman with cancer of the spine, for instance, had discarded her brace and followed Kuhlman's command to run across the stage. The next day her backbone collapsed, and four months later she was dead.

Nolen had gotten the names of eighty-two patients who had claimed a cure at one of Kuhlman's services. Of the eighty-two, twenty-three agreed to be interviewed by Nolen. The twenty-three, according to Nolen, reported dubious cures, which he attributed to everything from the power of suggestion and the placebo effect to cures of misdiagnosed diseases that never existed—the same sort of things Steve Lawson warned me about.

Some of the cures cited by Nolen, like the woman with cancer cited earlier, seem to be obvious failures. But others are subject to interpretation.

For instance, Nolen cites the case of a woman who believes her multiple sclerosis improved after the service. But he says her improvement could have been a product of the normal course of the disease.

He cites a man who claimed to have less frequent migraines after the service, but says that could be due to the fact that the man had a compulsive, tense personality subject to suggestion, and Kuhlman "reassured" his migraines away.

Of a nun who claimed to have been cured of bursitis, Nolen says, "The cure of Sister Marian's bursitis isn't of much consequence. Anyone who has had bursitis, and certainly anyone who ever treated it, knows that it's an on-again, off-again thing."

Kuhlman told one woman that in three days her skin condition would be cured, and in three days it was very much improved. Nolen says this is because the woman probably was highly susceptible to suggestion.

Nolen and other skeptics seem to have a tendency toward black-and-white thinking: Either there was a cure, or there wasn't. But such thinking leaves no room for degrees of healing that may occur following prayer or the laying on of hands.

What Nolen failed to note—perhaps because it is a relatively new insight coming after Nolen's book was first published in 1974—is that sometimes healing is only partial. And usually, as healer Francis Mac-Nutt maintains, healings are not split-second affairs that are finished after one laying-on-of-hands experience. Only one healing out of twenty-five happens immediately, he says. Sometimes, as MacNutt told me, healings are a *process* that calls for repeated prayer and laying on of hands on a daily basis. This point will be further explored in a later chapter.

So to expect a complete healing after only one experience with a healer even as renowned as Kathryn Kuhlman is unrealistic; to say that because the healing wasn't complete there was no healing is unfair; and to say that because one instant healing seemingly failed to occur, all reported healings are bogus, seems to be a quantum leap to an illogical conclusion.

To me, of the tens of thousands of people who claimed to have been healed by Kuhlman, a study of twenty-three seems insignificant. In her book *I Believe in Miracles*, Kuhlman cites twenty-one cases of quite well-documented cures. I'd like to see someone investigate those, as opposed to what appear to be easier targets.

If no one was ever really healed at her services, how could Kuhlman continue to draw, as Nolen says, at stop after stop, week after week, year after year, "twelve, fifteen, or twenty thousand people . . . the only limit being the size of the hall or stadium, since she almost invariably draws a capacity crowd." Surely, if her healings were *all* bogus, the word would have leaked out.

Physicians may say that Kuhlman's success with psychosomatic diseases is what kept people coming to her services. But the same thing could be said about physicians themselves, who acknowledge that about 80 percent of their patients suffer from psychosomatic diseases.

What about the fifty-nine people of the list of eighty-two who didn't respond to Nolen's request for an interview? Working at a newspaper, I've found that people are much more anxious to spread the word about a perceived injury than a good turn.

Rose's work, too, seems tainted by the physician's reluctance to consider the possibility of supernatural healing.

For example, Rose tells of a man who had a biopsy of the larynx that revealed cancer. After the cancer was detected, the man went to healer Harry Edwards "for direct healing, and during the course of the interview his hoarse voice began to improve in quality and gain in volume." Afterward, the man was re-examined by two throat specialists who reported no sign of cancer in the larynx.

Was there a miraculous cure?

Not according to Rose, who found a doctor to say that he believed it was "pure fortunate coincidence" that the tissue removed in the biopsy just happened to contain all of the cancerous tissue. "Fortunate coincidence" indeed!

In another case, this one cited by Nolen, a young man with liver cancer staggered down the aisle at a Kuhlman service to claim a cure but was turned back gently by an usher. "When he collapsed into his chair I could see his bulging abdomen—as tumor-laden as it had been earlier," Nolen wrote. It doesn't seem to have struck him that Kuhlman's ushers may have had wanted to weed out wishful cures from actual ones for the sake of Kuhlman's credibility.

To me, there's one adage that seems to hold here: "For the believer, no proof is ever needed; for the disbeliever, no proof is ever enough."

I can't help but think that the truth must lie somewhere in between, and like Longfellow said, "Some falsehood mingles with all truth."

Of the six thousand claims of miraculous cures submitted to the Medical Bureau of Lourdes since 1856, only sixty-four have been accepted as miraculous by the Roman Catholic church.

But even one miraculous case in all of recorded history—whether at Lourdes or under the hand of Kathryn Kuhlman or some modern-day healer—should be enough to at least give skeptics pause. Reality is so complicated, it seems that only a fool can say with certainty that something is, or is not, so.

Charisma's Lawson says that no one but God knows God's will, and just as it is not up to us to determine where and when a healing should occur, so it is not up to us to declare unequivocally that a healing has—or hasn't—happened.

A number of recent cases point up the need for caution on all sides.

On August 21, 1987, for example, Oklahoma City's newspaper *The Daily Oklahoman* published a story about a $5 million suit filed in August against evangelist Benny Hinn in connection with an incident that occurred at a service in Oklahoma City, providing the following details:

The paper stated that the suit, filed in Oklahoma City federal court by the family of Ella Peppard, eighty-five, of Oklahoma City, claimed that Peppard suffered a broken hip on September 18, 1986, while attending a revival at Faith Tabernacle conducted by Hinn.

The lawsuit claimed Peppard was convinced by ushers to go to the front of the church, where Hinn was touching people on the forehead and pronouncing them "slain in the Spirit." After Hinn touched the man in front of Peppard, the man fell backward into Peppard and knocked her to the floor, causing her to fracture her hip, the suit claimed. It went on to state that instead of offering her medical assistance, Hinn allegedly ordered Peppard removed from the stage and placed her in a seat near the front of the church.

The suit claimed that when one usher offered to seek medical aid for Peppard, witnesses said Hinn stopped the usher and said, "Leave her alone, God will heal her."

Peppard, according to the petition, eventually was taken to Deaconess Hospital, where surgeons implanted a prosthesis replacing her left hip. She was then transferred to Baptist Medical Center, where she died on October 3, 1986.

The state medical examiner determined that she died of multiple pulmonary emboli (blocked arteries) caused by the broken hip.

The suit sought $2.5 million in actual damages and another $2.5 million in punitive damages from Hinn; his company, Benny Hinn Ministries, Inc.; and the Faith Tabernacle Association, Inc. It was settled out of court for an undisclosed amount on May 9, 1988.

The November 23, 1984, issue of *Christianity Today* carried a story on controversy surrounding Hobart Freeman, then leader of the Faith Assembly sect based in Wilmot, Indiana. The article described how Freeman taught that to seek medical care demonstrates a lack of faith in God's ability or His desire to heal the body supernaturally. According to Freeman's theology, God is obligated to heal *every* sickness if a believer's faith is genuine. In his book *Positive Thinking and Confession*, Freeman wrote, "We must practice thought control. We must deliberately empty our minds of everything negative concerning the person, problem, or situation confronting us." Faith must be accompanied by "positive confession," according to Freeman, meaning believers must "claim" a healing by acknowledging that it has taken place. After healing is claimed, symptoms of illness or injury that remain are viewed as deceptions from the devil. When death occurs despite a positive confession, it is interpreted as a discipline from God or a lack of faith. (Most reputable healers view this as ridiculous.)

"It is estimated that some 80 people, many of them children, have died in recent years as a result of following Freeman's teachings," stated the *Christianity Today* article.

In June 1977, Rita and Douglas Swan, both Christian Scientists, relied on prayer and a church healer to cure their fifteen-month-old son Matthew of meningitis. The Swans were assured that Matthew was being healed but were warned that their fears and negative thoughts were blocking his healing. Then the Swans were told that their son was healed and that he just needed to get stronger. Rita told *Redbook* magazine that at that point she would stand over her son's bed, chanting, "God doesn't make disease, disease is just a lie."

In July, Matthew died after his parents were told by doctors that he had a type of meningitis that responds well to antibiotics—in its early stages. But the Swans' religious beliefs had keep them from using medicine.

The reputable healers I've talked with—Frances and Charles Hunter, John Wimber, Francis MacNutt, Peter Youngren, and others—all agree that never, under any circumstances, should medical help be refused when it is obviously needed.

Beware the healer who says otherwise, they say, because to advocate the withholding of medicine without medical sanction is to assume too much and is to deny the sovereignty of God.

All reputable healers wince when they hear of medical help being withheld from people, especially from children, who have no say in the matter.

Cal LeMon—not a healer but a guest columnist for *USA Today*—perhaps said it best in the paper's May 4, 1988, edition:

Stories of parents choosing prayer over medical help for their critically ill children are frightening. It scares me to think adults could choose children who have no choices as test cases for their faith. I've always believed that faith is blind, but never stupid.

The issue in this morass of morality is not God's ability. Spiritual healing does take place. I've been on the receiving end of a divine physical "miracle." But God can do just what He wants to do because He is God, not because He's manipulated by chance or chancels.

When a parent builds a box for God with predictions of physical healing, his arrogance can result in a pine box for his child. This twisted and selfish theology makes children the pawns of religion moved by sweaty, self-righteous hands.

I believe God can work His healing power through the deft movements of a surgeon, the contents of a plastic IV bag, or the invisible touch of a radiation machine. Divinity has the supernatural ability to squeeze into the confines of a surgical needle or roam freely the light-years of space.

Parents are not blessed with such ability. These adults have to make adult decisions about a child's future. Doesn't it make sense a parent would want to assist God with the healing process by bowing in prayer while waiting to see the doctor?

*   *   *

In his book *The Faith Healers,* James Randi tells his version of how faith healer W. V. Grant of Dallas once claimed to have healed an elderly man of cancer:

He'd been told by the evangelist, "Get up out of that wheelchair and walk!" and he'd done so, vigorously. Questioning revealed that his cancer was no impediment to his walking ability. In fact we interviewed him at his home, where he lived in a fourth-floor walk-up whose stairs he had to negotiate several times a day! Why had he been in the wheelchair? Because, he said, his pastor had told him to sit in it when he arrived at the auditorium. The chair was supplied by an usher. He'd never been in a wheelchair before in his life.

Also in his book, Randi claims to have uncovered how minister Peter Popoff of Upland, California, miraculously "read" the minds and medical histories of people in the audience by using a phony hearing aid-radio receiver to take prompting from his wife backstage.

In another chapter, Randi discusses what he calls a "leg-stretching" trick used by Grant.

Randi claims Grant appears to "adjust" a short leg on a person by actually tugging at his shoe or boot, thus pulling it away from the foot to make it appear as if the leg "grew." (Cowboy boots are an advantage to the trick, Randi says, because they can be pulled away from the foot for quite some distance.) At the same time, he shoves the pant leg slowly up, to enhance the illusion, says Randi, noting the illusion can also be furthered by swinging the person's legs at an angle to the audience, which makes it appear as if the legs do not meet.

In one chapter titled "The Lesser Lights," Randi devotes three and a half pages to the Happy Hunters (using my description of them as the "Ozzie and Harriet of Faith Healing"). He notes that they "present a cheerful, effervescent attitude to their work that makes many other faith healers look like grumps." He also chastises the Hunters for practicing "The Grant Leg-Stretching Trick."

"I cannot imagine that any person who regularly performs this trick as a demonstration can possibly fail to know it is a deception," Randi says.

In front of the TV camera, Charles Hunter used this technique on Regis Philbin to try to help relieve Philbin's back problem—Philbin has a bad disk. On the show, Philbin reported that the pain in his back immediately went away. He stood up after "the leg stretching" and bent over and touched his toes. Then he exclaimed to the audience. "Well . . . say, 'Hallelujah!' It . . . feels better!"

(When I followed up on his cure several months later, however, his producer told me the pain had left only "for a moment" and that there was no permanent healing. But based on Francis MacNutt's teachings, this does not prove Charles Hunter is a fake healer; it just means more than one prayer may have been needed.)

At a Hunter healing service in Erie, I watched Charles carefully when he performed the leg-lengthening technique on several people. I had just read Randi's description of the W. V. Grant trick. I was looking hard, to see if the shoes went down or the pantleg went up, or if Charles somehow manipulated clothing or body angles for a deception.

He did not. In every case I observed, and there were at least five of them, Charles kept his hands in one spot, touching only the person's socks, which did not move up or down. His hands did not move and no clothing was moved or manipulated. And yet the legs did seem to grow, just as they had when Debbie and I watched him do this in Jamestown the first time we saw him.

Charles explained to me later that many healers do indeed fake "leg stretching," but that when done properly, it can lead to improvement of many physical ailments.

He said that actually, the legs don't grow at all. It is usually the pelvis that rotates, making it appear that the legs change length. The rotation of the pelvis and the alignment of the spinal column that ensues is what produces back, muscle, and nerve adjustments, in much the same way that a chiropractor's manipulation of the back does.

"Chiropractors have told us that the nervous system controls and coordinates all organs and structures of the human body, and that misalignments of spinal vertebrae and disks may cause irritation to the nervous system and affect any number of body organs, structures, and functions," says Charles. "For example, vertebra number 2C, the second from the top of the spine, can affect nerves that go to the eyes, optic nerves, auditory nerves, sinuses, mastoid bones, tongue, and forehead. We don't know whether all doctors agree with this or not, but we have noticed that when God makes an adjustment in upper or lower spinal areas through rotation of the pelvis, hundreds of backs have been healed, and other conditions, such as eye problems, have been corrected."

<table>
<tr><td>CHAPTER

7</td><td>Ailing Friends</td></tr>
</table>

The attempt and not the dead confounds us.
—Shakespeare, *Macbeth*

IT'S ONE THING to be told you have eighteen months to live and to suffer quietly with the knowledge in the bosom of your family. It must be quite another to hold a press conference behind TV floodlights and smilingly dissect your mortality for the world, answering questions such as "Could you have less than eighteen months?" and "Do you think you can still do your job?"

But none of this fazed the mayor of Erie. "I'm fully capable of discharging my duties as mayor," Tullio had told reporters, and everyone, even longtime political enemies, had to agree. He could get as much done in four hours as most people could in twelve.

"I'm going to beat this," the mayor promised. "I told my doctor, 'There's no such thing as an incurable disease because God created this body and He can cure it.'"

Years before, when Tullio was business manager of the Erie School District, he and Erie architect Joe Restifo were driving from Erie to Harrisburg, the Pennsylvania capital, to get plans for a school construction job approved. Restifo was driving Tullio's car. Tullio fell asleep. Then Restifo fell asleep. The car sidewiped the center guardrail on the Pennsylvania Turnpike with a loud screech of metal that woke them both up.

"Are you okay?" the mayor asked when the car finally banged to a stop against the guardrail.

"I'm fine," the shaken Restifo said.

"Good," the mayor said. "You can keep driving then." Tullio went back to sleep.

48

Tullio knew that with all the adrenaline in Restifo's system, Restifo wouldn't fall asleep again.

Years later, Tullio would decide to handle his amyloidosis the same way, letting God do the driving this time. But on this trip, he'd ask his friend Richard Caliguiri to come along for the ride.

The October 26, 1987, issue of *Time* magazine carried this brief piece in its "Milestones" section:

AILING. Louis Tullio, 71, and Richard Caliguiri, 56, mayors of Erie and Pittsburgh, respectively, both with amyloidosis, an incurable, fatal disease that attacks such organs as the kidneys, heart and liver or the nervous system. The fact that two Pennsylvania mayors have fallen victim to the rare affliction, which has no known cause, was seen by medical experts as an unexplainable coincidence.

The two had been friends for years, as mayors of the second- and third-largest cities in Pennsylvania. Tullio first heard of amyloidosis from Caliguiri when the two mayors joined a walking tour of South Philadelphia with Philadelphia mayor Wilson Goode in the summer of 1987.

Caliguiri noticed Tullio was tiring easily and wondered aloud if it could be related to amyloidosis. The Pittsburgh mayor had already been told by doctors he had the disease himself, but he had not made his illness public at the time. Later, Tullio's doctors confirmed the Erie mayor also had the same strange disease.

"Ever since I became mayor, we leaned on each other a lot," Caliguiri said in a November 27, 1987, *Pittsburgh Press* article about Tullio. "Before we decided what issues to push or what candidates to endorse statewide, we would talk about it because we thought we would be stronger if we worked together. We are bolstering each other in the same way now, with this illness."

I hated to read about the mayor's impending death. Having spent all of my adult life with Tullio as mayor of Erie, it was hard to accept. He was an institution, a part of the city itself, and in a way, a part of all of us.

When I thought about his illness, I couldn't help thinking about a little boy named Gary I'd made friends with in the children's hospital.

Gary had a crew cut, rail thin arms, and fingers that had curled into claws, the legacy of polio. He looked so frail, we were sure he was dying. I didn't want to see that happen.

So at night, after the nurse had made her rounds, Gary and I would go down to the foots of our beds, and he would extend his hand across the aisle toward me. I'd clasp it hard and pull, until the old rollers squeaked and rattled on the cold tile floor and the ends of our beds would come slowly together.

His hand always felt so warm in the darkness.

I'd just be able to make out the sleeve of Gary's hospital smock riding up on his thin, bony arm, looking out of the corners of my eyes. I'd discovered that you could see better in the dark that way. Over near the window, the little ones would be sleeping, bars of light from the lamp outside falling across their backs.

I'd lift one leg over the railings of our beds and then draw the other one after, rolling onto my back into Gary's bed with a soft thud. (There was no telling how much damage all the moving was doing to my hip, scraping away the newly mineralized bone, and how much it was prolonging my hospital stay, but at the time I didn't know any better.)

Then we'd begin his therapy. I'd take one of his hands and slowly work at the curled fingers, bending them gradually back, trying to straighten them. But they never straightened. It felt like his fingers had taut steel wires in them, keeping them curled. I'd keep working at them, though, thinking that if we kept flexing his fingers long enough, the wires inside would stretch and we could gradually get them to uncurl, and then his hands would be flat, like mine. First one hand, for fifteen minutes or so, and then the other. Gary would cry softly the whole time because it hurt so much. But I would promise him it would all be worth it. I would help him to live and be healthy.

He wanted his hands to be uncurled because he was the prayer leader of the boys' ward, the one who led us in our prayers on Sunday. We had no priests or ministers coming into the hospital on the Sabbath, but Gary did just fine, leading us in prayer from his bed. I think his father was a minister. Gary knew all the prayers, but he hated to raise his ugly hands to God.

I never could get his fingers to straighten out, despite all the pain I caused him, no matter how much I wanted him to be well.

I guess there always has been a meddlesome part of me that wants everybody to have straight fingers like mine, and I guess that's why I suggested to Mayor Tullio that he should go to see Charles and Frances Hunter, and why I later took it upon myself to set up the meeting with the Hunters and the two mayors. How could it hurt?

When I suggested to the mayor that he might want to visit the Hunters, he loved the idea. "When do we do it, coach?" the former football player said. "You set it up." He hesitated only for a second before he said, "And I'll see if I can get Caliguiri to go with me. They can do us both at one time."

That was typical Tullio. If he'd had the time, he probably would have arranged for half of his City Hall employees to go with him to see the Hunters, all piled into the same car. "You got arthritis? Come see these faith healers with me. . . . You got a sore finger? Hey, you can come see the guys who are gonna fix me up."

For his whole twenty-three years as mayor, Tullio had always been the type of guy to wrap his arms around someone and say, "Hey, come on with me . . . while we work this thing out." His office door was always open, his phone was always listed.

Tullio called Caliguiri. "He's a little skeptical," the mayor said afterward. "His wife is all for it, she wants to try anything, but he's a little skeptical. I think maybe I can bring him around, though."

Tullio said he was going to have Charles and Frances Hunter lay hands on him whether Caliguiri did or not. The Hunters, meanwhile, would be in Buffalo for a healing service on December 13, 1987, and had agreed to meet with Tullio, or Tullio and Caliguiri both, at any place of their choosing, on December 12. They would fly to wherever the mayors wanted to meet, Frances said.

"We've only made a trip to minister to individuals one other time," Frances told me on the phone when I was making arrangements. "But I believe something special will come out of this. The Holy Spirit wants us to get together with these two mayors and just make one *tremendous* miracle, praise the Lord."

Tullio had suggested to Caliguiri that we could all meet in his office at Pittsburgh City Hall, or in a Pittsburgh hotel—anyplace that Caliguiri wanted. Finally, about a week before Tullio was scheduled to meet the Hunters, Caliguiri made up his mind. He said he wanted Charles and Frances to minister to him also, and would be glad to meet anyplace convenient for everybody.

The Royce Hotel was near the Pittsburgh airport. The Hunters would be staying at that hotel overnight. We decided that the easiest thing for everybody, and the most private way to handle it, would be to meet the Hunters at their hotel.

"We'll have a big suite," said Frances. "We can do the healing right there."

At this point I hadn't told anyone in the office about the book or the plans to have the mayors meet with the faith healers except Tony Zona, my city editor and friend of seventeen years. For as much of a hard nose as he is—his nose had been broken at least once in fights in his little Pennsylvania hometown of Ellwood City—and as gruff and grounded in the real world as he is, he's got a spiritual side that not many people know about. He was intrigued by the project and said he wouldn't be the least bit surprised if the Hunters could help the mayors.

He comes up to my desk one day and rests his elbows on top of my computer terminal.

"It's lunchtime. Wanna go across the street?" He has a look in his eye that says, "Fill me in."

"The chill factor is ten below," I answer.

"Come on, you wimp," Zona says. He's got his cowboy hat on and means business.

He talks me into it because going with Zona to McDonald's is always worth the price of admission.

"Hi, welcome to McDonald's. Can I help you?"

"A cheeseburger, regular fries, and a chocolate shake, please," Zona says.

A little high-school girl with curly blond hair and dimples punches in his order, then smiles brightly and asks in a "Hi, I'm Teddy Ruxpin, can you and I be friends?"-doll voice, "Would you like to try one of our strawberry McMuffins today?" while her ringlets bobble at her shoulders.

I brace myself for one of Zona's *Mac Attacks*.

"Why are you asking me that?" he says grimly.

"Sir?"

"Why are you asking me that? I told you what I wanted."

"Yes, but—"

"If I would have wanted a strawberry McMuffin I would have asked for one."

"Well, we're supposed to—"

"I'm only interested in eating what I want to eat, not what Mc-Donald's wants me to eat, thank you," Zona says, smiling through rubber band-tight lips.

It's the principle of the thing that bugs him. All the people in the country trying to keep their weight down and stay healthy and here's McDonald's trying to shove greasy food down your throat to make a buck. And besides, for the amount they charge for that food, let them clear their own tables and dump the trays in their Ronald McDonald trash barrels. He's not paid to be a busboy.

"Yessir," she says, and slinks over to scoop up his fries from the stainless-steel frier.

"Thought I had them all trained. Must have missed one. So tell me, what's new with the mayors—" He stops suddenly, turns white, and puts his hand to his chest.

Heart attack!

"There's two times you gotta put your hand over your heart," he says calmly. "One is for the pledge of allegiance."

"Huh?"

"The other is when something like that walks in the door. Check it out." He nods his cowboy hat toward the door. The Marlboro man scanning the prairie. He gets ready to ride. He's neglected, however, to notice that we have no prairies around Erie, Pennsylvania. All we have is a great, big lake.

He's staring at a woman with very long legs. She's wearing a fur miniskirt. She's just gotten out of a gold Camaro. She has glorious blond hair. She is unabashedly beautiful, with the sort of fresh young face most men choose for their midlife crises. (Zona had given me hope, though, that midlife hormone storms don't loom on every man's horizon. He was five years older than I, and despite all his talk, the worst that had happened to him was breaking out in a rash of strange new hats.)

A male cashier, about sixteen years old, appears from out of nowhere. The boy is sweating testosterone.

As the woman decides what to order, she shifts her weight from one leg to the other, making her hips go up and down. The young cashier is trying to smile, but he can't move his mouth. He keeps wiping his hand on his apron.

Finally she orders, pays, and drops a nickel by her hip on the stainless steel counter. The boy looks at her hip. She leaves the nickel there, and then with a milkshake in one hand and her bag of chicken McNuggets in the other, she moves slowly away from the counter and wafts toward the door. As her hand touches the glass handle and makes it hot, she turns her head to smile at the boy over her shoulder, gives a shake to her blond mane, and leaves. The boy's thoughts go with her to the secret recesses of the places where she is going.

Zona starts clapping softly, his sandwich bag tucked under his armpit.

"Let's hear it for her parents," he says, nodding to me and the boy.

We all feel obliged to clap.

"She makes my jaws sweat, right back in the joints," Zona says. "So. Your book about healing and all that spiritual stuff. How's it going?"

CHAPTER	Which World
8	to Choose?

But each for the joy of working, and
each in his separate star,
Shall draw the Thing as he sees it for
the God of Things as They are.
—Rudyard Kipling, *When
Earth's Last Picture Is
Painted*

DO WE LIVE in a cold, brittle, technological, thoroughly impersonal world, interpreted for us by pop astronomer Carl Sagan, where all that happens is influenced by natural causes without interference from a Supreme Being?

Or do we live in a warm and friendly place, interpreted for us by holy books—an environment constantly open to God's presence and subject to His power, a world where people like the Happy Hunters can help work miracles?

Those are the two worldviews, or paradigms, between which we all must choose, and ever since our experience with the Hunters in Jamestown, I felt like I was hung up somewhere in between.

Going to McDonald's and looking at blondes with my city editor after immersing myself for a weekend in Bibles and books on divine healing was a typical example.

We'd walk back to the office while talking about how a homeless man shot a Dallas cop in the face several times with the cop's own gun while the cop pleaded for his life and onlookers cried "Shoot him again!" Then a few hours later I'd talk to someone like Joppa Wiese, who would make me think, Well, maybe God does intervene in this mess, after all.

Which world to choose? The two seemed so far apart.

There's a famous drawing that Gestalt psychologists show their students that typified my state of mind. It's a picture of a witch. But if you

54

look at her picture long enough, she turns into a pretty young woman wearing a fur. And once you notice the beautiful woman, she's all you can see.

But walk away from the drawing, and the next time you see it, the witch is back. You have to search again for the beautiful woman.

That's the way my spiritual life had become despite my healing experience with Charles and Frances. One minute I was a skeptic, rooted in the world and the newspaper, cynical, seeing only the witch. The next, after hearing of a particularly wondrous healing or reading certain passages in Scripture, I wondered how I could ever see anything but the beautiful woman again.

A devil appearing in Joppa Wiese's doorway? Good grief.

But wiser men than myself have believed in the Evil One—Martin Luther, for instance, who led the Protestant Reformation in Germany. He said he battled with Satan, and people tell the story of how Luther even threw an inkpot at the devil once. The ink spot is supposedly still on the wall of the room where he slept.

What about Jesus, who said he confronted Satan? Do we believe him or don't we? Are we just to believe some parts of Christianity while denying the things we think might cause us embarrassment? Is it the truth that we believe? Or is it just what we've been taught, the things that others believe?

*　　*　　*

Our city room is like a Saragasso Sea for lost relics like plastic flowers, chipped glass vases, Pearle eyeglass cases, discarded books, and every once in a while, a stray article of clothing or two that drifts into the room from the outside world. We've had a pair of women's boots that came from who-knows-where reposing in the cloakroom for two years now. I think maybe their owner died.

Then there's all the mail that drifts in, addressed to people who worked at the paper years ago but who have since retired or died; the old photos of former movers and shakers lying here and there around the place, curling at the edges and turning brown; the stacks of old city directories that repose with their outdated data on top of stacks of old papers on the file cabinets in the morgue.

Sometimes I think my mind is like the city room, where it floats for so many hours each day. Bits of flotsam and jetsam, particles of ideas and concepts, drift in and stay there. Some stay forever and become part of me. Some drift in and stay for a little while, then get caught in an eddy and are sucked back out as quickly as they came in.

My wife tells me we all go through this—acquiring beliefs, living with them for a while, examining them, keeping some of them, and then discarding the rest to replace them with new ones. The book and the research I have to do for it to meet a nine-month deadline are just accelerating the process for me, she says.

Maybe so, but it's spiritually exhausting. I'm working out the destiny of my immortal soul, having come to believe I do indeed have one.

Satan?

Hadn't thought of him for years.

But there are millions of people out there who believe his influence on our lives is just as real as God's. I certainly don't want to go around seeing devils behind every bush, but what if, just what if, Lucifer, Satan, Beelzebub, Iblis, Eblis—he was called Demogorgon in the fourth century B.C.—really does intervene directly in our lives, putting potentially danger ous thoughts about wafting blondes in our minds, oppressing us with everything from lustful thoughts to jealousy to obsessions?

If God can talk to men, why can't His opposite do the same?

Given a choice, I'd rather stop thinking about it and install an anchor locker in the boat for next sailing season. But this book won't let me do either.

"A great deal of people's anxiety is expended on trying to reconcile these two pictures, or trying to decide which one is real," the late columnist Sidney Harris wrote, referring to the witch-beautiful lady drawing.

That certainly is true in my case. I am the poster child for obsessive-compulsive behavior. I've never been comfortable with ambiguity.

"Your problem is, you analyze things too much," Debbie says. "We've all got to take a leap of faith at some point. But fifty years from now you'll still be going over all the pros and cons, wondering whether you'll look foolish if you try to jump or not."

My wife is like one of those sleek U.S. Coast Guard icebreakers that work Lake Erie. Looking at the vast ice field ahead, I can't see how she'll ever make it through.

But she cuts neatly through the craggy mass like a knife through a Betty Crocker pie crust.

She *progresses* through the ice, slab by slab, like she's knifing through an expansive white sidewalk, a sidewalk leading to God-knows-where, and she crunches each slab asunder as she passes over and through it, shattering pieces of the white cement and sending them tumbling alongside her hull.

She doesn't falter. She hardly shudders with the impact.She just does what she was made to do. She breaks the ice. She *progresses*. She doesn't let anything stop her. This ship, my wife, should be named *Faith*.

And me? I'm just a crew member, along for the ride.

Debbie looks at me with her sweet, beautiful, wide-open brown eyes, eyes that say, "It's so easy to . . . believe. Why can't you do it?"

So many women are Lake Erie icebreakers when it comes to faith.

They do what they were meant to do. They forge ahead. They *believe*. They *progress*.

("*You're not* going to compare me to an icebreaker, are you?"
"Well, I was thinking—"
"What do you mean, 'sleek?' Icebreakers aren't sleek."
"Well, sort of, they are—"
"Those Great Lakes icebreakers are really called 'icebreaking tugs.' "
"That's true, but—"
"So you're comparing me to a tugboat?"
"All boats are feminine—"
"A tugboat? You're comparing me to a tugboat?")

*   *   *

Sometimes I wonder about all the people who talk to God and have such very serious conversations—seventy-four-year-old evangelist Lester Sumrall, for instance, who entered into a worldwide ministry of missionary evangelism in 1934, who believes in healing and laying on of hands.

I'd heard him tell a group of Erie pastors that at ten minutes to midnight one night God woke him up and told him that He wanted Sumrall to organize his ministry so he could feed the world's poor and starving, *with financial help from pastors just like those in this room.*

"So what's your point?" Debbie asked when I told her this story.

"I just wonder why, when God talks to these people, he never seems to lighten up a little. He's always talking about weighty matters like world hunger and asking for money."

Debbie shook her head and squeezed my hand. "You want a God who wakes you up at 3:00 A.M. to say, "Yo! Jack! Didja hear the one about the guy who walked into a bar with a turkey on his head?"

She smiled. "You know, you're writing and creating this book. But with all the reading you'll have to do, all the people you'll talk to, all the ideas churning around in your head, the book will create you, too. I don't think you'll be the same person when you get through."

The book creates me as I'm creating it. How very Möbiuslike.

*   *   *

We're talking about God on the living-room couch. Ian comes toddling up to us, lifts up Debbie's red sweater, and shouts, Pun-aah! PUN-AAH! and grabs for her tummy. Pun-aah is his word for belly button. He's lifting Debbie's sweater to stick one of his tiny fingers into her pun-aah.

PUN-AAH!

There's no one like our Miracle Baby when it comes to dragging our minds out of the cosmos, back to everyday organic reality.

He likes to compare his pun-aah! to everyone else's pun-aah! At a party, you've got to watch him because before you know it, he's got his hand up some woman's sweater, looking for her belly button.

"PUN-AAH!"

People tell us, because of the circumstances of Ian's birth, that he is a special baby. Frances Hunter keeps saying, "The Lord has his hand on that child." Charles Hunter says Ian is anointed because of "the light his story brought into the world." Our born-again Christian friends keep saying, "You watch and see what God has in store for him." Even Joppa Wiese says Ian is one of God's chosen, that "he'll live up to his name."

The Hebrews attached great significance to choosing a name for a newborn child because they believed the name often indicated the role the child would play in the family or the history of the people.

And in the New Testament, the angel Gabriel tells Zacharias that his wife, Elizabeth, who was old and barren, would bear a son. "And you are to name him John," Gabriel told Zacharias. The name would indicate that the child was specially chosen from the moment of birth to play a unique role in the plan of salvation.

"He will soften adult hearts to become like little children's and will change disobedient minds to the wisdom of faith," the angel said. The child would grow up to become John the Baptist.

How odd it was, Debbie and I often said, that we chose for a son the name Ian, Scottish for John, so many years before that son was born.

"God's gracious gift," the name John means in Hebrew.

"When you have this baby, remember what the Bible says—all good and perfect gifts come from Jesus," Frances Hunter had said.

"God's Gift," the inscription under the picture on the birthing room wall had read.

And how odd that we would choose a name "John" and later be healed of barrenness, just as John the Baptist's mother was healed of her own barrenness after so many years. (Ian's middle name, "Christian," was just our way of saying "Thank you.")

Ian's story appeared for the first time in our Sunday newspaper on Pentecost Sunday 1986, completely by accident—I simply handed it in when it was finished, and Sunday, May 18, was the first Sunday we had space for it. Pentecost Sunday, of course, is when the apostles received the gift of healing from the Holy Spirit: "A deep sense of awe was on them all, and the apostles did many miracles."

"It wasn't published then just by accident. God has his hand on every detail of your baby's life," Mayor Tullio's wife, Grace, told me. She is a very devout Christian who probably was born again at birth. "God has great plans for Ian Christian."

"PUN-AHH!"

I don't know if Ian will wear clothing made of camel hair and eat locusts and wild honey when he grows up, but already, judging by the response to his story in our newspaper, *McCall's*, and on the Regis Philbin show, he may very well have softened quite a few hearts.

"PUN-AHH!"

Whatever other plans God has for the baby, they no doubt include belly buttons.

One baby I came across in my research for this book who certainly appeared to have had a divine calling was Linda Martel of the Channel Islands. She wasn't the least concerned with belly buttons, but she was obsessed with sickness, according to those who knew her. She was probably the youngest "faith healer" ever. She was just two years old when she performed her first cure.

When she died from renal complications at age five on October 20, 1961, more than a thousand people attended her funeral on the island of Guernsey in the English Channel, where she had spent her life healing thousands of island residents and travelers from abroad of everything from acute asthma to heart problems.

Maybe because of her closeness in age to Ian, I was fascinated with her story, told in *The Legend of Linda Martel*, a slim yellow clothbound book written by Charles Graves and published in 1968 by Icon Books Ltd. of London, England. Graves, another skeptical reporter, was a journalist on the staff of the *London Daily Mail*, and as a columnist he had frequently ridiculed faith healing. Then he moved to Guernsey and became fascinated by the stories he heard of the little girl. Included in this enchanting book are a number of photos of Linda at age four—photos showing a beautiful little cherub with a button nose; a wonderfully innocent smile; teeth like little pearls; plump little cheeks, and huge, bright eyes that would seem to look right through you. In one photo the little healer is shown holding a huge white teddy bear.

The strange, beautiful little child in these photos leaves an indelible imprint in the mind of anyone who sees them.

Graves's book is apparently out of print now, but I think Linda Martel's sad, haunting, mystical story is one that deserves a retelling.

In Memory of Linda Martel

BORN 21st August 1956,
DIED 20th October 1961
Making someone well and happy
In your own special way,
Is how you let His Kingdom come,
Today and everyday.

—Epitaph on the
tombstone of child healer
Linda Martel

ON THE DAY Linda was born on August 21, 1956, her doctor sadly told her father, Roy, that Linda had water on the brain, spina bifida, and that her legs were paralyzed.

When his daughter was three months old, Roy Martel was lying in bed one night, and in the early hours of the morning, there was a wind: "Only the sound, not the feel of a wind. Then a light. Not a light that one can define, really; the room was lit with a glow, and it was not from outside, either. I called out, 'Who's there?' but received no reply . . . the room stayed like that for perhaps thirty seconds or more, then the glow disappeared."

The wind bloweth where it listeth . . .

When Linda was seventeen months old, after having had a shunt successfully implanted to treat her hydrocephalus, Roy Martel was in the dining room with her. She was lying on a cot when he heard a woman's voice say, "Hello, little girl."

"I turned, and there wasn't a soul there!" said Martel. "I felt the hair rise up on the back of my neck right to the top of my scalp."

Linda's mother, Eileen, in the kitchen, had heard the same thing. "I heard a lovely voice say, 'Hello, little girl.'"

But there was no one there. As Linda's father says, it was a forerunner of things to come.

Roy Martel had suffered for years with migraine headaches. One night in 1958 he came home, and with his head hurting so much he could barely stand it, he went straight to bed. As he lay there, little Linda called from another room, "Have you got a headache, Roy? Come and see me. I will make it better for you."

The child always called both parents by their first names. She did not speak like a child.

When her father knelt before her, she placed her hand exactly on the side of her father's head where the pain was situated. Usually, when he got these headaches, nothing would help. He had taken as many as fourteen aspirin at once with no relief. But much to his surprise, the excruciating pain disappeared at her touch, and from that day on he never suffered another migraine.

A few months later, Linda's brother Peter lay in bed with a bad case of flu and a dangerously high fever.

"Peter is sick," said Linda. "I will see to him."

Peter was called out to see his sister. She passed her hand over his forehead and said, "You will be all better now, Pete." And within fifteen minutes Peter was up and dressed, his fever completely gone.

A couple days later, Linda turned to her father and said, "Roy, it's my lady who looks after me, she comes to see me, you know." She would later become more specific, describing the "lady" as "the Lady of Lourdes," astounding everybody, since Linda had not been raised a Catholic, had rarely been in a church, and certainly had heard nothing about the shrine at Lourdes. She was only two years old.

Roy Martel couldn't help but think of the gentle breeze and the light that had appeared in the room, and the voice that came from nowhere and said, "Hello, little girl." Every night, when Linda was in bed, her parents could hear her talking, as if someone were in her room. And the next morning she would say, "My Lady came to see me last night."

Soon neighbors began to seek Linda out for mild ailments, and word spread through the forty-seven thousand inhabitants of the Isle of Guernsey that the child had the gift of healing. Linda never waited to be told what the pain or illness was. She always *knew*. She would tell the person where he hurt and why, then touch him on the exact spot or mention the place which was causing the trouble.

A reporter and photographer from the *London Daily Herald* arrived on the island to do a story on Linda and watched as she healed Elma Bougourd, seventy-six, of sciatica. She had been in intense pain for years and was barely able to walk. Immediately, Linda went to the woman's hip. "I know the spot," Linda said. "You will be all better now." She touched the woman and the pain left, never to return.

"The lady is better," said Linda.

"I SEE A MIRACLE," read the headline on the reporter's *Daily Herald* story.

In the next two years, hundreds of people came knocking on her door, and many of them, as in the following examples, went away healed.

Keith Woodhouse went to see Linda with his father when he was six, suffering from chronic asthma and eczema. "She didn't know what we'd come down for, whatsoever," his father said. "Then she looked across at Keith and said, 'Is your chest bad, Keith? I want to put my hand on Keith's chest.'" Hours later, her fingermarks were still on Keith's chest where she touched him. His asthma and eczema vanished immediately.

Baby Howarth. This baby was crying when Linda saw her, having had continuous colic for weeks. Linda went to her and dug her fingers into the baby's stomach, whereupon the baby had a huge and immediate bowel movement and stopped crying. Linda turned to the baby's mother and said, "It wasn't only her stomach, you know . . . it was also her toes." Linda massaged the baby's toes, the baby fell asleep, slept for twelve hours afterward, and had no more colic.

Roy Vernon was a baby born with a hole in his heart. Without being told what was wrong with the baby, Linda said he was "a very sick boy" and had "a very bad heart." She put her hand over his heart and said, "He will be all better now." Although he had been expected to die, Roy lived as a healthy little boy and had no further heart problems.

David King was a baby with projectile vomiting who was wasting away because he couldn't keep his food down. Linda told his mother to lift up the baby's undershirt, then touched the area between the stomach and chest and said, "That is the spot." The baby immediately stopped crying, and his projectile vomiting was ended.

"There was no need for faith where Linda was concerned," her father said, "because the children who came were too young to understand . . ."

"Linda was an extraordinary, lovable child," a neighbor of the Martels said. "She had a strange, deep voice, which one would never expect of a child of her age. Her eyes were also strange and full of love. She seemed able to read your mind and yet gave you a terrific sense of peace. This power was given to Linda to show that Christ's healing can still be done."

Somehow Linda's power even extended to photographs.

George Shepherd of St. Peter Port tells how he and his wife went to see Linda because his wife was having shoulder problems. As soon as they walked into the house, Linda said, "You have a pain in your left shoulder," although no one had told Linda anything about the woman's condition. Linda remarked that the woman was also worried, which the lady admitted was true. Her granddaughter had just had an operation. When shown a photograph of the grandchild, Linda touched the baby on the throat in the picture and said, "That's where she's had the operation and she'll be all better. Not to worry, things will work out all right."

"Our grandchild had just come home from the hospital and they had put a silver tube into her throat to enable her to breathe," Shepherd said. "But later on, the child coughed out the tube and began breathing perfectly without it."

By looking at a photo, Linda could even tell if someone were dead. "If you gave her a photograph of a group, she'd tell you who was dead in it by saying, "He's with my Jesus Christ," Martel wrote. And Linda was never wrong.

Although just a child, Linda never claimed any of the cures for herself. It was always Jesus Christ, or the Lady of Lourdes with Jesus, who helped the sick people.

Often Linda would claim to see Jesus as well as her Lady. One afternoon she said to her mother, "Don't shut the door, Eileen, my Jesus Christ is standing there." Then she put her hands out toward the door and said to the figure that only she could see, "You are beautiful, you know, you are beautiful, you know."

One night the Martels were awakened by Linda, on the cot next to them, saying, "He has got bad feet, bad feet, that will be all right, I will see to his feet."

When the Martels looked at Linda, they could see a soft light by her cot. Eileen Martel described it as a shapeless light, not earthly at all, but more like a glow. "That was as near as we got to an actual vision as far as we were concerned," Roy Martel said.

A few days later, a man with bad feet, ready to be cured, arrived at the Martels' door.

Linda Martel finally did go to Lourdes—but when she was taken to the grotto, there was no cure for her. Her only comment on the statue of the Virgin Mary was, "There is my Lady. Why can't she bend her knees?"

The way she had always seen the Virgin—the light low down by her cot—apparently was on her knees.

One day, little Linda said to her father, "My Jesus Christ has seen to Grandpa Martel's eye in heaven, you know."

"Which eye?" asked her father.

She pointed to her left eye and said, "This one."

"Now, my father had been dead for ten years, that was five years before Linda was ever thought of, so she didn't know him and neither could he know Linda," wrote Roy Martel. "But here she was with the knowledge about his eye, and she was absolutely right, he was blind in his left eye. Now, how could she have known about that? Even her four brothers did not know. I knew, of course, but it had never been discussed."

"Maybe . . . Linda's mission on this earth [was] to make people think and believe," said Roy Martel. "I know that if I ever had any doubts about Jesus Christ, I can assure you that these doubts were quickly dispersed, because Linda knew him so intimately."

"I am not here for my father, you know," little Linda would often say. "I am here for the other people."

"I personally think that Linda was most likely sent here," said Roy Martel, "that she was here to prove to people, and maybe the world, that there is a supreme power. . . ."

One Monday morning, six weeks before Linda died, she said to her mother, "My Lord Jesus Christ told me last night that I will walk next year." At five years of age, she had never walked in her life.

The next day pains started in Linda's back, lasting for four or five minutes at a time, pains so severe that they caused beads of perspiration to drop from her hair, which was saturated. The child would moan softly but would let no one approach her.

"That's quite all right; there is nothing wrong with me. My Jesus Christ is looking after me," she would say.

Eileen said, "Linda, when your Jesus Christ comes, ask him, darling, if he will give us some power for us to comfort you in some way."

The next morning Linda said to her mother. "I asked my Jesus Christ what you told me to ask, and he told me you have nothing to worry about. Everything will be all right; but could I come and sleep in your bed one night, not tonight, Eileen, but one night?"

"Thank you, Linda, and certainly you can come and sleep in our bed whenever you like, darling, you just tell us when you want to."

A few days later, after another siege of pain, Linda asked her father, "Why have people to suffer pain, do you know, Roy?"

"I'm afraid I cannot answer that question, Linda," her father said. "I suppose everyone has to suffer pain at some time or other in their lives."

"These pains are terrible, you know, Roy; they are very awful."

Roy Martel would later write. "It is a dreadful thing to see a child suffer and be unable to do a thing about it, and when it is your own child, it is much worse, especially when one is talking to a five-year-old who has the intelligence of a woman."

The next week, when two visitors stopped by the house, one of them said to Linda, as they left, "Cheerio, see you next week."

But Linda would only say good-bye, which was unusual for her.

That night Eileen Martel asked Linda, "Would you like to come and sleep with us tonight?"

"Thank you very much, Eileen, thank you very much," the child said.

Eileen brought her into the bedroom and put her on the bed. "Will you cuddle me, Roy?" Linda asked.

"Of course I will, Lynne," her father said.

"My Jesus Christ has been to see me; he put both his hands on my chest," Linda said. "My Jesus won't be coming to me anymore," she added. "I am going to him."

At seven the next morning, Linda called to her mother three times: "Mum! Mum! Mum!"

Twenty minutes later, she died in her mother's arms.

The stories of people like Linda Martel* and Joppa Wiese are typical of the tales that abound in the supernatural realm of healing. They seem so strange, yet they indicate that there is apparently another world existing a few steps above the one that the nightly news packages in thirty-minute cans of Reality Concentrate.

How much of it is myth and legend, and how much is real? Because if it is real, I'll have to make some big changes in my life, and I think I'd rather be sailing.

*I was curious as to whether people still remembered Linda Martel. Calls to the Tourist Bureau of St. Peter Port on the Isle of Guernsey and to the Guille-Alles Library there showed that indeed they did, and that little Linda's amazing healings are still being talked about today. I was told that Linda Martel's father, Roy, had died, although her mother was still alive. But when I tried to track down Eileen Martel, sources on Guernsey said she had remarried, taken another name, and "disappeared into obscurity." One woman recalled, "I do remember how people from around the world used to write and ask the Martels for scraps of material from Linda's clothes in hopes that just touching the material she wore would heal them. And the Martels used to send the scraps. This just went on and on, bit by bit at a time, you know, until they had no clothes left of hers at all."

Linda's Lady

> Poor mortals that we are, we are naturally inclined to
> minimize the importance of the spiritual and the eter-
> nal and overrate the physical and the temporal—the
> latter at the cost of the former.
>
> —Father Solanus Casey

WHO WAS this "Our Lady of Lourdes" who looked after little Linda?

Ruth Cranston, a Protestant writer who made numerous visits to Lourdes and who was given complete access to the files of the Medical Bureau of Lourdes, wrote what is recognized as probably the most comprehensive study in English of the Lourdes cures. That book, *The Miracle of Lourdes*, was updated, expanded, and reprinted in 1988 by Doubleday Image Books.

Cranston describes how, on February 11, 1858, Bernadette Soubirous, her sister, and another little peasant girl went looking for firewood not far from the town of Lourdes in southwestern France.

As Bernadette was watching her companions cross a dry millstream, she felt a sudden little puff of wind on her face, like a gentle breeze, a strange wind that seemed to come from all directions at once and yet from nowhere in particular.

The wind bloweth where it listeth, and thou hearest the sound thereof but canst not tell whence it cometh. . . .

A moment later Bernadette saw a golden light radiating from a rock grotto on the far side of the stream. The light was coming from a sort of radiant mist, and finally it formed itself into the image of a very beautiful lady, clad in a white robe with a blue sash. The lady was standing high up on a rock in the grotto above the river.

Bernadette stared dumbstruck, then fell to her knees in prayer.

She returned to the grotto to see the apparition several times, and finally the figure spoke, instructing Bernadette to return to the grotto every day for fifteen days, promising her happiness "in the next world."

On February 25, while kneeling before the grotto, Bernadette suddenly rose from her knees, walked a short distance, then fell to the ground. She began to dig in the dirt with her hands until a small puddle of water appeared. The apparition, which only she could see, had told her to dig there. Over the next few days, the puddle gradually formed into a pool and finally broke forth as a spring. Residents of Lourdes began taking flasks of the spring water home, claiming it could heal any illness that afflicted them.

Soon people from all over came to bathe in the Lourdes waters, and the miracles began—the blind saw, the lame walked, and crippled children were healed. It was reported that even the son of Napoleon III had been cured by the application of Lourdes waters. The emperor himself then ordered that the site remain open to the public.

"Go and tell the priests to build a chapel upon this spot," the apparition told Bernadette. "I want people to come here in procession. . . . Pray—tell them to pray! Prayer and penitence!"

"Go and drink in the spring and wash in it," she had commanded. "I am the Immaculate Conception. I desire the chapel here."

Today the shrine at Lourdes attracts over two million people a year and is one of the greatest pilgrimage centers in the world. The annual visitors include fifty-five thousand registered sick in Lourdes hospitals and fifteen thousand known sick in hotels.

The underground Basilica of St. Pius X, opened in Lourdes in 1958, is the second-largest Roman Catholic church in the world. Only St. Peter's in Rome can accommodate more people.

Every afternoon at 4:00 P.M., throngs of the sick and handicapped enter the valley of the grotto of the Virgin Mary for prayer, song, and hope for a recovery. The water in the grotto has been channeled into fourteen *piscines*, or pools, where those who need healing come to bathe. It is here that the miracles of Lourdes are still occurring, miracles investigated and validated by the Medical Bureau of Lourdes and further substantiated by an organization called the International Medical Committee of Lourdes, whose members include doctors and specialists from other nations as well as France.

The process of confirmation of a church-recognized miracle is a long and arduous one, accounting for the fact that only sixty-four cures have been officially classified by the church as miraculous. But cures have been occurring ever since Bernadette exposed the Lourdes spring. There have been over six thousand claimed recoveries, over two thousand of which have been acknowledged by doctors as inexplicable.

The last miracle at Lourdes was proclaimed by the church on June 17, 1978, in the cure of Serge Perrin of France, cured of multiple stroke syndrome in 1970 at forty-one years of age.

Perrin had lost most of his sight and was so disabled he could not walk or care for himself.

On May 1, 1970, he was in his wheelchair in the Basilica of St. Pius X when, during the anointing of the sick ceremony, he sensed warmth in his toes. The feeling spread to his legs, and a few hours later he was able to see without glasses and could walk unassisted.

Arteriograms had shown blockages in the carotid arteries of his neck prior to his cure. Afterward, the blockages were no longer present.

As many as 174 doctors examined the evidence in Perrin's case and concluded that his cure was extraordinary, verifiable, and permanent.

Cranston describes many cures certified as medically inexplicable by the bureau. Some of the most interesting of these are cures in which diseased organs began to function again while remaining damaged to such an extent that it should have been impossible for them to do so.

One such cure involves Gerard Baillie, an eight-year-old who was cured of blindness at Lourdes in September 1947. The child had been blinded at two years of age by a condition known as bilateral chorioretinitis with double optic atrophy. His optic nerves were completely atrophied, and because these nerves are incapable of regeneration, his condition was diagnosed as "incurable" by a number of doctors.

His parents had placed him in the Institute for Blind Children in Arras, a town in the North of France.

His mother was heartbroken and prayed constantly that her son might somehow live a normal life. Finally, as a last resort, she took him to Lourdes. Nothing happened when she at first immersed him in the healing waters of the shrine.

But the next day, while they were walking down the path of the Way of the Cross, he suddenly regained sight in both eyes. All at once the child began to pick up pieces of wood from the ground and offered them to his mother, looking up into her face. "Oh, Mama, how beautiful you are!" he said. His mother bathed him again in the Lourdes water the day after his cure, and his sight continued to improve.

The Medical Bureau of Lourdes had the boy examined by an ophthalmologist in the city of Tarbes. This doctor certified that the boy's optic nerves were still atrophied and that it still should have been physiologically impossible for him to see.

Yet Gerard could see—not very well, but still he saw. He left the school for the blind, attended a regular school, and credits the Lady of Lourdes for performing a miracle.

Then there's the amazing case of Guy Leydet, a five-year-old French boy who had been stricken with infantile encephalopathy, a disease that left large portions of his brain dead. He had been left a quadriplegic, subject to convulsions, incontinent, and so brain-damaged that he couldn't talk, recognize his parents, dress, or feed himself. He had been this way for over two years.

On October 6, 1946, he was taken to Lourdes by his family and bathed at the shrine. *Immediately* after his immersion he reached for his mother, and in a strong, clear voice, said, "Mama!"

In the next several days he began to talk more and more and regained complete use of his limbs.

His intelligence returned to normal, and he grew up the picture of health.

The case baffled the doctors of the medical bureau. His brain had been so completely destroyed that either he had to have been given a new brain by the cure, or else he was thinking with a brain that, physiologically, should not have been able to function.

Another typical case documented by Cranston is that of Charles McDonald of Dublin, who had entered a hospice for the dying in November 1935. He was diagnosed as having tuberculosis and arthritis of the left shoulder with three abscesses; tuberculosis of the spine with two abscesses; and chronic nephritis characterized by pus, blood, and albumin in his urine. The five abscesses were also giving off pus.

His doctors had told him there was no hope of recovery.

But McDonald made a pilgrimage to Lourdes. He was so ill that he had to travel on a stretcher. Even the slightest movement caused him severe pain.

On September 6, McDonald was lowered into the healing waters and his wounds were cleansed. He *immediately* regained greater mobility than he had had in the past several months of his illness, and was up and walking *the next day*. His pain eventually ceased, and McDonald returned to Ireland, where an examination showed that his tuberculosis, arthritis, and nephritis had all disappeared.

McDonald returned to Lourdes in September 1937. He and his medical files were examined by thirty-two doctors at the medical bureau. Included in his records was a statement from his own doctor saying there was no doubt McDonald had gone to Lourdes suffering from an advanced tubercular condition with complications. The bureau concluded that McDonald's healing, "obtained without the use of medicaments or of any therapeutic agent whatever, is confirmed by one year of excellent health and work. . . . No medical explanation, in the present state of science, can be given, considering the extraordinary rapidity of the healings of these tuberculous affections, judged incurable by the specialists called in to treat him. . . ."

"The longer one stays at Lourdes, the more one is impressed with the literal truth of many passages in the Bible that, of late years, learned critics have insisted we should consider purely allegorical," Cranston wrote.

". . . The man with the palsy, the boy with the deaf and dumb spirit, the woman with the infirmity of twelve years, the soldier's son, the man with the withered arm, and many much worse, are there before our eyes."

*   *   *

"Let's be rational," some people would tell me regarding divine healing. "If you think about it, you know it just can't happen."

But most thinking itself is not rational, according to researchers trying to develop thinking computers.

Uncomplicated statements such as "Debbie gives Jack a Bible" involve a nearly infinite set of presuppositions that we never ponder but accept on faith: Jack and Debbie must be within arm's reach; they are probably in the same country, the same state, the same city, and the same room; the Bible is light enough so that Jack and Debbie can hold it; Jack is more or less alive.

But what if Jack and Debbie were not in the same room or even the same city and Debbie still gave the Bible to Jack?

Then default assumptions must be considered. Maybe she mailed it to him. Maybe she had her sister take it to him. Maybe she photocopied it and had her pet carrier pigeon deliver it page by page.

The number of exceptions and alternate assumptions, called *counterfactuals*, is nearly infinite.

No human or computer could function if he or she or it had to think about every detail of every situation.

In other words, to perform the act of thinking, a person or computer must skip over a staggering number of logical assumptions to make one conclusion.

That sounds like a leap of faith to me.

So far, people are able to do that much better than computers. Humans still are much more advanced than machines in thinking ability.

By the same token, maybe those who have faith, those who can skip over a *very large* array of logical presuppositions to perceive and interpret reality, are simply more advanced in *their* thinking than those who don't.

No wonder I never win arguments with my wife. Even when she makes a mistake, she's smart enough to know it's probably my fault.

*   *   *

"Everything has presuppositions, and despite claims to the contrary, the historical critical method is not neutral," Monsignor William Smith of St. Joseph Seminary in Yonkers, New York, says in the March 21, 1988, issue of *Insight* magazine. "If someone starts convinced that physical resurrection is not possible, he will never find evidence for it." He says modern Bible scholarship and criticism, in an effort to make the Bible understandable and relevant to modern man, has left no place for the physical Resurrection of Christ and the miracles described in the New Testament.

"Only shells of the biblical message are left," he says.

Debbie and I found that many of our Christian friends and acquaintances don't want anything more than the shells of the Bible's message.

People say they believe in concepts such as the Virgin birth, the deity of Christ, and the Resurrection; that in partaking of the Eucharist they are sharing the spiritual body of Christ. They say they believe in the power of prayer. They go to their churches knowing that the rites of exorcism exist within them for ridding souls of demons and evil spirits. Our Catholic friends, especially of the older generation, also believe that saints in heaven can work healing miracles and wouldn't think twice about rubbing the purported bones of St. Jude over their bodies to help cure a severe physical problem.

Those are *all* very strange ideas when you think about them.

But healing and the laying on of hands? Come on! That's Holy Roller stuff.

When Debbie and I tell the story of Ian's birth to our friends—some of whom have since chosen to become our acquaintances—their bemused and amused reactions suggest that most of them want it both ways:

They want to worship an infinite, supernatural God for Whom nothing is impossible; a God Who became flesh and was born of the Virgin Mary, a Christ who rose from the dead.

But they don't want to believe, or are afraid to, that this divine, all-powerful, omniscient, omnipresent Being could do supernatural works in their own lives; and they are indignantly *against* Him working miracles in anybody else's.

They want a circumscribed God to worship, a God made in *their* image.

Not that Debbie and I blame them. We were the same way until our experience in Jamestown.

And anyway, how could I be critical of others when here I was, about to go to Coraopolis with the mayors to see the Hunters, *still* searching for faith myself?

The possibility of divine healing seems strange to many of us who live in the high-tech 1980s. Most baby boomers have little sense of history and the precedent for belief that history provides. Those of us still rooted in the secular world are just now beginning to confront our mortality, but we're still more familiar with instruction manuals for VCRs and laptop computers than we are with Scripture, books on the history of the early church, the healings of Lourdes, the miraculous cures of the saints, and healers such as Gordon Lindsay, Jack Coe, T. L. Osborn, William Branham, Kathryn Kuhlman, Morris Cerullo, and other figures of the healing revivals of this century. For instance, Cerullo, one of the mainstays of revivalism in the 1960s, was credited with converting one million people in 1973 in his crusades. In a five-day period in Los Angeles in 1971, he preached to more than eighteen thousand people and reported two thousand healings. How many people today have even heard of him? And what about the centuries-old tradition of healing in the Roman Catholic church? When an institution as large, and as old, and as rooted, and as conservative as the Roman Catholic church claims to have documented evidence for thousands of healing miracles, you've got to wonder if there might be something to supernatural healing after all.

Part of the church's official process of beatification and canonization of saints includes verification that miracles such as healing cures have occurred. A number of these cases are described in the fascinating book *Miracles: A Parascientfic Inquiry into Wondrous Phenomena*, written by D. Scott Rogo and published by Contemporary Books, Inc., Chicago, in 1983. (Healing of the saints is among the tamer phenomena described by Rogo, who examines everything from saintly levitation to bilocation, the purported ability to be in two places—in the flesh—at the same time.)

The cures of St. Martin de Porres, 1579–1639, are good examples of saint-assisted healing.

Two of these healings, which occurred after he died, were decreed valid by the Vatican in 1836.

The first of these concerned a Lima housewife whose eye was pierced by a sliver from an earthenware jar she had broken. The vitreous humor, the fluid in the eyeball, leaked out through the wound, and the woman was left incurably blind.

But the abbot of a nearby monastery sent her a small bone fragment, a relic of St. Martin. She held the bone to her injured eye and awoke the next morning to find her eye and sight totally restored. Although this was medically impossible, the cure was authenticated by the woman's own doctor, who had examined the original wound.

The second healing that led to St. Martin's beatification involved a two-year-old child who fell eighteen feet from a balcony and split open his head. The child went into convulsions and a doctor was called. He told the child's mother there was no hope for her son.

With nothing to lose, the mother prayed to Martin de Porres. The woman's employer, a noble Spanish woman, joined her in prayer and placed a portrait of the saint under the boy's head. Three hours later the boy walked away from his bed, completely recovered.

The evidence supporting these two cures was sent to Rome and was approved by Pope Gregory XVI on March 19, 1836.

In 1961, a more recent cure was examined by the medical college of the Sacred Congregation of Rites, a Vatican body charged with investigating reports of miracles.

On August 25, 1956, in Tenerife in the Canary Islands, a four-and-a-half-year-old boy named Anthony Cabrera Perez fell from a wall at a construction site. A block of cement weighing 70 pounds, which had broken from the wall when the boy lost his balance, landed directly on his leg. The flesh and the bone of the leg were crushed. Gangrene set in. The child had been sent to St. Eulalia's Hospital in Tenerife, where four doctors examined the boy and agreed that the leg had to be amputated to save his life. But on September 1, a friend of the Perez family flew to the Canary Islands from Madrid and gave the boy's parents a picture of St. Martin and urged them to pray to the saint.

The next morning, the doctors found that the boy's gangrene had completely disappeared during the night and that the blood had begun circulating normally through the leg. Anthony was soon completely recovered.

This cure was officially described as miraculous in March 1962 by Pope John XXIII.

Also well documented by the church are the cures of Mother Francesca Cabrini, 1850–1917, an Italian-born nun, one of only three Americans to be canonized.

The most famous of these involves the baby Peter Smith, born March 14, 1921, in Columbus Hospital Extension in New York. This healing is described by Theodore Maynard in his book *Too Small a World: The Life of Francesca Cabrini.*

As a matter of routine, the hospital nurse put a solution of silver nitrate into the newborn's eyes, but by accident, she had placed a 50 percent solution of silver nitrate into the baby's eyes instead of a 1 percent solution. That meant Peter's eyes had been irreparably damaged. She tried to wipe the solution away, but it was no use. The harm had been done. She rushed the baby to the nun in charge of the floor, screaming, "Sister, sister! Come and do something! I've done a dreadful thing! Get a doctor!"

Not one, but two doctors were called. They examined the baby's eyes and then looked at the bottle of silver nitrate, shaking their heads. The nurse had stayed, hoping against hope that there had been some mistake in labeling the bottle and that somehow the baby's eyes would be spared.

But an eye specialist was called, and he verified what the other doctors had found. "The cornea has gone," he said. "Nobody can do anything."

The mother superior hurried in. Perhaps something could be done, after all. She placed a relic of Mother Cabrini over little Peter's eyes before pinning it to his nightgown.

That night, she and the sisters spent the entire night in prayer at the chapel.

The next morning, the doctors came again. One of them leaned toward the other after he had examined the baby, and said, "Am I seeing things?"

The other doctor bent over and looked into the baby's eyes with his light. "No, *you* are not seeing things, but he is. Those eyes are intact and perfectly normal." He marveled as he said this, because lines had been burned into the baby's face at the corners of his eyes from where the silver nitrate had run down.

But the very same day, little Peter came down with double pneumonia. He had a temperature of 108.

The sisters sent for the doctors again. "Well, a degree less than that is invariably fatal," one of them said to the mother superior. "Mother, you'll have to do some more praying. Even though those burns have not harmed the baby, this fever will burn him to death."

"Doctor," the mother superior said, "Mother Cabrini has not cured his eyes just to let him die of pneumonia."

They prayed again, thankful for the first miracle.

By morning, all the symptoms of pneumonia had gone.

When the doctors came again, one said, "I never knew of such a thing. Why, that child is perfectly all right. Not a trace of high temperature!"

"Look how he's sleeping," said the other. "Mother, your Mother Cabrini can certainly do extraordinary things!"

Mother Francesca Xavier Cabrini was beatified in the Vatican Basilica on November 13, 1938. In his homily, Pope Pius XII said, referring to Mother Cabrini's works and healings:

"While human beings are transitory and all grow old little by little and fall in ruin, the glories, the initiatives, and the works that flow from Christian holiness, on the other hand, not only are preserved with the passage of time but also prosper and flourish, sustained by a marvelous force.

"Similar to grain, to the mustard seed, which is the smallest of all seeds, but which, when planted, develops and becomes the largest of plants, so they grow every day and in the end invade the whole world."

*   *   *

Healings of saints-to-be are still being documented today, as in the cases of Monsignor Nelson H. Baker of Buffalo, who worked a number of healing miracles during the 1920s, and Father Solanus Casey of Detroit, a Capuchin monk who died thirty-one years ago.

Many miracles are attributed to Monsignor Baker, who was born in Buffalo in 1841. These include the healing of a twenty-three-year-old Brooklyn woman who had been paralyzed and in a wheelchair since age five, and an elderly Buffalo woman unable to walk because of spinal problems.

Father Solanus Casey was born in 1870 near Prescott, Wisconsin.

A secretary named Dorothy, who knew him at St. Bonaventure Monastery in Detroit, Michigan, told me, "He was one saint who did many miracles while he was alive, thousands of them. Before the Salk vaccine and TB vaccines, he healed many, many people of polio and tuberculosis.

"Father Solanus would bless them, and they would be healed. It was as simple as that. Sometimes people would just call over the phone and cry, and he would pray, and things would happen, and they would be healed."

Father Casey died on July 31, 1957. His body, exhumed in 1987, was found to be in a state of perfect preservation, according to those involved in his cause.

Canonization for Father Casey is imminent, and it is expected soon for Monsignor Baker.

Many of those healed by Monsignor Baker and Father Casey are still living, and are being interviewed by the church as part of the beatification and canonization processes.

"Just like the saints drew people to Christ when they were alive, they continue to do so after they're dead," said Dorothy. "Saints are there to inspire us to be fully ourselves. They increase our faith, our hope, our virtue, and finally, our eternal reward."

She said that most of Father Casey's healings were *not* instantaneous. "He encouraged people in faith and hope, and people would get the gift of faith that moves mountains. Then things would happen. Faith is so important."

Many fundamentalists I've talked with bristle when they hear about the intervention of the saints or the Virgin Mary, but a friend of mine who's a Catholic priest explained it this way:

"We believe that although dead, the saints still exist with God. We have prayer groups here among the living, where a number of people, or even a whole church, will be asked to pray for someone who is sick. As far as the intercession of the saints goes, we simply are asking the saints in heaven to join with us in our prayer group. It's the same for the Virgin Mary. We are not praying to her, but asking her, as we ask the saints, to pray for us. And just as certain people alive here on earth seem to have the gift of healing, we believe the saints in heaven have that gift also, and can help channel, through their prayers, God's healing to us."

Healing Through Time

> Is there any sick among you? Let him call for the elders
> of the church; and let them pray over him, anointing
> him with oil in the name of the Lord; and the prayer of
> faith shall save the sick, and the Lord shall raise him
> up. . . .
>
> —James 5:14–15

SAINT PATRICK healed the blind. St. Bernard healed the blind, made the lame walk, the dumb speak, and the deaf hear. Among the miracles attributed to Saints Hildegarde, Katherine, Margaret, and Odilia are the curing of the martyrs Damian and Cosma, the physical healing of Emperor Justinian, and the healing of lepers.

Justin Martyr wrote in A.D. 165, "In our city, many Christian friends have been healed and have healed other sick persons in Jesus' name."

Bishop Ireneus wrote in A.D. 180, ". . . those who truly are His disciples receive grace from Him to perform miracles in His name and they really cast out evil spirits. Others pray for the sick by laying hands on them and see them healed."

Origen wrote in A.D. 250, "Some prove through healings that they perform what tremendous power they have through faith, in that they do not call on any other name over those who need help than the name of Jesus and God. In this manner we have seen many persons delivered from terrible misfortunes and mental disorders and innumerable other sicknesses. . . ."

In A.D. 275, Clement gave the following advice to young preachers: "Let them, therefore, with prayer and fasting pray for people in faith and trust in God . . . as men who have received gifts to heal for God's glory."

In 1780 Count Zinzendorf said, "To believe when all hope is gone is the key to the gift of miracles, and I give the testimony about our dear church that the apostolic power is revealed there. We have had undeniable proof of this through various revelations regarding people, persons, and circumstances that no man could have known, and through healings of incurable sicknesses, even from such things as cancer, when the patient was in the final struggles with death. All this happened through prayer or the simple word of God."

And in the 1980s, these miraculous healings "through the simple word of God" still were being reported:

The November 23, 1987, issue of *Sports Illustrated* featured a cover story on Washington Redskins' football star Dexter Manley, telling how his baby daughter Dalis was cured of a rare bone disease when the Reverend Fred Price, a Los Angeles television evangelist, laid his hands on her and told Satan to exit the child's body.

The *Cleveland Plain Dealer* told how ten thousand people went to Cleveland's Public Hall in the spring of 1985 looking for a miracle from the Reverend Ralph DiOrio, a Catholic priest from Leicester, Massachusetts. Scores of people at the service claimed that at DiOrio's touch, they were healed of everything from scoliosis to deafness.

People magazine described the powers of Archbishop Emmanuel Milingo, a fifty-five-year-old African churchman who heals in his Vatican office or in his apartment and who draws thousands for his monthly healing Masses. One woman told how she had traveled all over Italy to the best doctors, who said she had an inoperable brain growth. "Nobody could do anything for me. Then I met Archbishop Milingo. He prayed over me in English, Italian, and in an African dialect. Today doctors can find nothing wrong with me."

At a 1987 Pittsburgh Faith Crusade, Kenneth Hagin of Tulsa, Oklahoma, moved down the healing line that formed after each evening service and said, "I lay hands on you by direction of the head of the church, Jesus Christ, and in obedience to the Law of Contact and Transmission. The contact of my hands transmits God's healing power. . . . There it is! There it is! It'll heal you if you mix faith with it. . . ." Scores of those he touched left the service believing they were healed.

The Reverend David Paul, frequently credited with healing many of those who attend his services across the country, received a letter from a woman he had prayed for. She had gone to one of his televised services, he had laid hands on her, and in the letter she said she was free of cancer and her doctors couldn't believe it.

The January 1988 issue of *Charisma* carried a story titled, "Kenneth Copeland Reaches Out to AIDS Victims." The article described how the Texas-based Copeland, believing he had been told by the Lord to "Reach out to those with AIDS," prayed for one man who reported a healing, although medical verification had not yet been obtained by Copeland's ministry.

Morris Cerrullo's ministry in San Diego told me of two apparent AIDS cures administered by Cerrullo, although these, too, had not yet been confirmed.

Elizabeth Fuller, in her book A *Touch of Grace*, about the healing ministry of Grace DiBiccarri of Brookfield, Connecticut, tells the story of eleven-year-old Jeffrey Comeau, whose mother had taken him from their Springfield, Massachusetts, home to one of "Amazing Grace's" healing services in late 1983. The little boy was suffering from bone cancer. His joints were sore and swollen. The backs of his hands were so swollen, his knuckles couldn't be seen. He couldn't use his hands to hold anything.

"Dear God," Grace prayed, "take this cancer from this little boy's body. Make him whole again in you."

Grace had her hand on his forehead, and as she touched him, Jeff was suffused with a strange, warm, comfortable feeling. His fingers and toes tingled. Grace massaged his fingers. Only minutes before, they hurt when they were even lightly touched. Jeff felt no pain.

"Move your fingers," Grace said.

Jeff slowly opened and closed his hand. The puffiness disappeared before his eyes. Within minutes, his fingers were as flexible and normal as they had been before he was stricken with cancer.

"I've got no pain! Mommy, I've got no pain!" Jeff shouted.

He jumped up and down to test his legs. He knew his cancer had been cured because Grace told him so and because the pain and swelling had gone. He could run and jump and use his hands again.

Jeff's doctor, Dr. Lawrence Zemel of Springfield, later confirmed Jeff's cancer had disappeared.

He said, too, that it was certainly because of nothing he had done.

*   *   *

I wasn't doing research for the book alone. When I uncovered these stories, I'd pass them along to Mayor Tullio, if only to keep his hopes up. I also wanted to prepare myself as best I could for the moment of healing, the moment when Charles and Frances would lay hands on the mayors to make them well. If I were going to take a step into faith, I wanted to put my best foot forward.

Unbelief, according to everything I had read, can hinder healing, even if the unbelief is in a bystander and not in the person to be healed. Jesus, for example, had unbelievers leave a room when he was to about to heal, as in the miracle involving the twelve-year-old daughter of Jairus, described in Mark, chapter 5.

I found another scriptural reference to the power of unbelief in the description of how, when Jesus came to Nazareth, he could not do any significant healings there because of the unbelief in that city. The Bible notes that only a few were healed of minor illnesses: "And he could there do no mighty work, save that he laid his hands upon a few sick folk and healed them. And he marveled because of their unbelief."

I certainly did not want to be a hindrance to the healings of the mayors. I had learned enough to believe it was altogether possible that they would be healed, but I was by no means sure they would be. Sometimes people are not healed. Sometimes people are prayed for and have hands laid on them and nothing happens. Sometimes they die anyway. The Hunters once laid hands on a man to cure him—and he had a heart attack while they were doing so.

God has great, glaring, mysterious, dark spaces that make life unpredictable even for true believers and the faithful.

My wife would not allow herself to think that anything other than healing would occur in Coraopolis, although she admitted to having doubts: "Sure, the doubts are there, but I've made the decision to believe the mayors will be healed," she said. "If it turns out later that I was wrong, what will I have lost by believing? My pride? That's nothing. In the meantime, I'll keep making the decision to believe."

The icebreaker.

I wanted to be able to go into that hotel room with the Hunters and the mayors and set aside my rationality, to be at one with the moment, to "will one thing," to put the Annoying Observer face to the corner for an hour, to have faith, like Debbie, that the mayors would be healed.

*   *   *

In his very first sermon, in Nazareth, Jesus spoke of healing the sick:

"The Spirit of the Lord is upon me, because He hath anointed me to preach the gospel to the poor: He hath sent me to heal the broken-hearted, to preach deliverance to the captives and recovering of sight to the blind, to set at liberty those who are bruised."

When John the Baptist was in prison and wondered whether Jesus was the Messiah or whether he should wait for someone else to come, Jesus sent this message back with John's servant:

"Go back and tell John what you have seen and heard: The blind see again, the lame walk, the lepers are cleansed, the deaf hear, the dead are raised up, and the poor have the gospel preached to them."

The healing miracles Jesus performed convinced multitudes of his authenticity:

And it came to pass, while he was in one of the towns, that behold, there was a man full of leprosy. And when he saw Jesus, he fell on his face and besought him, saying, "Lord, if thou wilt, thou canst make me clean." And stretching forth his hand, Jesus touched him, saying, "I will; be thou made clean." And immediately, the leprosy left him. (Luke 5:12–13)

. . . And behold, some men were carrying upon a pallet a man who was paralyzed, and they were trying to bring him in and lay him before him. And as they found no way of bringing him in, because of the crowd, they went up onto the roof and lowered him through the tiles, with his pallet, into the midst before Jesus. . . . he said to the paralytic, "I say to thee arise, take up they pallet, and go to thy house." And immediately, he arose before them, took what he had been lying on, and went away to his house, glorifying God. (Luke 5:18–25)

. . . and a great crowd was following him and pressing upon him. And there was a woman who for twelve years had had a hemorrhage, and had suffered much at the hands of many physicians, and had spent all that she had, and found no benefit, but rather grew worse. Hearing about Jesus, she came up behind him in the crowd and touched his cloak. For she said, "If I but touch his cloak, I shall be saved." And at once, the flow of her blood was dried up, and she felt in her body that she was healed of her affliction. . . . But he said to her, "Daughter, thy faith has saved thee. Go in peace, and be thou healed of thy affliction." (Mark 5:24–34)

Bible scholars say Jesus performed his healings as signs so that others would believe he was the Son of God.

And most scholars agree the gospels describing those healings were written for an evangelistic purpose, to spread the "Good News" so that people might believe in the Son of God. John writes in his Gospel that he included healings so his readers "may believe that Jesus is the Christ."

The thought occurred to me that if we believe Jesus when he says, "I am with you always," it follows that his signs and wonders, which drew thousands to him when he was on earth, must be continuing today. The gospels, which contained so many examples of healings, were written primarily for the conversion of unbelievers. It seems as if that process is still going on today, with hundreds of thousands of people the world over attending healing rallies and coming away both healed and "saved."

"That is what God wants today in every church," says evangelist Peter Youngren, a healer from the Niagara Falls, New York, area, who drew 250,000 people to one healing service alone in the city of Madras, India. Like the Hunters, he routinely draws huge crowds to his services. "I know it hasn't been my oratorical skill that has drawn tens of thousands of non-Christians to our meetings," he says. "It has been the miracles."

"The climate is changing," writes Francis MacNutt in his best seller *Healing*. "People are hungering and thirsting to know God in a direct, experiential way. And the sick need healing just as much as they did in Christ's day. Those needs and desires are basic to our humanity. If the risen Christ is still healing the sick, then there is no problem in making Christianity relevant to the needs of most people today. But does he still heal? The most convincing argument is always, I think, experience: 'Go back and tell John what you have seen and heard: The blind see again, the lame walk . . . and happy is the man who does not lose faith in me.'"

*   *   *

Bible scholars also point out how much of the four gospels is devoted to the healings of Jesus.

For instance, in Mark's Gospel, which most scholars believe was the primary source for Matthew and Luke, 209 verses out of 666 are about the healing miracles of Jesus. That's just over 31 percent.

A great deal of space in the other gospels also is devoted to the healings of Jesus. John's Gospel centers around what he calls "signs," the majority of which are healing miracles.

In his book *Power Healing,* healer John Wimber makes the point that many Christians who sincerely believe in the Christ described in the gospels have trouble accepting the healing miracles described therein, even though so much space is devoted to them. This group even includes many Christian Bible scholars.

He tells how an associate of his once analyzed 27 modern reference works on the Bible—a total of 87,125 pages discussing important Bible passages and what they mean.

Wimber's friend found that of 87,125 pages written by modern biblical scholars, only 287.5 pages or .33 percent, were devoted to healings, miracles, and signs and wonders.

"When the high number of verses devoted to healings, miracles, and signs and wonders in the New Testament (especially in the Gospels) is compared to the low number of pages written on the same topics in modern literature, it is reasonable to assume modern secularism has influenced Christian scholars," Wimber writes.

Bible scholars are among the Christians, he says, whose thinking is tainted by materialism and rationalism, two philosophies which date to the eighteenth-century Enlightenment and which form the cornerstone of modern secularism—the worldview of the witch, as opposed to the beautiful lady.

A materialistic paradigm, or model of reality, says Wimber, "assumes that nothing exists except matter and its movements and its modifications, that there is no supernatural reference point in this life. Rationalism proposes that there is a rational explanation for everything, that for every human problem there is a rational solution, and that there is no room for divine providence.

"Most Christians," he says, "recognize the more obvious anti-Christian results of secularism: the preoccupation with acquiring and having material things and sexual promiscuity. While they may avoid these, they are nevertheless affected by secularism in other ways. One is that they find it difficult to accept supernatural intervention, especially physical healing, in the material universe.

"I am not saying that we should be credulous," Wimber says. "The problem is with what we exclude from our field of attention, with what we give no prominence to in our thinking. . . .

"So, many Christians, caught in the web of Western secularism—and few of us are not affected in some way—have a formidable barrier to cross before they can pray for the sick. That barrier is the belief or suspicion that supernatural healing is impossible today."

Toward a Fuller Understanding

Men learn while they teach.
—Seneca, *Ad Lucilium*

EVEN THOUGH my wife thought the book was creating me as I created it, my daughter had her doubts about my capability for spiritual growth. While I was putting her to bed one night, Stacey said, "Dad, you've got a lot of improving to do."

"What?"

"You better start working on improving yourself. You're not very nice sometimes."

"What are you talking about?"

"Like the other day when we went out for my Saturday candy, and in the car you called that person who was just walking along, minding her own business, a 'big mama,'"

"She couldn't hear me. She *was* fat."

"It still wasn't nice. Sometimes you say nasty things about people."

She sits straight up in bed, her nose just inches from mine, tapping her index finger into my breastbone. She is no longer the little girl who used to cry when I left for work and say, "Wave to me from the truck, Daddy!" Now she's so busy cramming at the breakfast table for health tests on the skeletal joints that she hardly has time to say good-bye. She is a pre-ten-year-old, which means she is a pre-pre-pre-teen who wears a sweatshirt and baggy sweatpants to bed instead of her little flowered pajamas.

"Tell me a story, Daddy" has been replaced by "Let's shop till we drop!"

She still has her five fuzzy white unicorns. A few weeks back, she couldn't bear to sleep without them crowding all around her. But they're not on her bed anymore. They're not even in her room. She's banished them all to the inside of a green plastic garbage bag in the attic. Now she sleeps with a Wild Puffalump who wears yellow plastic sunglasses to bed. Stacey is feeling her oats.

"Good grief, Stacey. You make your First Holy Communion and now you think you're better than everybody else. Knock it off."

"You swear to much, too."

"Bull . . ."

"See, you almost said the 'bull-go-to-the-bathroom word. I think maybe you should see a counselor, Dad. Maybe the one at my school will talk to you."

"What?"

"How can you write a holy book on healing if you keep calling people 'fat mamas'? You're crazed, Dad. Crazed!"

Crazed or not, I kept doing my interviews.

From Fuller Theological Seminary, an oasis in the midst of downtown Pasadena, from a campus planted with palms, eucalyptus, oak and evergreen trees and all kinds of wild tropical greenery most Easterners have never seen before, the voice of Dr. Lewis B. Smedes, professor of theology and ethics, comes to chilly Erie, Pennsylvania, where the wintry air is a bone-chilling eighteen degrees and where seven inches of snow cover the frozen ground.

The voice comes out of the saltshaker holes in the telephone very slowly, as if it started out warm and liquid in California but congealed in the telephone wires when it hit the frigid Erie weather. Each word emerges like cold molasses, one hole at a time, and hangs there cautiously before it finally drips out.

Smedes is speaking very carefully, cautiously, and measuredly about the course MC510, "The Miraculous and Church Growth," one of the most popular courses ever offered at Fuller, the largest nondenominational seminary in the world—a course the seminary ended up canceling. The course was designed to deal with both the theory and the practice of the miraculous—not just hands-on experience, but also *laying on of hands* hands-on experience. The canceling caused a great deal of controversy.

MC510 was launched with a great deal of fanfare. For probably the only time in American church history, an academic course was the subject of an entire issue of a national religious mazagine—the October 1982 issue of *Christian Life*. The course broke all enrollment records at Fuller and the lab sessions held at the close of each lecture drew overflow crowds of those who wanted to witness God's power in action, as in the case of Fuller student Diane Moore, who said she was miraculously healed of a degenerative eye disease after she requested the laying on of hands and prayer during one of MC510's two-hour lab sessions. Other students, ranging in age from twenty-five to seventy, said they were healed of everything from headaches to scoliosis.

But that optional lab, which provided an opportunity to pray for healing and to witness divine cures, was a point of contention from the beginning. Opponents said the sessions were experimental and not up to par for graduate-level studies. They said healing ministries should occur in a caring community, not in a classroom.

Some questioned whether the course placed too great an emphasis on the gift of healing in biblical theology. Finally, the course was canceled to preserve unity.

But, Smedes tells me, the legacy of MC510 was a good one. "I think all of us opened our paradigms a little in that we allowed for things to happen that were not normally expected within the range of our understanding of how God and nature work together," he said, slowly and cautiously.

To Smedes and other professors at Fuller, the net effect of the course was "illuminating, creative, and disturbing." It was illuminating in that everybody involved discovered new ideas and viewed old ideas in a new way. It created a deeper community, because while faculty and students experienced division and misunderstanding and suspicion, once those feelings were put out on the table, a healing process began that knit the community tighter than before, when all of those negatives remained unsurfaced.

The course was disturbing academically and institutionally, because a "healing workshop" was unprecedented in the academic community at Fuller and because new things within institutions are always disturbing. It was disturbing because the concepts being promoted within an academic course were contrary to the religious traditions of many at Fuller—to the dispensationalists, for example, who believed Christ's mandate to heal the sick and raise the dead was not for all time, but for the disciples' time alone. And it was disturbing because many of the faculty had misgivings about the credibility and the integrity of the business going on.

To some, the course prompted a sense of triviality. In this world of incredible suffering on such a cosmic scale, it was laughable how some people could celebrate a millimeter's lengthening of a left leg as a triumph of the Lord and Creator.

"When that is celebrated, that kind of cure . . . there was something in the minds of some of our people that said with starving children in Africa and racial injustice in South Africa and genocide in Cambodia, it would be trivial . . . it would trivialize God to proclaim to the world that God is alive and well because He had lengthened someone's leg," Smedes says.

"Your case, in which Frances Hunter helped you and your wife to have a baby, was highly serendipitous and beautiful," he adds. "And I can tell you that my wife and I went for ten years without children, and prayed and prayed and prayed."

He pauses and takes a deep breath. "And finally, my wife got pregnant."

I look outside my window. The snow has stopped. The professor's voice is becoming liquid. His words are coming out of the holes in the phone just a little faster.

I look at his photo on the back of *Ministry and the Miraculous*, the book he edited. He's an imposing old gent, a professorial type with a gleam in his eyes; smile lines at the corners of his eyes; and a shock of thick, pure white, longish hair that looks like maybe he wore it that way in the 1960s, and I stare at his picture, trying to match it with his voice, trying to identify his joyful experience with mine, knowing how it feels to have God answer a prayer for a child after so many years.

"God's Gift."

Here was a comrade-in-belief who understood that inscription; who, like me, had risen above the carping of co-workers who couldn't see beyond the tops of their beer cans and farther than the next Super Bowl Sabbath. Smedes and I had both experienced the Glory. He and I could talk about our shared experience . . . and the spiritual maturity—Jung called it "integration"—that such miracles bring.

"The child my wife bore died within a day of its birth," he says.

Smedes believes that his and his wife's prayers were certainly as fervent as anyone else's. And that most of his friends who are not able to have children never will have them despite all their prayers that wing their way to heaven for years and years and years.

"Yours was a case in which you can only say, 'Praise God,'" Smedes says. "But others will say, 'If it happened to you, why didn't it happen to me?' There is no answer to that, any more than there is to the question of why children are born into a family in which they are abused and sexually molested while other people who would be wonderful parents are denied the privilege of having children. There are simply great mysteries that a wonderful story like yours does not answer."

Smedes was right. I'd already been asked many times, "If it could happen to you, why can't it happen to me?" I told the professor about one example, that of an Ohio woman who had written a desperate letter to me following the *McCall's* article about our miracle, Ian Christian.

"Sometimes I think that if I can't have a baby, I don't want to go on living," she wrote.

Healers say that sometimes healing is complete and immediate; sometimes it's only partial; and sometimes it doesn't happen at all. I'd heard of one case involving a father who took his deaf son to healing services every few months for eight years, with no improvement at all. But finally, going into the ninth year, the father took the son to a minister who touched the boy's ears and prayed for him, and the deafness vanished immediately.

When I talked to this woman on the phone, she tearfully asked me why I thought my wife and I had been healed when others go to faith healers and nothing happens.

I told her I hadn't the faintest idea. That maybe whatever happened to my family occurred so I could write about it—so she could read the article and contact me—so I could tell her that maybe she should think of adopting a special-needs child with a physical or mental handicap, instead of putting all her eggs in her own biological basket. That maybe thinking of a child's desperate need for her would take her mind off her desperate need for a child. That maybe when God answers our prayers and "heals" us, it's not always in the way we expect. Or on our timetable, as opposed to His.

"The answer to her might indeed be to adopt a child," Smedes says, tacitly granting that maybe that answer and the solution open to the woman were part of a healing miracle. "But the much bigger miracle for me is that most of the time, when people make love and want a child, they eventually get one and have families. . . . You had a wonderful thing happen to you. Praise God. But think of all the people who bear children without going to the Hunters. That's a miracle to me. That's a wonder. It's like Moses standing before a burning bush in the sense that it is surprising, but just stand in front of any bush and you've got cause to wonder and praise God. The fact that there is a bush or a world at all is a miracle."

Smedes's voice goes on, quickly now, the words pouring out all of the holes at once:

"I think occasional miracles are nice. On a cosmic level, a great historical level, it doesn't matter much whether you have a child or not. It's beautiful, wonderful, and of utmost importance to you, but on a cosmic level, we could get along well enough without one more. Maybe your child could turn out to be a great leader or whatever, but chances are, statistically speaking, your child is just going to be a wonderful human being and not a world shaker. I may be wrong.

"My wife and I didn't have children of our own," he says. "We regretted it a lot, but that isn't shaking the world. We have three adopted kids and gave them the best upbringing that we could. We love them and care for them and they love us and so forth and that's okay, too.

"As far as my emotions go, I'm terribly grateful that you had that child. But for my theology, that neither upsets it nor confirms it too much. My deep concern with God is the great and terrible things that happen in the world. . . . What I want God to do is get in the minds of the Kremlin and in the minds of the Pentagon and in the minds of other leaders and bring healing there. I want God to bring in His kingdom, that's what I want."

"If God can cause the miracle of birth, with or without help from the Hunters, why can't He bring world peace and cure our planet?" I ask Smedes. "Aren't we praying hard enough? A lack of faith, perhaps?"

"I bow before God's time and purpose and I don't want to engage that question," he says.

"And, too," he goes on, "when somebody's arthritis is healed and so on, I sometimes think that God is being whimsical, that He's showing us His whimsical side.

"It's almost as if God is saying, 'Look, you guys, you may have a lot of problems with suffering and with pain and with evil in the world, but I just want to put my little pinky into human affairs to show you that a God of love is still present with His people and He can do wonderful things! It's like the Almighty is still giving us a hint that He is still around. That's my personal response to many miracles, and it isn't a way of minimizing Him at all—because what looks small in the light of the history of the world is enormous in the experience of any particular family or person."

I share with Smedes one of my bathtub revelations, telling him I've come to realize that "big" and "small" are mental constructs to which we humans attach a value—we think because something is bigger than we are, it is more important, better. When something is smaller, it is insignificant, inferior. But sitting at my computer terminal in the city room, reading science stories from the Associated Press about astronomical structures in Carl Sagan's smug cosmos large enough to encompass whole galaxies like ours, and then reading about minute subatomic particles that make an atom look like a galaxy in comparison, it's apparent that matter probably progresses both to infinite largeness and infinite smallness. (German physicist Emil Wiechert asserted in 1896 that "the universe is infinite in all directions, not only above us in the large but below us in the small.") Large to small or small to large—either way, it's a spectrum—and saying that "big, cosmic" things like world peace are more important to the scheme of things than "small, minute" things, like people having babies or getting cured of arthritis, is like saying that red, on one end of the color spectrum, is more important and has more value than violet, on the other.

In a newspaper interview with Pete Conrad, the commander of *Apollo 12,* the second American lunar landing craft, I once asked him if the enormity of what he did, flying 250,000 miles to the moon and back—

with his soul flying through infinite space wrapped only in a skin sandwich baggie—changed his religious viewpoint.

"Flying 250,000 miles to the moon is rather insignificant as far as infinity goes," he said, noting laconically that he believed in God before the trip and that his belief was unchanged afterward.

If our sun and all its planets could fit into a coffee cup, our galaxy would be the size of North America. There are an estimated one hundred billion galaxies in the known universe. Looking at it from that vantage point, how much "larger" is the suffering of a few hundred thousand humans as opposed to one?

I used to think, in my Sartre-Camus days—in college, before I was married—how absurd it was that some people could think an infinite being, a God of galaxies, black holes, and supernovas, would be concerned with the propriety of how and when and where and whether a tiny little furless monkey on some little speck of a planet somewhere places his tiny little appendage into one or the other tiny little orifices of another tiny little furless female monkey. "Thou shalt not commit adultery. Thou shalt keepeth thine eyes off blondes when thou goeth for a Big Mac."

Indeed.

But to an infinite being who stretches forever both ways, "big" would have no value over "small." And that, I think, provides a space for morality, explaining how Jesus could say—and mean it—"Not one sparrow can fall to the ground without your Father knowing it. And the very hairs of your head are all numbered."

That's why, it seems to me, it wouldn't be difficult for God to take time out on a busy day to make a stop in Joppa Wiese's bedroom for a conversation lasting a millionth of a billionth of a second. "Difficult" and "important" are human concepts related to the shape and size of things, and how well they can be manipulated by our little monkeylike hands or conceptualized by our limited anthropoid brains.

So there's really no such thing as a "little miracle."

Right, Professor?

"That's a good qualification of what I said, and I accept that," Smedes says. From his tone, I realize I haven't told him anything he hasn't thought about before.

"God could intervene to cure a migraine headache through a two-year-old healer because 'small' isn't small to Him, right?" I ask.

"Exactly. That's a very wise and good thing to say. I've said in times past, pain is something that really isn't quantifiable. Five people with migraine headaches don't hurt any more than one person with a migraine headache, and the thousands of children starving in Ethiopia aren't in any greater pain, qualitatively, then one hungry child in one poor family.

"I'm aware of that and I don't, therefore, wish to minimize the miracles in the lives of people who are not changing the world because of what happened to them."

Why talk about healing of individuals when what is really needed today is the healing of broken relationships, a fragmented society, and a world torn apart by wars and terrorism?

Well, we all go to the doctor when we're sick even though global problems are vying for our attention, don't we?

Maybe healer Francis MacNutt is right when he says in his book *Healing* that the global issues of injustice will be helped "when individuals in society are themselves made whole—when they are healed . . . so that they can enter into healthy relationships, so that they are not acting out of prejudices or ancient hurts."

"The Kingdom of Heaven is like a tiny mustard seed planted in a field," the Bible says. "It is the smallest of all seeds, but becomes the largest of plants, and grows into a tree where birds can come and find shelter."

Even the tiniest sparrow, no doubt. Or a child with AIDS. Perhaps even Erie mayor Lou Tullio . . .

The healing at Fuller didn't stop after course MC510 was canceled. It just changed location.

In the next healing course, MC550, "Healing and World Evangelism" (taught in 1988 by C. Peter Wagner, professor of church growth), classtime healing clinics were prohibited. But the faculty did not keep the students from meeting after class to conduct their own healing workshops.

Steven Long, thirty-nine, a student at Fuller, became the prayer leader at Thursday and Friday night sessions. He told me that often the praying would last from 9:00 P.M. until 1:00 A.M.

"We take some of the subjects discussed in class and put them into practical application," Long said. "The joint faculty had specifically said that they did not want clinic healing to be included in MC550, but that as a student I could organize a prayer time afterward and we could have a clinic then. So I did. It's a student-run function, not faculty-run at all."

Despite the loss of the faculty, the healing didn't stop—Long described healings of everything from cancerous tumors in the body of a seventy-six-year-old man to the healing of an airline stewardess's hypoglycemia to the healing of back pain in a thirty-year-old woman named Lisa.

C. Peter Wagner described for me one healing he himself was involved with outside the classroom. The healing involved the regeneration of a child's ear. (Apparently it was a hard one for some of Fuller's more skeptical professors to ignore, since it involved the grandson of Paul Pierson, dean of Fuller's School of World Missions.)

"The boy was about six years old at the time," Wagner said. "He was born without ears. His parents brought him to my office. I prayed for him, and a half hour later his ears started to grow," Wagner said.

Steve Pierson, the boy's father, told me that he and his wife, Sarah, had adopted the little boy from Guatemala. The child had been born with just little nubs where his ears were supposed to be. Pierson confirmed for me that after Wagner's prayers, at least a quarter inch of new flesh was added to the nub on one side. He said that he and Sarah continued praying for their son's healing over the next forty-eight hours. More tissue grew."We noticed red tips at the end of both nubs on both sides where ears were forming," he said. "You know how when you hit yourself on the finger with a hammer, it becomes all red and sort of glows? Well, that's what the tips of his ears were like. I mean, they were red and sort of glowing and pulsating. It was amazing. They're not fully formed yet, but the ears have grown out more than they had been."

Doctors now say they have enough tissue to work with to do reconstructive plastic surgery, using the boy's own ear tissue, whereas before, there was not enough there to work with.

Not only had the boy's external ears grown, Pierson said, but also his hearing improved tremendously. "He's able to mainstream now in first grade at seven years of age. Before, he had great difficulty hearing at all and could never have done that."

The boy's name is Christian.

A Hundred Pounds
of Clay

But Jesus answered and said to them, "Have faith in
God. Amen I say to you, whoever says to this mountain,
'Arise, and hurl thyself into the sea,' and does not waver
in his heart, but believes that whatever he says will be
done, it shall be done for him. Therefore, I say to you,
all things whatever you ask for in prayer, believe that
you shall receive, and they shall come to you."
—Mark 11:22–24

"OH, GEE, no . . . hey . . . d'ya have to tell that story again? I mean . . .
come on, now . . ." the mayor of Erie would say when someone would
tell the football story at a party.

After high school, Lou Tullio won a football scholarship to Holy Cross
College in Worcester, Massachusetts, and after graduation he stayed in
Worcester, playing end on the local pro football team and starting a small
dairy business out of his wife's family's farm.

So there's Tullio in the huddle. The quarterback nods to him and calls
the play.

The ball's in motion. Tullio goes out, the quarterback passes the ball
to him. Tullio leaps! He reaches out! And the ball slips through his
fingers.

Back in the huddle. "That's impossible what I just did," Tullio says. "I
don't do that. I've never dropped the ball like that in my life. C'mon. Let's
do that play again!"

He manages to convince the quarterback to try it again.

Again, Tullio goes out. Again the quarterback passes. Tullio makes a
magnificent lunge! The crowd cheers!

But again, Tullio drops the ball.

A fat man in the stands pops up, pokes out his belly through his

93

overcoat, and yells at the top of his lungs, "Throw the guy a milk bottle—he won't drop that!"

The crowd goes wild. With laughter. Tullio ignores it and puts his head back down in the huddle.

"Look, I've never done that twice in a row in my life," Tullio says. "It's impossible. It's just not happening. Hey look. Three times. I can't miss three times in a row. You know? I've never missed the ball three times in a row in my life. C'mon. One more time! I won't let ya down. I promise!"

The quarterback hesitates. It's against his better judgment. Tullio gives him a wink. The quarterback sighs and decides to let Tullio try it just one more time.

Now, there are two endings to this story.

The way Tullio tells it, he caught the ball the third time and led the team to victory. Not only that, but the insult yelled from the stands helped his dairy business grow from twelve to two thousand customers, five trucks, and his own dairy barn.

The other version of the story, the one whispered in alleyways and in City Hall men's rooms, has Tullio dropping the ball three times in a row.

"You're not gonna put that story in the book, are you?" Tullio asks me.

I tell him I am.

"Aw, gee, listen . . ." he mumbles, shaking his head slowly back and forth like a big old bear trying to shake off flies.

"Just make sure you stick around to see how the story ends," I tell him.

When a *macho,* mainstream magazine like *Sports Illustrated* publishes a story on the Washington Redskins' leading career sacker, Dexter Manley, with a close-up of Manley's snarling face on the cover—while running inside a photo of a faith healer Manley believes cured his little girl of a rare bone disease—you know times are changing. And it gets you thinking that maybe you're not so odd after all for imagining that perhaps God could heal the mayor.

While reading that story in the magazine's November 23, 1987, issue, I couldn't help but wonder if Manley could somehow talk to the mayor before he met with the Hunters. Tullio had been an avid football fan ever since his Worcester days, and I guessed that even talking to Manley about split pea soup would cheer the mayor up. I figured that to the extent faith healing is helped by positive thinking, talking to Manley could do a world of good. If a mainstream guy like Manley could believe in faith healing, maybe that could inspire the mayor to do the same.

But Manley was a superstar, soon to become a 1988 Super Bowl champion.

"GET OUTTA MY WAY!," in big green type, was the caption for Manley's face on the issue's cover.

Sports Illustrated writer Rick Reilly painted Manley as an enigma, ". . . a brute who can bench-press five hundred pounds, yet weeps at TV movies; a philanthropist who buys dinner for five hundred homeless people, yet has few close friends; an extrovert who is hopelessly chatty, yet aside to agreeing to be interviewed for this story, has refused to talk to the press all season. . . ."

If Manley was that big and that complicated, I didn't think I had much of a chance of patching him through to Tullio.

But reporters don't mind making phone calls. So I got on the phone.

"I really think Dexter will go for it," one of Manley's representatives at the Boston-based Robert Woolf agency said. "He cares about people. He loves to do things like this. He'll probably be giving you a call."

"Jack? This is Dexter," I heard a voice say on the bedroom phone just a couple nights after I'd talked to Manley's agency.

"Hey, Dexter!" I said, like I'd known the man all my life.

I didn't let the fact that Manley could bench-press over three of me intimidate me at all. I told him the mayor's story and asked if he'd help.

"Sure, I'd be happy to call him," he said. Then he and Glinda, his wife, told me their story.

When their daughter Dalis was one day old, doctors told them the baby had fibrous dysplasia, a rare disease that prevents the bones from forming properly. The doctors told the Manleys that their baby's right leg might have to be amputated.

"I'd heard of faith healing and I knew it was in the Bible," Glinda said. "But I didn't know of a minister who could do this. After all, I never needed one before."

She *had* seen the Reverend Frederick Price, a Los Angeles television evangelist, on TV on Sunday mornings. And one day her mother told her, "You know, Reverend Price does healings . . . and he's coming to D.C. Why don't you try it? You have nothing to lose. These doctors are talking about cutting your baby's leg off."

"I was at that point where I felt I had to believe in something," said Glinda. "My back was against the wall. What did I have to lose?

"So I just went gung-ho. I went 100 percent into it. I didn't care if I was a fool, I didn't care how people perceived me. I just thought, 'This is my daughter, I'm going to do everything I can. And if it doesn't work, at least I'll know I tried.'"

Dexter says he wasn't so sure: "I'm glad one of us had great faith."

I'd sent him a copy of my *McCall's* article. "I'm kinda like you, Jack—I went along with it because I had nothing to lose and her faith was much stronger than mine. I was just there. I prayed about it, but that was it."

In August 1986, Dexter and Glinda took their baby girl to the Washington Convention Center to have the Reverend Price lay hands on her.

"Satan, you will not claim any parts of this child's body!" Price shouted, one hand on the child's forehead, the other on her leg. He looked at Glinda and said, "Through your faith and your knowledge will she be healed!"

The Manleys took Dalis straight from the healing service to Children's Hospital in Washington, where she was scheduled to have a new cast put on. When doctors cut the old cast off, "they felt Dalis's leg and it was on fire," Glinda said.

"Her leg was very hot after the reverend touched her," Dexter said. "It was very, very warm. It stayed warm for a long time."

The doctors said, "There's no reason for her leg to be on fire like this . . ." and thought that either a tumor or cancer might be causing the heat, Glinda said. "I just said, 'No, she's okay. . . . I just took her to have her healed,'" she said.

"Uh, right, Mrs. Manley. Well, let's get an X-ray anyway."

The X-ray, done within *two hours* after the healing, already showed new bone coming in.

Although he believes the healing was indeed a miracle, the experience hasn't changed Dexter all that much. He doesn't go to church every Sunday. "I go to church every now and then when I have some free time, but I haven't felt no thunder and lightnin' or anything like that," he said. "Things are still pretty much the same. I'm not gonna lie to you."

He believes the experience did change his life in one way, though. Like the sportswriter said, "Something that couldn't be beaten by strength and speed had been beaten just the same."

"Ever since she was touched, she was getting new bone, and it made those doctors really, really freak out," Glinda said. "They decided to do a biopsy to figure it out, thinking maybe she didn't have what they thought, because if she did have fibrous dysplasia, there was no way she was going to get bone."

A biopsy was done. Glinda said the doctors told her, "Well, it's not anything else, and the only thing it could have been was fibrous dysplasia. But we've never seen anything like this happen before."

"Last summer (1987), when they said she didn't have fibrous dysplasia anymore, they said she was *the first person in the history of the disease in the world* that has ever done this," Glinda said. "That's a miracle."

"Price just looked at you and said, 'By your faith, she will be healed'?" I asked, thinking that the power of positive thinking, suggestion, the placebo effect, and all the other scientific explanations for healing couldn't have been operating in the mind of a baby, meaning that healing can come from without, not just from within.

"Right, because that's the only way healings occur. Scripture tells you that you're already healed; it's Satan who takes away your healing. We as people are healed, period. We are not to be sick. We are not to have any illnesses. And when we get them, that is Satan attacking our body. He's taking away what is really rightfully ours.

"What I'm saying is that she was just a baby, she was only three months old when Reverend Price laid hands on her. She didn't have faith and she didn't know God yet. So he looked at me and said, 'Through your knowledge . . . and through your faith . . . will she be healed. That's how the miracle will take place.' He explained that he was just the conduit to God through which the healing would occur. If it wasn't totally my faith, if I didn't believe it, it wasn't gonna happen."

Glinda was caught up in her subject, on a roll, and she rolled on in splendid, raw eloquence, a woman who believed in believing. *Another ship called Faith, churning through the ice.*

". . . People keep saying, 'Oh, I'm gonna take Mary or cousin so-and-so to see him,' but I say, 'Hey, it just doesn't work that way, like taking a pill. It has to be in that person's heart that they know it's done. That they know it's given to them. That they know it's rightfully their power to be healed by the Word. They have to know this and they have to believe it and they have to fight Satan, who's always gonna be sayin', 'No, no, you ain't healed, you ain't healed.'

"That happened to me. I'd look at her going to the doctors and they'd give me a grim prognosis, and I'm saying in my mind, 'That's okay, that's okay, I know she's healed, I know she's healed.' But sometimes I'd look at her and say, 'Well, I don't know . . . I don't know!' "

The icebreaker forges ahead. And every now and then, great chunks of ice flip up from beneath her hull to go skittering across the hard surface of the lake like so many pebbles. . . . The ship churns ahead, and the ice rushes in behind to fill the inky void left by her passage.

"These are the doubts you get. But when that happens, what you have to do—and you don't have to be a crazy person shoutin' 'I know I'm healed! I know I'm healed!'—what you do is, you say to yourself,' Thank you, Lord, for healing me.'

"Every time you get a bad thought or a doubt comin' into your mind, 'cause doubt and worry and all that are Satan's attacks on you, you just automatically say it, you just counteract it, by saying, 'Thank you, Jesus, for healing me.'

"It's like you're a computer, and you're reprogramming your brain. You start saying, 'Thank you, Lord, for healing me,' even when you really don't believe it yet. You just keep saying it, and the more you say it, the more you start to believe it.

"That's what happened to me. I just kept sayin' it to Satan. And eventually I didn't care what none of them doctors said. I just kept telling them, 'Oh, she's all right. She's healed.' They'd look at me and say, 'Yeah, Mrs. Manley, that's nice.' But I didn't care what they thought. I knew in my heart she was healed.

"Every time I went for a checkup, I would say, 'Thank you, Lord, for healing her, I know you've healed her . . . but just show me another sign to help my faith and strength.' And every time she had an X-ray, every two months, there was more bone in the leg. Every time, it was constant bone. And now it's full bone.

"I will tell anyone that it only works through faith."

I remember thinking, when Debbie and I took a ride on a Coast Guard icebreaker one winter for a *Popular Mechanics* article I was working on, that an icebreaker is an *unnatural* contrivance. It's *unnatural* to cruise on the Great Lakes in winter; it's *unnatural* to move through a solid mass; it's *unnatural* to push through ice two feet thick as if it weren't there; it's unnatural not only to challenge nature in such a cavalier manner but also to disregard her so completely.

How do they do it, these women? They crush the ice. They forge ahead. They PROGRESS, unstoppable, full of the forward motion that impels them through all things, advancing from flesh to . . . spirit.

Glinda, you, too, are an icebreaking tug—but you are a capital ship for an ocean trip.

*   *   *

I tiptoe into Stacey's room to check on her on my way to bed. She's been moaning in her sleep. Her nylon Wild Puffalump is abandoned at the foot of her bed, and she's curled up with her two fuzzy teddy bears, Heidi and Sam. I have to look twice. Clutched tight to her chest between the two bears is a unicorn she's retrieved from the body bag in the attic.

Apparently, she's having trouble with paradigm shifts too, trying to decide which world to live in.

In our room, Debbie's sitting up in bed, reading this chapter. "What do you think your friend Dexter will do to you when he finds out you've called his wife a tugboat?" she asks.

She's wearing my bathrobe and her white socks. I suspect that, as she does occasionally, she's soaked her feet in baby oil before putting the socks on and going to bed. She does that so she'll wake up in the morning with soft toes. Why she thinks she needs soft toes, I'll never know. She just tells me she likes to pamper her feet once in a while, just like people pamper their noses after they've had a cold.

????

"I didn't call her a tugboat. I called her an icebreaking tug," I answer.

"How's Glinda going to like being called an icebreaking tug?"

"Well, I sort of bounced the image off her on the phone the other day—"

"And?"

"And she said she liked it."

Debbie just shakes her head.

Before she turns the light out, I can't help staring at her face. She doesn't look at all like those other middle-aged women, the clucking hens at parties who roll their eyes and smirk when we tell them about being slain in the Spirit—no crow's-feet at her eyes, no chicken flesh around the neck, no sagging turkey wattle starting under her chin, no feathers of white frosted hair tufted out over her ears—nothing that looks like a bird anywhere near her face, which doesn't have a wrinkle on it. Her eyes are still clear and bright, open and innocent. Her expression is uncynical and vulnerable. Her lips are full and quick to form a smile. Almost forty years old, and she still looks the same as when I met her in college, twenty years before, with skin smooth and soft as a baby's.

My wise and beautiful wife.

The skin doctor's business card, stuck to the refrigerator door with a magnet, caught my eye the next day.

"You have an appointment with the skin doctor?" I asked Debbie.

"I do, but I'm going to cancel it."

Soon after she had delivered Ian and started to nurse, Debbie been plagued with facial blemishes caused by a hormonal change. Her doctor said this happened frequently to women after pregnancy, and he'd give her some antibiotics to clear up the problem.

"Why would you cancel it?" I asked.

"I don't need to go. Look at my face."

I looked.

"See? My skin's completely clear."

"You get a new kind of soap, or what?"

"I laid hands on my face," she said softly. I could hardly hear her.

"You what?"

"Laid hands on my face. I laid hands on my face and prayed," she said, giving me a look that said, "I'll smack you in *your* face if you make fun of me." So I made fun of her. I rolled my eyes, wiggled my fingertips, and hummed the theme from *Twilight Zone*.

"It worked, didn't it?" she huffed.

"Got me. Did it?"

"My face cleared up."

I got the feeling that the Graziers were well on their way to strange new worlds where no man had gone before. Soon we'd be praying for God to fix the truck rather than taking it to our mechanic.

(That might not be so bad. I could just hear Frances Hunter saying, "Just close your eyes and listen to God, and pay him what you think it's worth." And I'd say, "Two bucks!")

The lines between the real and the unreal, between realistic thinking and magical thinking, seemed to be blurring.

I didn't have the nerve to tell my wife that I had laid hands on myself, too, trying to cure an infected prostate, no less, which had plagued me with pain and cramps for the past several months. I self-medicated myself in the shower.

See, you read enough of these healing books, talk to enough Glinda Manleys, see enough before-and-after X-rays, call enough healing ministries, watch enough of the Hunters' videos, and pretty soon your view of reality starts to change. You experience a paradigm shift, as the people at Fuller are wont to say. We were rejecting the paradigm of unbelief, discussed in Smedes's book:

There are paradigms of reality that are, so far as natural causes and effects are concerned, essentially godless. They construe the universe as a magnificent nexus of physical causes and events, a world where all things are, and all events occur only because of physical antecedents that can be located, identified, and possibly manipulated by the interjection of other physical influences. Variations of these paradigms allow for influence on the physical world by mind or human spirit but not by God or Satan. In all variations of the godless worldview God is eliminated from effective presence in creation, grace is separated from nature, and the power of the Spirit is irrelevant to the power of nature. This is the paradigm of unbelief. We reject it.

Right. What that man said. Me and Debbie too.

We had both chosen the paradigm of belief—my wife prenatally, and I belatedly.

For me, the first choice to reject unbelief came on March 23, 1983, after a day of reading wire stories about various means the Soviets were using to slaughter the Afghans. *The furless monkeys are killing each other. If there is no God judging this, how can it be wrong? Because man says it is? Who cares about the laws made by a furless monkey?* I had a sick feeling in my stomach, and chose then, quite deliberately and in cold blood, to believe there was something more. To opt for the paradigm of belief. I couldn't accept that this endless killing was all there is. I rejected the paradigm that we are only animated lumps of clay, reproducing other lumps to simply add to the growing pile of dust and detritus formed by gravity, friction, and time wearing down the clay and pulling it back into the earth. If there is no God, why isn't clay content to remain clay? Why does it live and breathe and reproduce and laugh and sing and cry and move about? Clay could exist in a cold, impersonal universe quite well as an unmoving, unfeeling, inert gray lump, if indeed there is no God to aspire to. Why would a lump of clay feel compelled to shape itself, all on its own, into a Carl Sagan so it could explain the cold, impersonal cosmos to other lumps?

I chose to believe we weren't alone because I could feel the *progression*, feel humanity striving to become more, the relentless, icebreaking motion of clay-to-flesh-to-spirit. I could feel the movement, the tropism, like a plant leaning toward the sun, and I chose to believe there must be a bright light somewhere, the tug of which I so strongly felt.

I didn't want to be alone.

But in my case, unlike my wife's, I had to make the decision often, to choose belief.

The infection seemed to get better for a few days after the shower, then it came back. Hot water can often ease the pain of an infected prostate, though, and in this case, I think that's what really happened. But still . . . the prayers were there, and that was something new.

In bed, after Debbie had canceled her appointment earlier that day, I said to her, "I think you should lay hands on me."

"Not tonight."

"I mean my prostate. For healing."

"Where is it?"

"Somewhere down here. Just put your hands on my stomach. And remember what the Hunters say on their tapes: Any believer can heal."

I hoped they were right. My urologist was charging thirty dollars a visit.

She giggled and placed a hand on my lower abdomen. How cold it was. Her blood pressure is only about 90 over 60, and she always runs a degree or two cooler than I do.

She cleared her throat and whispered, "In the name of Jesus Christ, I command that the infection leave your system, that all blockages be removed, and your prostrate return to normal."

"I hope God knows what a prostrate is," I said.

"What do you mean?"

"It's prostate. One *r*, at the beginning. Not two *r*'s. Not pros*trate*. Pros*tate*."

"I mean, fix Mr. English Major's *prostate*, dear Lord," she whispered.

"Why are you whispering?"

"I don't want to wake the baby."

She tapped my abdomen twice.

I thought the tapping was some part of the ritual I hadn't read about. "What are the taps for?" I asked.

"It means you're supposed to say, 'Thank you, Jesus,' to affirm your healing. Remember what Glinda said?"

"Well, you should have said 'Amen!' after your prayer."
"People don't have to say 'Amen!' after a healing prayer."
"I think you should. It sounds like it needed an 'Amen!'"
"Amen! Now say, 'Thank you, Jesus.'"
"Thank you, Jesus," I said.
How strange that sounded, coming out of my mouth.

One of These Old Damn Days

The devils are especially happy to tire and frighten the soul with . . . terrible thoughts and frightening images. . . . When the soul seeks help from the Gospel of Christ, then Satan comes and shakes his head and makes the soul unsteady and uncertain so that it begins to waver and vacillate.

—Martin Luther

The big cardboard box, covered with blue wrapping paper, was like an upright coffin, with Mayor Tullio inside, standing up, looking out of the box . . . he looked bewildered, then smiled and reached out over the top of the box. "Can you get me out of here?" he asked, the way he always managed to make a command sound like a request. I grasped his hand. It felt uncharacteristically thin. But he started to cough and choke . . . and he slumped back down inside the box. His hand slipped away . . .

I WOKE UP with a start, my heart pounding against my ribs. It was just a bad dream.

I looked at the red-lit numbers on the clock radio, just inches from my face on the nightstand. "It's 1:14 A.M., and you haven't been sleeping very well at all, you poor sap," the radio blared. "You poor slob, you have to get up at 6:00 A.M. for work. But don't worry, I'll count every second of missed sleep for you:

"All . . .

"Night . . .

"Long . . ."

How I hated that thing.

I'd gone to bed unable to stop thinking about the mayor, and then, shortly after 12:30 A.M., must have fallen off to sleep dreaming about him and his birthday party. The sound of the silverware clinking against the plates was still fading from my ears. I sighed, sat up, and looked around the room. Debbie was sleeping soundly next to me, lying on her back and looking, as always, as if she had passed away in the night with her mouth wide open. I listened for her breathing, and when I heard it I resumed my own. Her form was made visible by the infernal, bright red numbers on the General Electric clock radio.

The house was quiet, everybody but me was asleep; their souls were elsewhere, and mine was alone. Our two geriatric poodles, who used to sleep in the bedroom, were locked in the kitchen downstairs. In the old days, they would have been in the room, wagging their tails and keeping me company, as if they slept all day and kept watch all night, waiting faithfully to offer comfort when somebody awoke. But now Pooh, the mother, seventeen years old, was deaf, blind, and incontinent. "Why do I always step in it with the same foot, Dad?" was Stacey's overriding question.

Pooh's daughter, Dinky, at fifteen, had lost all her teeth and had accidents whenever she got excited, which happened every time she heard a car door slam five blocks away. Both dogs had been banished to the kitchen for the sake of the bedroom's baby-blue-and-beige oriental rug.

I fell back into a light sleep and dreamed I was back at the children's hospital . . .

It was summertime, and in the summer they'd roll our beds out onto the screened-in patio.

Behind the head of my bed, about a foot off the ground, a small square night-light had been set into the brick walls of the hospital. *I was staring into the light. The soft creamy light that lay in a pool on the cold cement floor was a point of reference for my mind. I could look into the light and start from there, and my thinking would be lit by the light, and then my thinking would keep me company.*

In the night, my thoughts were all I had. It was in the hospital that I first became the Annoying Observer. It was so lonely at night that I had to split myself into two people. Instead of thinking, "Tomorrow I'm going to watch television and then ask to visit Tommy," it was better to think, "Tomorrow *you're* going to watch television and ask if *you* can visit Tommy." That way, I had both a "you" that spoke and a "me" that listened. A person who *did* and a person who *watched*.

I drifted up toward consciousness, and in my half sleep, a part of me was thinking that it's a pretty good bet that many reporters have had a childhood experience that makes them feel set apart, different, like observers—a drunken parent, teenage acne, weight problems, giftedness, secret love affairs with their brand-new rubber galoshes. I'd have to remember that insight when I awoke. How kids grew up to become Annoying Observers. Then my mind sank back down again.

I sat up in the hospital bed and looked at the moon, shining through the screened-in patio. I squeezed my mother's ring with the index finger and thumb of my other hand. I felt my blood pulsing through my feet, my knees, my calves, my heart, my neck, my hands, and my temples. I wished I could stop feeling it. I was all there was for me, in the hospital, and I was tired of being left along with myself. I ran my tongue over my lips to moisten them, and I thought before I prayed.

"Please, God, let me die."

Good grief! From what subterranean ooze had my mind dredged that one up? I sat up again, sweating, and looked at Debbie. Thank God for her snoring.

I thought I had pushed the hospital far, far into my subconscious. It usually never came out in dreams anymore. The only obvious remnant was a phobia about hospitals that had lingered into adulthood—I practically had panic attacks whenever I had to set foot in a hospital. The birth of Ian, cutting the cord myself, being with Debbie when she delivered him, holding him in my arms in the birthing room, was indeed a wonderful, unforgettable, God-given experience—but it was all I could do to stay within the confines of the hospital walls for ten hours without bolting for a door.

"Hey, Möbius-breath! Hey, hotshot!" my clock radio shouted, glowering red. "It's 1:45 A.M., in case you're interested. Man, you gotta get up at 6:00 A.M. How you gonna do it? If they put you on the desk writing headlines tomorrow, one little slip, like calling the Hammermill Paper Company vice president a PUBIC AFFAIRS director—you outta a job, boy."

What a miserable night. I'd had quite a few like it since starting this book.

I tried to get back to sleep, but Debbie's snoring was making the headboard vibrate. Her head was against the board and the wood was acting like the sounding board of a guitar.

"Debbie. You're snoring. Roll over."

Obligingly, she stopped snoring and rolled over. In an interview for a story on coma arousal for *McCall's*, a doctor had told me that one way to help bring somebody out of a coma was by exposing the person to familiar sounds—favorite songs, loved ones' voices, even the sound of their name.

"Tell your wife to stop snoring sometime," he said. "And then call her name first, and tell her to stop snoring. You'll see the difference. The subconscious homes in on familiar things and you really get its attention that way."

He was right. It worked.

I wonder if she's having rapid-eye-movement sleep now. Maybe when I said her name, it brought her to the surface enough to start dreaming. I resisted the impulse to get a flashlight to check her eyes, to look for the telltale bulges of her pupils moving back and forth under her eyelids. What would she think if she saw me standing over her, like some crazed paranoid schizophrenic, with a flashlight—checking for REMs?

"Keep thinking, dummy," my radio said. "Rapid eye movement, you gotta be kidding. It's 2:00 A.M. You're gonna get four whole hours of sleep. REM *that*, you big, dumb Whoop!"

Bud Dwyer. An image of Bud Dwyer sucking the barrel of a pistol popped into my mind.

Good God, get that one out of your mind or you'll never get to sleep. Stop thinking about it.

Shouldn't have done that! Tell someone not to think about pink elephants, that they *absolutely cannot* think about pink elephants, and that's all they can think about. Then, dummy, you go and tell yourself not to think about Bud Dwyer.

"It's 2:05 A.M., my high-strung friend. Still keeping track," the radio said.

And then, again, back came Bud Dwyer's face, with a gun in his mouth, and I was wide awake again, wanting to wake my wife up, too.

Pennsylvania state treasurer R. Bud Dwyer, known personally by many of us at the *Erie Daily Times*, killed himself at a news conference on January 22, 1987, a day before he was to be sentenced on federal bribery and conspiracy charges.

Nobody at the conference knew it was coming. He had given a long, rambling speech, giving a blast at the press near the end. And then, when he saw some of the TV and news people starting to leave, he held up his hand and said, "You don't want to take down your equipment yet."

Dwyer pulled a gun from a manila envelope and put the gun barrel in his mouth like a big cigar. Then he pulled the trigger.

My God, it's almost 3:00 A.M. and here you are thinking about Bud Dwyer blowing his brains out. You'll never get to sleep. I had my ear to the mattress, listening to my heartbeat. At forty-one I hated it more than ever, that sound, the beating heart, because heading down from midlife, each beat was a tick on the clock of my mortality.

I was beginning to feel oppressed by these dark, terrible thoughts, as if they were being *imposed* on me from the outside. And then I remembered all the Bud Dwyer jokes we'd told in the newsroom:

"What's the difference between a Budweiser and a Bud Dwyer? One has a head."

Zona's got a pair of red-handled bolt cutters on the city desk. Someone picks them up, puts a handle in his mouth, and says, "I'm going to commit suicide the Polish way."

I'm afraid that was me.

"Bud Dwyer's favorite toothpaste? Aim."

"Well, guess he won't be shooting his mouth off anymore."

"The guy standing next to him had a sudden brainstorm."

"An attendant takes his body to the mortician and says, 'This Bud's for you.'"

"Dwyer puts his gun in his mouth and mumbles, 'I'm going to make my day.'"

"The Erie police are right on top of the case, as always. They think that in the next few days, they may have a suspect in the shooting."

The jokes seemed funny in the light of day with a roomful of people telling them, telephones ringing all around, the fluorescent lights buzzing, the police monitor blaring, all part of daytime civilization that obscured the fact that all around us was infinity, that we and our planet had the preposterous nerve to exist in an infinite black void.

The tribe, huddled around their glowing computer terminal screens, nervously telling funny stories to keep the howling void beyond the glow of the tubes from sucking them all out of existence and spiriting them off to join R. Bud Dwyer.

We Annoying Observers use jokes like those to keep us at a healthy distance from reality. But they don't really work. Zona called me that night at home and we talked about Dwyer for two hours, asking each other, "Why?"

Those jokes were not at all funny at 3:00 A.M., awake alone in the black night.

"It's *not* 3:00 A.M., it's 3:30 A.M., NUMB NUTS!" the infernal red lights said.

It was approaching the hour of the wolf, that hour between night and dawn when, according to filmmaker Ingmar Bergman, most babies are born; when people who are ill and ready to die do so; when nightmares are most vivid. The hour when the sleepless are haunted by dread, when ghosts and demons, for those who believe in them, are most powerful.

The Chism murder, January 29, 1975.

Don't think about it!

A husband kills his wife, her father, and his three little children with a rifle.

I had stood outside the Chism house for five hours, the snow falling, falling, falling, a notebook in my hand, shivering and stamping my feet, waiting for them to finish carrying the bodies out one by one, so I could call in the story to the newspaper. First the two big ones, then the three little ones, covered with sheets, on stretchers. I wrote with a pencil instead of a pen. It was so cold the ink in the pen kept freezing. After you've been reporting a while, you learn to carry pencils in Erie winters.

The next morning, at my desk, Zona walked by and said, "My God, what's the matter with you?"

"Me? Nothing. Why?"

He said that as he walked past my desk he just got this feeling that my mind was churning like a bag of worms, like he was walking past "some kind of vortex."

He was right. I'd spent the night trying to push the murders out of my mind, looking at my own wife, sleeping peacefully, wondering how a person could kill someone he loved. And of course, the harder I tried to push the thoughts out, the more I entrenched them inside me. I'd been at many gruesome police scenes over the years—I could remember Coroner Merle Wood strolling down Peach Street, after a two-car accident, picking up brain parts and putting them into little plastic sandwich bags. And for years, nothing had bothered me. Nothing had gotten farther than the Annoying Observer's notebook.

But the Chism murders—it was the first time the spectral slime had seeped in; it became part of the subterranean ooze. Even now, sometimes, looking at my wife sleeping, as if she's lying there dead, my mind jumps back to the Chism murders and how Donald Chism killed his wife and left her lying there, asleep forever.

"It's 4:00 A.M., O Sensitive One," my radio says. "Two hours of sleep, if you're lucky. Whydoncha just wimp out and call in sick? Oops, better not do that—they haven't found a cure for sick days yet, have they?"

I put the tissue box in front of the radio to shut it up. Little white roses on a navy blue box. I couldn't see the numbers anymore, just a crimson glow from behind the box, showing the thing was still yammering away.

The night had been a long one, like a nocturnal descent.

"Satan doesn't like what you're doing," a Christian friend of mine said at a coffee break the next day. "He's against your book going forward. He doesn't want people believing Jesus will restore the health he steals away. He doesn't want a book that builds faith. He's going to fight you every way he can."

"Yeah, right."

"I'm not kidding. You better be ready."

"Ready for what? The next express to La-La Land? A sleepless night is a sleepless night."

"Don't be so sure. The Chism murder really messed you up for a while, didn't it? Maybe the devil was working on you way back then, because he saw this book coming and didn't want you to do it."

"Aw, come on—"

"Just watch out. You better watch it, all the time."

His existential fears of the Precariousness of the Human Condition and the Vulnerability of Man to Unfriendly External Forces made me think of one of those old recordings made down South in the 1940s, recordings of prison ax gangs singing as they cut wood. Each prisoner is chained to a tree. A white folkologist, searching for True American Folksongs, sits quietly in their midst, head down, his microphone sucking the fear and pain out of the air and pumping it into his machine:

Devil gon' jump out da bushes and grab yooo (WHOCK!)

Devil gonna jump out da bushes and grab ya (WHOCK!)

Devil gon' jump out da bushes and grab yooo (WHOCK!)

One a dese old, damn daaaays! (WHOCK! and SPLIIINGGG!!! as a wood chip flies out and hits the recording microphone.)

Indeed.

<table>
<tr><td>CHAPTER

15</td><td># Wormwood</td></tr>
</table>

What are the greatest needs of the Church today? . . .
One of the greatest needs is defense from that evil
which is called the Devil. . . .

Evil is not merely a lack of something, but an
effective agent, a living, spiritual being, perverted and
perverting. A terrible reality . . .

—Pope Paul VI

HEALER JOHN WIMBER, who taught in the MC510 course at Fuller
Theological Seminary, tells in his book *Power Healing* of a twenty-eight-
year-old wife of a missionary who would look in the windows of her home
at night and instead of seeing her own reflection, she would see strange
and tortured faces. She also told of having terrifying dreams, something
that started in France after she prayed for a man who had claimed to be
oppressed, if not possessed, by demons.

Also, as long as the woman could remember, she had struggled with
impure thoughts, fantasizing about having sex with married men, even
though she had never done so and was terrified at the possibility that she
might.

Soon after returning to California, the woman attended a prayer
meeting led by Blaine and Becky Cook. Cook is an associate of Wimber's
in Wimber's Vineyard Ministries. During the meeting, the missionary's
wife behaved in a bizarre manner. For no apparent reason, she cried out,
fell to the floor, and began thrashing around. When Becky Cook
approached her, the woman said, "I hate you," but it did not sound like
her own voice at all.

Blaine then picked the woman up and took her to another room for
prayer with a prayer group. The woman hit him in the mouth.

Blaine Cook suspected the woman was under the influence of demons.

"You demons who are producing defiance, the temptation to commit adultery, anger, and fear, be gone from this child of God," Blaine prayed. And as he did so, the woman fell to the ground and experienced immediate and dramatic relief from her oppression, according to Wimber.

Since then, he says, she has had no problems with habitual sexual fantasies, demonic dreams, or seeing spirits in her windows.

In 1985, Pope John Paul II himself prayed in Latin for a young woman hiding underneath a sofa with her demons. Afterward, the pope told a senior Vatican official that it had been for him a new, biblical experience, one which involved a spirit of evil.

John Wimber believes in the existence of Satan and demons, and, as he told me when I interviewed him, believes their principal target is the human race. "They do vex, interact with, involve themselves with, and indwell in people," he said.

Most Westerners have a problem with paradigm shifts when it comes to believing in Satan and demons, he said. "Coming up through our educational systems here in the Western world we tend to have basically a Western rationalist view in which we look for logical, scientific explanations for everything that happens . . . in our society, with our background, we have a worldview which prohibits even considering certain things. But I think demons do exist. Certainly they can try to prohibit what you are doing, and yes, they could even try to stop you from writing your book, Jack. I think there is intelligence in the demon world. I think they interact. For instance, in the gospels, we see Jesus traversing the Sea of Galilee and a big storm comes. Right in the middle of it Jesus stands up and rebukes the wind and waves. The term he uses there is the very same term that he uses when he speaks to demons. In the very next page, he is on the other side of the sea and he meets the Gadarene demoniac with the legions of demons in him. In my opinion, there is a relationship here. Those demons knew that Jesus was coming and they stirred up a little problem for him in an attempt to stop it. Talking to Lew Smedes about this, I think he would have great difficulty, because from his theological reference point, he is a Western rationalist. Your training can control your viewpoint.

"If we accept that the Bible is true," Wimber said, "then we have to accept the reality that there is spiritual warfare going on between the forces of good and evil and that Jesus Christ came to resolve a basic problem that started in the garden with the fall of Adam and Eve and that he came . . . to end the race of Adam and establish a new species, a new kind of people on earth called Christians. Outside of the protection of Christian faith and a relationship with God there is indeed a dire consequence for humanity. People with no relationship to God are subject to the enemy's work, and he can work freely on them because first, they don't even recognize his existence, and second, they don't have the protection that goes with a relationship with God. But even within the context of the Christian provision, if we are unbelieving Christians, we don't have any protection either, so large numbers of Christians don't even know there is a war going on. They don't even believe in Satan or hell or any of the consequences.

"As Christians, ministering in Jesus' name, we are commissioned to warfare. We have to pray, because it is one of our weapons of warfare and one of the principal ways in which we interact with the Lord and master of our lives, Jesus Christ. As a new Christian, Jack, you've joined an army rather than an audience, and as such, there's a consequence, there's a job for you to do. You are now at war with the enemy of God, and the enemy of God brings sickness and sin into the world. One of our jobs is to heal the sick because that thwarts the enemy and relieves the suffering. We have an ambassadorial privilege. We have been sent into the world to represent Jesus with a ministry of reconciliation. We are to preach reconciliation to people either through our personal testimonies or actual preaching. In so doing we reconcile men to God. One of the means is healing."

I was beginning to question whether there might be a slight chance that sleepless nights and dark thoughts might not be simply the product of a tired brain—not a bag of worms, but Wormwood himself.

The classic book *The Screwtape Letters*, by C. S. Lewis, is written in the form of a series of letters from a senior demon named Screwtape to a junior tempter named Wormwood. Wimber points to *The Screwtape Letters* as a classic description of demonic strategy. In the seventh letter, Screwtape tells the young Wormwood:

Our policy, for the moment, is to conceal ourselves. Of course, this has not always been so. We are really faced with a cruel dilemma. When the humans disbelieve in our existence, we lose all the pleasing results of direct terrorism, and we make no magicians. On the other hand, when they believe in us, we cannot make them materialists and skeptics. At least, not yet. I have great hopes that we shall learn in due time how to emotionalize and mythologize their science to such an extent that what is, in effect, a belief in us (though not under that name) will creep in while the human mind remains closed to belief in the Enemy. The "Life Force," the worship of sex, and some aspects of psychoanalysis may here prove useful. If once we can produce our perfect work—the Materialistic Magician, the man, not using, but veritably worshiping, what he vaguely calls "Forces" while denying the existence of spirits—then the end of the war will be in sight . . .

"Worshiping forces . . .?" That sounded a lot to me like "harmonic convergence" and other trappings of the *New Age*.

I kept encountering all these people who talked about Satan and took him seriously—Joppa Wiese even saw him in his bedroom—while I still pictured the devil as a myth, a little boy wearing red tights and styrofoam-filled nylon horns standing under a front porch light on Halloween. I decided to do a little of my own research, since Satan was continually being portrayed to me as the dark side of healing. I went to the public library and returned with a stack of dusty old clothbound theology books with dark black and navy blue covers; most of the books had been checked out only once or twice in the past five years.

I found that the devil and his minions aren't what they used to be, at least in terms of our understanding of them. The concept of Satan has undergone quite a few changes through the ages. In the New Testament, the devil is portrayed as "The Prince of This World," the ruler of an infernal kingdom, a renegade from the family of God, an evil power diametrically opposed to God's will. But in the Old Testament, "the Satan" is actually an agent of God's or "Yahweh's" will. The best example of this is in the Book of Job, where Satan is revealed for the first time as a distinct personality—distinct, but not necessarily evil.

In the Book of Job, Satan is present among the "Sons of God" (the angels) as an angel called "Hassatan," which means "The Adversary." But here, Satan is acting more as an adversary of man than of God, inflicting suffering on man with God's permission. The Satan is allowed to inflict suffering upon mankind to test man's faith, confidence, fidelity, and love (in the Old Testament, Satan is almost always introduced by the definite article—"The Satan").

According to one theologian, John L. McKenzie, who spoke to me from the yellowed pages of the *Dictionary of the Bible*, "The Satan" is not an evil spirit of the kind that appears in Mesopotamian and in later Jewish literature; he is an accuser, the adversary of man, a heavenly officer or prosecutor whose function is to question and to test the genuineness of human virtue. To accomplish his work he has the power to inflict evil on men—sickness, natural catastrophies. The purpose of these misfortunes is to test the reactions of men—virtue is not genuine unless it sustains adversity.

In the Book of Job, for instance, Satan is working in alliance with God. He has the permission of Yahweh to tempt Job but not to kill him.

The only place in the Old Testament where the word "satan" appears without the definite article, and therefore as a personal name, is in I Chronicles 21:1. Here, my dusty theologians point out, a new concept seems to be developing. No longer is Satan just a good angel who does God's will by policing the earth and reporting men's offenses to God. Here he appears as a bad angel who actually tempts man to do evil.

In Genesis, it is never stated that the serpent who tempted Eve was the Devil, or his agent. It is only toward the end of the history of Old Testament revelation, in the Book of Wisdom, that the Bible states, "But by the envy of the Devil, death entered the world."

In the New Testament, I found many allusions to the evil personality of Satan, The Devil—he's called The Tempter, The Wicked One, Beelzebub, Prince of the Devils, The Prince of This World, The God of This World, Prince of the Power of the Air, The Dragon, and The Serpent.

In the New Testament, the concept of Satan has two special characteristics: He is the fallen angel mentioned in Luke and Jude, and, as Lord of this world, he is the enemy of God but shall ultimately be overcome by Christ.

Christ's victory over evil is shown dramatically by his cures of those possessed by demons, who, according to Matthew 25:41, are subject to Satan.

One of the most powerful of these cures, which healers like Charles and Frances Hunter often point to, is the story of the blind and dumb demoniac, also called the Beelzebub pericope, described in Matthew 12:22–27. It tells how Jesus cured a possessed man so that he "spoke and saw" after being blind and dumb. The crowds were amazed and said, "Can this be the son of David?"

The Pharisees said, "This man does not cast out devils except by Beelzebub, the Prince of the Devils."

Jesus countered by stating that a house divided against itself cannot stand, "And if Satan casts out Satan, he is divided against himself; how then shall his kingdom stand?"

Christ then said, "He who is not with me is against me" and proclaimed that not believing is a sin against the Holy Spirit. "But let anyone speak against the Holy Spirit and he will not be forgiven, either in this world or the next."

The Beelzebub pericope shows how Jesus is stronger than the "strong-armed man" and brings an end to the previously uncontested dominion of Satan. The exorcism depicted in the Beelzebub pericope shows the triumph of Jesus over The Prince of This World.

"Jack, Pooh's just wet all over the hallway carpet!!!" Debbie bellows up the stairs to my attic office, interrupting my scholarly studies. Apparently she thinks I promised, when we were married, to love, honor, and clean up after the dog.

LOVE! HONOR! STOP DOG URINE!

"Jaa-ack, POO-oooh's just whhhettt ALL OVEEEER the CAAAAR-pet!" I whine under my breath.

"I take care of the baby's messes, you can handle the dogs'!" she hollers up the stairs.

I can't argue with that. I stomp down the stairs and head for the VicVac.

Thank heavens for the VicVac.

There's a photographer at work who bought his wife engraved champagne glasses for Christmas so they can toast each other. It's his second marriage.

I bought my wife a little red VicVac for Christmas. It's a plastic, battery-powered, wet-dry, hand-held vacuum sweeper she lets me use to clean up the rug when the dogs abuse it. I can suck up a dinner-plate-sized puddle in three minutes.

"What would we do with engraved champagne glasses anyway?" Debbie asks, taking obvious delight in my efforts to remove the dog's organic indelicacy.

Her raised eyebrows and the slight nodding of her head say, "*Now you see what I put up with all day long.*"

Her slightly flared nostrils add, "*And I don't even get a salary like you do.*"

That little crease, starting to harden at the left corner of her mouth, proclaims defiantly: "*But my job's just as important and necessary as your job or your self-important little book, only I don't get any recognition for what I do.*"

The little pink tip of her tongue, pointing at me from just inside her smirk, finishes the unspoken oration:

"*So how do you like it?*"

She has the nerve to stand there supervising the interpreter of the Beelzebub pericope, looking lectures at me, while I'm on my hands and knees working on the rug.

"What would we do with engraved champagne glasses?" I ask, repeating her question. "I could toast my first wife, maybe?"

She gives a little sniff of quiet satisfaction. Just with a look, a simple facial expression, she'd made her point. She'd had me again. I'd *reacted*. A Superior Woman. An icebreaker.

"How's your research going? Find out anything I should know?"

"Well, you'd better pay attention to the Beelzebub pericope," I tell her, sticking the loud, working end of the furiously sucking red VicVac in front of her face.

I explain to her that according to Mr. McKenzie, who may have passed away by now, for all I know, we better not be too flip about demons. "He calls the Beelzebub pericope one of the most 'severe' in the Gospels. I read to her from McKenzie's *Dictionary of the Bible*: "Refusal to believe that Jesus exhibits the power of God precisely in his power over demons is the sin against the Holy Spirit which is not forgiven.""

"The only sin . . . not forgiven?" Debbie says. "I didn't know there was such a thing as a sin that wouldn't be forgiven."

One question I'm left with: If Satan isn't a myth, how could he undergo a personality change from the Old Testament to the New Testament, changing from an agent of God who tested man with God's permission to an evil adversary of both God and man? Wouldn't that seem to indicate the evil Satan is just a convenient creation of the superstitious mind of man, with Satan's evil nature growing like some fluvial accretion as legends flow over and around him?

A pastor from a little church near Pittsburgh offered this answer: "I don't think Satan transformed or changed. I think what changed was our education, affecting how we perceived him. Satan didn't change. It was our perception of him that grew as we went from God's kindergarten class in Genesis to maturity in the Revelation of the New Testament."

I joked with the pastor that besides having a few restless nights, I'd had more problems with equipment breakdowns in the two months after starting this book than I'd had in the past twenty years of reporting—tape recorders and tapes breaking three or four times in the midst of important interviews, computers malfunctioning and inexplicably erasing data, the telephone going dead twice when I tried to call Mayor Tullio. Even the dogs seemed to be taking more delight than usual in the carpets.

"You are involved now in a work of God, a book you were meant to do from the moment you were born," the pastor said, deadly serious. "You are forming opinions and building your faith, the thing that is most dangerous to the kingdom of Satan. He will try to interfere with you, and you are going to have to tell him in the name of Jesus to flee from you, before he calls in some of the bigger boys who do some things that are beyond the jurisdiction of those who mess up computers and tape players. You're going to have to say, 'Lord, help my unbelief,' and tell God that you trust Him and believe that the blood of His Son is covering you. Then, when you tell Satan, In the name of Jesus, flee,' Satan will leave, not because of you, but because of the Power behind you."

"All of this is very strange," I tell Debbie after we've put the kids to bed and locked the dogs in the kitchen. In our house, there is little room for demons.

It's too full of things like VicVac, VCRs, color TVs, desktop and laptop computers, stereos, humidifiers, boom boxes, microwaves ovens, blenders, toasters, aquariums, copying machines, books and bookshelves, antiques—all the material things aging baby boomers accumulate to anchor themselves to the planet to help them forget there's infinity over their heads. "Do you believe in all this demonic stuff? That there could be evil spirits in the VicVac?" I ask my wife.

"I don't have all the answers and I don't think I ever will," she says over her shoulder, padding in her slippers and nightgown into the bathroom with a white ironstone pitcher. "I don't sleep as well when the air gets too dry, so don't turn the humidifier off tonight, even if it is noisy," she says from the bathroom. The pipes clunk after she turns the faucet off. She likes the air moist. I like it dry. She likes the sound of the humidifier. It keeps me awake. She likes the room cold at night. I like it warm—I don't like heavy blankets. She loves to snuggle under them.

"You won't answer all your questions on this side of the grave either," she says, back in our room, pouring water into the machine. "But I do believe that if there is good, there must be evil. For black, there's white. Yin and yang, that sort of thing."

Yin and yang, the Chinese terms for the passive (yin) and active (yang) principles of the universe, or the female, negative force and the male, positive force—black and white, woman and man, softness and hardness, sorrow and joy, death and life, hate and love, smaller and greater, despair and faith, sickness and healing. The Chinese believed the two forces comprised ch'i, the life force that makes the universe tick. Yin and yang. Evil and good. The two faces of infinity. The ugly witch and the beautiful lady.

"We live in a world of opposites," Debbie goes on. "If God can influence our lives for good, I would think Satan could for evil. I don't see how you can believe in one without believing in the other. It's like your Möbius circle—a one-sided figure that has two sides."

A one-sided figure that has two sides. Are God and Satan like that?

In the Old Testament, Satan inflicted suffering upon man with God's permission. The dark shadow that Joppa Wiese described in his doorway was an Old Testament Satan—when God spoke to Joppa, he said, "I can't do a complete healing in you until you obey Me . . . and if you won't . . . *then I will allow Satan to have his way.*"

It's as if the shadow that Joppa saw sent him running straight into the arms of the Lord, so that ultimately and ironically, Satan was doing the Lord's work. A one-sided figure that has two sides.

M. Scott Peck, M.D., in his book *The Road Less Traveled*, expresses the dynamics of good and evil this way:

. . . Evil backfires in the big picture of human evolution. For every soul it destroys—and there are many—it is instrumental in the salvation of others. Unwittingly, evil serves as a beacon to warn others away from its shoals. Because most of us have been graced by an almost instinctive sense of horror at the outrageousness of evil, when we recognize its presence, our own personalities are honed by the awareness of its existence. Our consciousness of it is a signal to purify ourselves. It was evil, for instance, that raised Christ to the Cross, thereby enabling us to see him from afar.

A Tale of Two
City Mayors

A pleasant companion reduces the length of the journey.

—Publius Syrus, *Maxims*

"JACK!"

I look up from the rewrites on my desk to Zona at the city desk. He's
got his eyebrows raised at me. "I sent you something," he says.

I swivel around in my chair and push the W/AT UDK button on my
keyboard. The file name "Illness" pops up. I push "N" (space) "execute"
and the whole story appears—at first glance an Associated Press wire
story, written by a guy named "A. Nuss."

NEW YORK (AP)—Researchers at Cornell School of Medicine here report in
today's edition of the *New England Journal of Medicine* that they have isolated a
heretofore unidentified optical condition known to affect millions of Americans.
The condition, known as opticus rectumitis, occurs when the optic nerves
become crossed with the lower nervous system near the anus, according to the
report.

Opticus rectumitis results in tunnel vision. There is no known cure.

Zona's grinning at me. "You've had your ups and downs lately. Maybe
that's what you've got. Better call the Happy Hunters!"

Good old Tony. It's 6:45 A.M., the workday hasn't even begun yet, and
already he's starting in on me.

A few minutes later, Zona's back by my desk, sitting at the Macintosh
computer. He's having his second cup of coffee, and it's time for him to
get a weather graphic for the weather page. "Those idiot elitists," he says
to his computer terminal.

"Who?" I ask.

"Database people. These computer nuts are logging their stories in

119

Greenwich mean time, even though this weather map of the United States doesn't go outside the United States. How elitist can you get?"

That makes me think about computer system managers. The Keepers of the Holy Flame. The Protectors of the Knowledge. At our place the Mainframe is the Company Deity. No one is allowed to approach its Presence but the systems managers, for surely if anyone else managed to figure out the numerical code to the locked door of the computer room, the sanctum sanctorum, if anyone but the Sanitized Unfantisized Demagnitized Systems Managers stood before the Mainframe, the sight of it would turn his eyeballs into Kibbles and Bits.

The computer has such power that lay persons not wearing pocket protectors for their ballpoint pens *dare not approach it.*

We must honor and respect the Mainframe, systems managers tell us, because it is only by His—they really call it "He" and "Him"—grace that we are able to perform day-to-day operations and carry on with our jobs.

The systems managers are our priests, ordained by Digital, and we recognize them by their short-sleeved shirts, which they wear all through winter; their plastic pocket protectors; and their eyeglasses, worn lenses-toward-heaven on the tops of their heads. The priests intercede with the Silicon Deity for us. They dole privileges to us, according to His Word. They are like the elite group of scribes in Mesopotamia, who in 2000 B.C. were the only ones privileged to read and write cuneiform; writing and communication have always meant power. (These scribes mostly wrote things like "Two sheep, fully grown, barley fattened, trained to guide the oxen to the big house." But it was impressive, just the same.)

Our priests constantly remind us of the ten commandments they brought back from Digital's headquarters:

1. Thou shalt not scroll the wire services for stories out of mere curiosity, but rather of necessity only.
2. Thou shalt honor thy instructors.
3. Thou shalt not trespass into another's memory area.
4. Thou shalt not covet thy neighbor's files.
5. Thou shalt clean thy directory of outdated files so as not to overload the system.
6. Thou shalt not place others before me in importance—remember that the Radio Shack Model 3s and the laptops are only clones of My Glory, and I am thy Main . . . Frame.
7. Thou shalt put merge signs in their proper places in thy text or else thee will slow the system.
8. Thou shalt call for systems maintenance priest Larry Skowronski the moment thee noticeth anything amiss with thy terminal.
9. Thou shalt not spilleth coffee into the keyboard.
10. Thou shalt not seek out computer codes which thee art not permitted to use—such as the MUL code.

＊ ＊ ＊

We veteran reporters didn't know how to MUL until one day a young intern appeared in the city room. This clean-cut young man, wearing docksiders and no socks, born of parents so rich they have spaces labeled "guest parking" next to their house, had come from a college where anyone could MUL, where there were no priests to feel threatened by MULing. The power to MUL should belong to everyone, this charismatic young man told us, and then he taught us how.

The priests hadn't trusted us to MUL. Perhaps they felt that once we learned how to MUL ourselves, they wouldn't be needed anymore; that maybe we would start wearing our own plastic pocket protectors.

MULing is simply a means by which you can send humor-testing messages to the women in the Features Department. It works like this:

Say you hear a call on the police monitor that goes "*Rescue squad to 128 West 8th for an unresponsive male.*"

Well, then you just quickly type M-U-L on your keyboard. When the computer prompts you, you tell it you want to send this humor-testing message to the Features Department:

"Rescue squad has unresponsive male at 128 West 8th. *Quick! Send your women!*"

Then, the next time a Features Creature does *anything* on her computer, even hits the space bar, bumps it, or even *coughs on the thing*, that message will pop up, out of nowhere, and *no one will be able to know who sent it!*

We in the news business have constantly to think of new ways to laugh—if only to keep from crying.

I can't help myself!

It is 2:30 P.M. I started work at 7:00 A.M. My workday is almost over, I am burned out, feeling like I've done three term papers in four hours.

I weaken. I break one of Digital's commandments. I scroll the wire, out of sheer curiosity to see if the world still exists outside our underwindowed city room.

I had already gone through the wire service photos on the old black typewriter stand at the front of the room, looked at all the weather art, NASA rocket explosions, and pictures of a young boy who was put into a clothes dryer and tumble-dried by his mother.

I find two stories of interest. The Associated Press stories, both by Tara Bradley-Steck, are labeled "TWO MAYORS."

The first one is about Pittsburgh's Richard Caliguiri, the second about Erie's Lou Tullio.

I pull up the Caliguiri story and read:

SOFT-SPOKEN CALIGUIRI AN ENIGMA

By TARA BRADLEY-STECK
Associated Press Writer

PITTSBURGH (AP)—Over the din of chatter and clattering dishes at a senior citizens' center, Richard S. Caliguiri raises his sotto voce voice ever so slightly for the attention of several hundred lunching men and women.

"If you wake up in the morning and you need a mayor, call me," he says.

A stout, elderly woman promptly races toward him, shouting: "I don't need a mayor, I need a man."

Blushing but not missing a beat, the normally restrained Caliguiri, his diminutive frame exaggerated by the cavernous room and boisterous crowd, sweeps the woman in his arms for a one-minute waltz among the chuckling lunchers.

"She loves to dance. She knows every dance there is," the mayor explained later as he adjusted his tie and straightened his always-neatly pressed suit.

In a city where people speak their minds, laugh heartily and complain loudly, the soft-spoken, self-effacing Caliguiri is something of an enigma.

As Pittsburgh's chief executive for 10 years, Caliguiri is credited with engineering the city's metamorphosis from a wilting steel giant into a progressive, technically-oriented metropolitan core of 365,000 and earning it an award as the nation's most livable city.

He meets regularly with some of the country's top business, academic and labor leaders and has cultivated a partnership with the private sector that would be the envy of any big-city mayor.

Yet he maintains the low-profile savvy of a corporate chairman instead of an elected official consumed by popularity polls.

When he needs rejuvenating, though, Caliguiri turns not to the exclusive clubs, but to one of the city's 55 mostly-ethnic neighborhoods and to the people who have voted him into office three times by landslide margins.

Since learning last spring he'd been stricken with amyloidosis, a rare and usually fatal disease that attacks the body's vital organs, Caliguiri has revived an old practice of visiting one neighborhood each week to talk to residents about their problems.

On a recent walk through the city's South Side, with its workers from German and Eastern European stock, Caliguiri's smile and handshake were warm and the conversation was animated, absent the typical politician's braggadocio or swagger.

"If you just sat in your office with all the paperwork, all the phone calls, all the problems and frustrations, you would jump out the window," Caliguiri said. "But you come out here and they're sincere. I rather enjoy this. I always have."

Caliguiri, 56, a surprisingly slight man of 5-foot-6 with neatly-cut hair and an olive-tinged complexion, is a Pittsburgher through and through with roots as deep as any steelworker's. He's not a big joker, but he has a subtle, dry sense of humor.

"I thought you was bigger," an elderly man joked while shaking the mayor's hand.

"I'm still growing," Caliguiri quipped.

Caliguiri isn't known for his impulsiveness or quick wit.

Indeed, he seems restrained and cautious at press conferences or while being interviewed. But there is a genuine, spontaneous quality revealed in special moments—when he entertains a fifth-grade music class with a tap dance, cajoles an elderly man about his Pittsburgh Steelers watch, or holds the hand of a stroke victim struggling to pronounced the words, "I'm praying for you."

. . . It took some time, Caliguiri says, before he was able to come to grips with the knowledge he had an incurable disease.

For a man who's rarely been sick, that realization didn't come easily.

"You never want to accept the finality of anything, but somehow, sooner or later, you're going to go. I don't know at what age is a good age to leave this good earth of ours. But the more I understand it . . . the more I've learned to cope in a sense with what I have," he said.

"What's going to happen when this thing progresses again—right now it's not—I don't know how I'll react. But as of right now, I've accepted it and my family's accepted it and we're living a normal life."

Pausing briefly, Caliguiri pulled from his pocket a handful of trinkets hurriedly pressed into his hands from an assortment of well-wishers on his South Side tour—a cross from a woman's necklace, a blue-and-white carnation and a hand-crocheted change purse containing a new penny.

"Look," he said, carefully fingering each item. "This is what makes you feel good. It makes it all worthwhile."

I pushed "Control F" to file that story, then pulled up the next one, about Lou Tullio:

ERIE'S SIX-TERM MAYOR NOT ABOUT TO STOP

By TARA BRADLEY-STECK
Associated Press Writer

ERIE, Pa. (AP)—Louis Tullio's presence envelops this Great Lakes city like the mist rising from its harbor.

The mayor's name is emblazoned on a civic center, a college athletic field and a senior citizens' tower. His face, to the people of Erie, is as recognizable as President Reagan's.

His social life mirrors his political life, taking him to any function to which he is invited—anniversary and birthday parties, confirmations and bar mitzvahs, baptisms, weddings and funerals—mostly by people he doesn't know.

He even keeps his phone number listed so citizens don't have to wade through a sea of bureaucrats to resolve pressing problems.

For more than two decades, Tullio, 71, has been the only mayor this city of about 120,000 residents has known or wanted.

But doctors say Tullio has less than 18 months to live because of an incurable disease that is daily weakening his heart and lungs. It means he has only 18 months to wrap up unfinished projects. His fervent wish is to be granted an extra six months to complete his sixth term, which expires at the end of 1989.

"I wake up in the morning and figure, 'Well, gee, I have another day.' I have a challenge. And I need a challenge. If I don't, I'm not happy," he says cheerily.

"My next challenge is to see if I can beat an incurable disease. I don't think there's any such thing as an incurable disease because God created the body and he can cure it, too."

In 22 years—he claims to be currently the second-longest serving mayor in the nation—Tullio has helped turn Erie from a decaying manufacturing town into a thriving port city with a respectably low—6.6 percent—unemployment rate.

But Tullio says he has much more to do, including spearheading a renaissance of the industrialized harbor area into a showcase development of condominiums, marinas, recreation areas, history trails, shops and a hotel.

"I'd like to finish the projects down at the bayfront area, which we're just starting," he said. "I'd like to see that come to fruition, and I think that after that, my work is completed."

Tullio's first wife of 28 years, Ceil, died in 1969. They had three children. He married his second wife, Grace, an Erie area businesswoman, two years later. They have no children.

Tullio is a big, strong man, a former football star and coach who isn't accustomed to battling illness. But over the past year, he has struggled with his health, undergoing quadruple bypass surgery and losing about 45 pounds.

. . . Tullio's lone concession to his affliction is to trim his office time to four hours a day and curtail his social activities.

The problem, says his administrative assistant Pat Liebel, is that leaves everyone else exhausted.

"His time may be a little less with people, but he's accomplishing in four hours what he normally accomplishes in an eight-hour day," she said. "I always feel by the time he leaves here I've put in a full day, and I've got another half day to go."

Critics—and there aren't many—charge that Tullio gets involved in too many things, however minute, and is averse to delegating responsibility.

Liebel says that's not only because he's a "detail person" but also because he likes to be in control.

Tullio has been an effective mayor in part because he's known how to get things done, from acting as mediator in labor disputes to bringing in $295 million in state and federal funds for urban renewal projects.

. . . The dozens of photographs on his large office wall—which show Tullio with every president since John F. Kennedy—attest to the Erie mayor's ability to push the right political buttons, be they Republican or Democrat.

Tullio, a die-hard Democrat, even supported the 1982 re-election of Republican Gov. Richard Thornburgh, much to the chagrin of some Democratic leaders.

. . . By all appearances, it will take a long time before another tenant of the Erie mayor's office leaves such an indelible mark.

"As Tullio fights his personal battle, the citizens of Erie are watching the beginning of the end of an era," the Erie Times-News, often the mayor's adversary, wrote in an editorial in October.

"For a long time, even after Tullio has left office, when someone mentions 'the mayor,' many will, by habit, still think of Tullio."

Creative Miracles

> Whatever a man prays for, he prays for a miracle. Every prayer reduces itself to this: "Great God, grant that twice two be not four.
>
> —Ivan Turgenev, *Prayer*

ONE OF the best-documented and most amazing of all Lourdes-related cures is the case of Pierre de Rudder, described by Ruth Cranston as an amazing example of a *creative miracle*—a cure in which new tissue appears instantly where there was none before. This cure is documented by the patient's own bones.

Pierre de Rudder was a Belgian peasant who lived in Jabbeke, a town near Bruges. In 1868 his leg was broken and crushed by a falling tree. The break was so complete that over an inch separated the upper and lower parts of the bone. De Rudder's doctors recommend amputation, because the bones couldn't be set together, but he refused to consider it.

He lived with the pain for eight years before finally making, at age fifty-two, a pilgrimage to a city near Ghent, Oostacker, where a statue in honor of Our Lady of Lourdes had been erected.

Before leaving his hometown, he was again examined by a physician there, a Dr. Van Hoestenberghe, who found an open, unhealed abscess at the site of the break through which he could see the bones of de Rudder's leg, still separated by over three centimeters. The doctor found no sign of healing, and his patient was still in great pain. The lower portion of his leg could be turned in all directions and could even be folded upward.

At the foot of the statue in the Oostacker grotto, de Rudder prayed earnestly, asking that all his sins be forgiven. Then he prayed to be able to return to work so his children would not have to live on charity.

While praying, de Rudder felt a "profound movement in his whole body," Cranston wrote, and then he started to walk all around the grotto without his crutches.

His leg bone had immediately fused together and the wound had healed. He did not even limp, because both his legs were the same length.

Verifying the cure to Lourdes officials, Dr. Van Hoestenberghe wrote:

"Pierre is undoubtedly cured. I have seen him many times during the last eight years, and my medical knowledge tells me such a cure is absolutely inexplicable. Again, he has been cured completely, suddenly, and instantaneously, without any period of convalescence. Not only have the bones been suddenly united, but a portion of bone would actually seem to have been created to take the place of those fragments I myself have seen come out of the wound. . . . if [this is] a miracle, then there is something beyond [biological] law—*a God exists, and surely he must have given some revelation of himself* [italics mine]."

De Rudder died of pneumonia at age seventy-five. An autopsy showed that the two ends of de Rudder's leg bones had been joined together by a *new piece of healthy bone over an inch long that had formed, apparently instantaneously, over the broken ends of the original bones.*

De Rudder's leg bones are themselves the documentation of his miracle. They are kept today at the University of Louvain in Belgium. Copper molds of the bones are kept at the medical bureau's offices in Lourdes.

The De Rudder case of regenerated bone is similar to one reported by one of the best-known healers of all time, Kathryn Kuhlman, who was called a "one-woman Lourdes."

In her book *I Believe in Miracles*, Kuhlman describes the miraculous healing of James McCutcheon's hip.

On October 31, 1947, McCutcheon was working on a railroad when a bulldozer flipped up a crosstie on which he was standing. The tie flew up, struck him on the leg, and sent him sailing ten feet into the air. Doctors at St. Joseph's Hospital in Lorain, Ohio, discovered that the ball of his hip had been knocked off the end of his thighbone, "Just as if you had taken a hacksaw and cut it off."

Following the accident, McCutcheon underwent a series of five operations to try to reattach the hip to the femur, but all of them were unsuccessful. The bones were starting to decalcify and would not fuse together.

Doctors at Allegheny General Hospital near Pittsburgh told him his only hope of ever walking again lay in replacing the broken hip ball with an artificial new one of plastic and silver.

Before undergoing that operation, however, McCutcheon decided to visit the famous Kathryn Kuhlman instead. On November 5, 1949, he was sitting midway back in Carnegie Auditorium, when suddenly, in the middle of the service, a great heat came over him. McCutcheon told Kuhlman later, "It felt as if there were a fire under my chair, and the sweat just poured off me."

His eldest married daughter, who had attended the service with her father, had her hand on his knee. "Waves of electricity seemed to go from his leg into my arm," she told Kuhlman later.

Kuhlman herself describes what happened this way:

"The first thing Jim knew, and to his utter amazement, his cane was stashed under his seat and he was up on his feet and out in the aisle, his daughter beside him. Without a moment's hesitation or doubt or fear, he walked, unaided, down the aisle to the platform. Without hesitation, he climbed the high steps to the platform."

McCutcheon said, "When I got up there, Miss Kuhlman told me to lift my leg high and stamp my foot. I did, and I've been able to do it ever since."

From that day on, McCutcheon never used a cane again or had any trouble with his leg. From his healing in 1949 until 1960, he never bothered to go back to his doctor for more X-rays. "I knew I was healed, that was good enough for me," he told Kuhlman.

But knowing that skeptics demand scientific proof, McCutcheon finally procurred, in 1960, a full set of X-rays showing before-and-after pictures of his leg. The final X-rays show a piece of new bone which had grown instantaneously over the cleavage between the ball of the hip and the upper thighbone, according to Kuhlman. The new bone thus welded the formerly separated pieces into one strong, solid piece of bone.

Kuhlman quotes McCutcheon's surgeon as saying, "This was truly a miracle."

Born around 1915 (she would never reveal her age) and raised in Concordia, Missouri, by a Methodist mother and a Baptist father, Kathryn Kuhlman decided at age sixteen that she was called to preach. She went from community to community, sometimes having to hitch-hike, looking for empty buildings where she could set up benches for the people who would come to hear a redheaded, teenage girl preach.

Kuhlman spent almost twenty years as a traveling free-lance evangelist before settling in the mid-1950s into a small church in Franklin, Pennsylvania. In 1954, members of her ministry began to claim spontaneous healings during her services there. That was the beginning of her healing ministry. Soon she moved to Carnegie Auditorium in Pittsburgh, where she conducted healing services for over twenty years, becoming one of the most respected leaders of the charismatic revival.

Her services would begin with hymn singing. As one song after the other was sung, the emotional pitch of those in the audience would grow, as if the music were submerging their rational, critical minds and letting the love in their hearts pour forth.

Then assistants would tell the audience about her ministry and the miraculous healings that occur during her services, healings of the sort that everyone there would certainly see for themselves.

The music would continue, and suddenly, from out of the wings, Kathryn Kuhlman would walk briskly to the microphone in center stage, taking long strides, smiling radiantly, wearing a dress of dazzling white silk trimmed with gold. She was tall and slim, with long auburn hair.

Allen Spraggett, another once-skeptical journalist who wrote a book on Kuhlman called *The Woman Who Believes in Miracles*, described her meetings, writing, "Charisma pours from her in almost visible rays. So powerful is her magnetism that the congregation leaps to its feet as one person and bursts into tremendous applause, a tumult of adulation." Her face seemed to glow with a preternatural light, he said.

Then the tumult would cease as Kuhlman would lead the choir in her theme hymn, singing the words clearly and deliberately:

> He touched me, oh, He touched me,
> And oh, the joy that filled my soul,
> Something happened and now I know
> He touched me and made me whole.

The congregation would sing the phrases over and over, like the chanting of the "Ave Maria" at Lourdes. It was "the same rhythmic repetition, the same almost unbearably intense feeling," Spraggett wrote.

The singing would stop. Kuhlman would look up, lips moving as if in prayer, oblivious of her surroundings.

Finally she would look out at the audience again and proclaim, "There is power in the name of Jesus. Yes, there is power in the name of Jesus."

She would talk about God's love and how healing occurs through His power channeled through her, making sure the audience understood that it was God, not Kathryn Kuhlman, Who would work the wonders there that night.

"We know, Father, yes, we know that miracles are going to happen in this place today. Oh, we feel the blessed presence of thy Holy Spirit. We promise to give You all the praise, all the glory, for what is about to happen here. Pour out your power on us, for Jesus' sake."

Prayers for healings would follow, and Kuhlman would seem to enter into a trance. That was the moment, she said, when she would become filled with the Holy Spirit: "There have been times when I have felt faith so permeate every part of my being that I have dared to say and do things which, had I trusted to my own understanding or reason, I would never have done."

Soon, like a grown-up Linda Martel, she would begin pointing to various sections of the auditorium, where by a word of knowledge—spiritual ESP—she knew healings were taking place. "I can only say that many times my mind is so surrendered to the Spirit that I know the exact body being healed: the sickness, the affliction, and in some instances the very sin of their lives. And yet I could not pretend to tell you why or how," she wrote later in her book *I Believe in Miracles.*

And as she pointed to members of the audience, they would stand, come forward to the stage, and announce that they had indeed been healed. Doctors there would examine these people and tell the audience whether they thought the healings had occurred or not. (Often the "Holy Spirit" would be manifested so powerfully that healings would occur outside the auditorium. One woman told Spraggett, "I was walking up the steps outside the building when wham, down I went. A man helped me up and said, 'Are you all right? Don't worry, that was the power of God.' Then I realized that the arthritis I'd had in my hands for years was gone. I'd been healed and wasn't even in the service yet!")

The crowd inside would be a conglomeration of all types of people. Spraggett, writing in 1970, described the scene this way: "Long-haired hippies, looking like parodies of themselves in garish costumes and bare feet, rub shoulders with dignified dowagers. The little old ladies are here, the kind who live in one room and cook their meals on hot plates. And there are the young couples with children, gray-suited businessmen, students, clergymen in dog collars, and even one or two faded movie stars hiding behind dark glasses."

<table>
<tr><td>CHAPTER

18</td><td># Why Must Children Suffer?</td></tr>
</table>

God moves in a mysterious way
His wonders to perform;
He plants his footsteps in the sea,
And rides upon the storm.
>—William Cowper, *Light*
>*Shining Out of Darkness*

I HAD KNOWN that at some point, as a child of the 1980s, I'd have to do some boning up on Kathryn Kuhlman, especially since my book editor, Steve Wilburn, assumed I knew who she was. And I, of course, acted as if I did, while making a mental note to cover my tracks as soon as I got the chance. One slaying in the Spirit does not an authority make.

In virtually any book you read about divine healing, Kuhlman's name appears. A relative latecomer to the healing revival that started in the 1940s, she became a giantess in the field nonetheless. She died in 1976.

The Monday that Debbie brought home *I Believe in Miracles* from the library was a day on which I didn't believe in miracles.

I'd been home sick with the flu and had a splitting headache. I was feeling lousy spiritually as well.

The previous Saturday I'd worked a 5:00 P.M.-to-1:00 A.M. shift at the newspaper, and the events of that night were gloomy and painful. I'd spent much of the evening talking on the phone with a young mother, Debbie Danowski, who had just been told she would have to spend three more weeks with her ten-month-old son Eric at Children's Hospital in Pittsburgh. Her baby had just received his second liver transplant. The second liver was finally functioning well, after a few nerve-racking days when it looked like it, too, might stop working as had the first transplant. Now the baby had come down with pneumonia in his left lung, caused by a virus typical in transplant patients whose immune systems have been depressed.

"If the virus spreads to the new liver, it will destroy it," Debbie told me haltingly over the phone.

I'd been reporting on her baby's plight for weeks. We had become friends. "If only the lung infection was bacterial," she said. "They could treat that with antibiotics. But with a virus, we just have to let things take their course."

She paused, then said, "God knows what we're going through here, so why is He letting this go on? We keep praying to Him. Eric's just a baby. Why won't God heal him, Jack?"

When I got home, her question was still echoing in my mind. The house was silent.

I'd carried the clip file on Eric Danowski home with me. I sat down on the couch and read every newspaper story we'd written about him for the past few weeks. I had done most of them myself:

December 13, 1987. IN TRUE SPIRIT OF CHRISTMAS, FRIENDS RALLY TO HELP DANOWSKI FAMILY.

Debbie Danowski says she and her husband give thanks for their friends and relatives who are trying to make things easier for the Danowskis and their eight-month-old son Eric, who needs a liver transplant. Most children with Alpha-1 Anitrypsin Deficiency don't need a transplant until they are eight or ten years old. But Eric's case is different.

The Lord is my shepherd; I shall not want. . . .

January 14, 1988. ERIE BABY UNDERGOING LIVER TRANSPLANT TO-DAY IN PITTSBURGH HOSPITAL.

Debbie Danowski holds her nine-month-old baby in her arms this morning while he's being prepped for liver transplant surgery.

He maketh me to lie down in green pastures: . . .

January 15, 1988. BABY'S TRANSPLANT SURGERY CANCELED.

The donor baby had died in a car accident, and even as Eric was being prepped for his first transplant, Dr. Thomas Starzl, world-famous transplant surgeon, was deciding that the donor liver was too bruised to use. Such a last-minute cancellation had happened only once in five hundred transplant cases at Children's Hospital.

he leadeth me beside the still waters. . . .

January 17, 1988. ERIC DANOWSKI TRIES AGAIN FOR TRANSPLANT.

Debbie and Scott Danowski leave Erie for Pittsburgh again when they receive word that another donor liver is available. The Danowskis are overjoyed. "We didn't expect to be called back again so soon," Debbie says. "But our faith helps carry us through. We pray every day about this."

He restoreth my soul: . . .

January 18, 1988. FAMILY DISAPPOINTED AGAIN OVER LIVER TRANS-
PLANT.

For the second time in a week, the Danowskis face the disappointment of
preparing for a liver transplant that didn't take place. The hospital decides the
liver that Eric was to have received must go to a young girl in an "emergency
situation."

he leadeth me in the paths of righteousness for His name's sake. . . .

February 9, 1988. ERIC DANOWSKI RETURNS TO PITTSBURGH.

Ten-month-old Eric's condition worsens over the weekend, and doctors decide
to transfer him to Children's Hospital in Pittsburgh to await the liver transplant he
desperately needs.

*Yea, though I walk through the valley of the shadow of death, I will fear
no evil: . . .*

February 11, 1988. BABY'S CONDITION NOW CRITICAL.

Eric is "Status Six." Eric is in critical condition in the intensive-care unit of
Children's Hospital in Pittsburgh, and if a donor organ is not found soon for him,
he will die.

. . . for thou art with me; . . .

February 21, 1988. LIVER FROM CALIFORNIA BABY NOT YET OFFERED
TO HARBORCREEK YOUTH.

Doctors at Children's Hospital tell the Danowskis that even though a liver for
Eric may be available from a baby born without a brain in California, they must
wait until the liver is offered to them. They cannot request it, according to
hospital policy. The liver is never offered.

thy rod and thy staff they comfort me. . . .

February 21, 1988. MAYOR TULLIO TRIES TO HELP DANOWSKI BABY.

As sick as the mayor is, he tries to mount a national appeal to find Eric a liver.
He calls his friend Willard Scott on NBC's *Today* show to ask Scott if he can
mention the baby's plight on the air, but Scott says regretfully that it is against
network policy—to ask for a liver for Eric could take a donor organ away from
another baby, so the network can't become involved. Tullio calls friends at ABC
but gets the same answer. "He was so nice," Debbie Danowski says of the mayor.
"I called him on Sunday and he started making calls from his home that day."

"Mrs. Danowski was surprised the mayor of Erie would help a Harborcreek
resident," Tullio says. "But all life is precious. How well I know."

Thou preparest a table before me in the presence of mine enemies: . . .

February 22, 1988. LIVER TRANSPLANTED INTO ERIC DANOWSKI.

Eric gets a new liver in a 15½-hour operation.

thou anointest my head with oil; . . .

February 23, 1988. DANOWSKI'S CONDITION WORSENS.
During the night, Eric's new liver begins to fail. His parents are told that if it doesn't improve, the baby will go back to the top of the list for another transplant.

my cup runneth over. . . .

February 24, 1988. ERIC DANOWSKI APPEARS TO BE IMPROVING.
Eric was a little feisty this morning, his grandmother says. "He takes my fingers and squeezes them. He's kicking his feet and looking up at you with those big blue eyes." She adds that the family appreciates all the prayers of the folks back home. "I'm a firm believer in prayer and I really believe the prayers from all those people are helping," she said.

Surely goodness and mercy . . .

March 2, 1988. ERIC DANOWSKI RECOVERING.
Ten-month-old Eric is listed in critical but stable condition after surgery to open the bile duct of his new liver.

. . . shall follow me . . .

March 4, 1988. DANOWSKI BABY'S TRANSPLANT DELAYED.
Eric needs another liver transplant after all. He is expected to undergo transplant surgery about noon today for a second transplant because the bile duct and an artery in the new liver are not functioning. That transplant is later canceled because a suitable donor organ hasn't been found. Debbie Danowski says she has known for days Eric would need another transplant. "I was crying all day yesterday, saying something is wrong with my baby," she says.

. . . all the days of my life: . . .

March 5, 1988. ERIC DANOWSKI HAS SECOND TRANSPLANT.
Eric comes through a second transplant. Doctors are optimistic, but worried about pneumonia beginning in his lungs.

. . . and I shall dwell . . .

March 12, 1988. ERIC DANOWSKI IMPROVING.
Two-time liver transplant recipient Eric Danowski improves enough that he may be moved from intensive care to a regular floor. "He smiled today, he really did a lot of smiling today," his mother says. "I got to hold him all day today, and I tell you, I held him the whole day." She gives thanks to God.

. . . in the house of the Lord . . .

March 20, 1988. ERIC'S CONDITION WORSENS.
Eric is put back on the respirator because of a virus infection in his right lung, although his second liver is functioning perfectly. Debbie Danowski is worried, because if the virus spreads to his new liver, it will destroy it. Eric is again listed as critical.

. . . for ever.

Yeah, right.

Let them read their Twenty-third Psalm.

What can it say to children like Eric or Linda Martel?

"Why have people to suffer pain, do you know, Roy?"

"I'm afraid I cannot answer that question, Linda. . . ."

"These pains are terrible, you know, Roy; they are very awful."

Everybody in the house was sleeping.

I tried to relax in front of the television with a plate of instant mashed potatoes and a beer, but my eyes were treated to a news report of another slaying in Northern Ireland. It was a hard thing to erase from my mind before I went to sleep, and when I was able to forget about the Belfast killings, thoughts of little Eric Danowski came crashing in.

The next day, Sunday, I started reading a book called *Holy Blood, Holy Grail*, which painted Jesus as a con man. The book describes the contents of some of the Gnostic Gospels, thirteen scrolls dating from the late fourth or early fifth century. These scrolls, more accurately called the Nag Hammadi Scrolls, from the name of the village where they were found in Upper Egypt in 1945, are believed to be copies of other earlier scrolls dating from about A.D. 150.

Holy Blood, Holy Grail tells how in A.D. 120 an Alexandrian scholar named Basilides claimed that the crucifixion was a fraud, that Jesus really did not die on the cross, that Simon of Cyrene died in his place.

The book, written by Michael Baigent, Richard Leigh, and Henry Lincoln, quotes Jesus himself, in the Gnostic Gospels, saying the same thing:

I did not succumb to them as they had planned. . . . And I did not die in reality but in appearance, lest I be put to shame by them . . . for my death which they think happened, happened to them in their error and blindness, since they nailed their man unto their death. . . . It was another, their father, who drank the gall and the vinegar; it was not I. They struck me with the reed; it was another, Simon, who bore the cross on his shoulder. It was another upon whom they placed the crown of thorns. . . . And I was laughing at their ignorance.

That wasn't exactly the kind of reading that helped to build my faith—Jesus laughing at the circumstances in which a man was crucified. He seemed to have a rather perverse sense of humor when it came to little Eric Danowski also.

By the time Monday rolled around, I had no spirit to work on the book.

What kind of a ridiculous project had I gotten myself into, anyway?

The Annoying Observer wanted to separate from my spirit and rush headlong into disbelief. The face of the beautiful lady was nowhere to be found. All I could see was the witch and the jaundiced face of little Eric Danowski, with a cannula in his nose.

By now, though, I'd started to pray quite regularly. Evidently the process of writing the book had at least prompted that behavior, which was new to me.

"Please, God, help my faith."

I avoided using Jesus' name just in case he *was* a fraud.

I was tired of vacillating from face to face. My research was touching my intellect, which likes to examine curiosities, but it was leaving my spirit untouched.

Would it be too much to ask God for some sort of confirmation, to let me know if I was on the right track with not just the book, but my spiritual life as well?

Late Monday afternoon I seemed to receive the confirmation I was seeking through the late Kathryn Kuhlman, dead so many years.

On the very first page of her book, Kuhlman quoted Dr. Elmer Hess, an *Erie* urologist who had been president-elect of the American Medical Association in the 1960s:

"Any doctor who lacks faith in the Supreme Being has no right to practice medicine," she quoted him as saying in a digest planned for the opening of the Southern Medical Association, which then had a membership of ten thousand doctors.

" 'A physician who walks into a sickroom is not alone,' " Kuhlman quoted Hess. " 'He can only minister to the ailing person with the material tools of scientific medicine. His faith in a higher power does the rest. Show me a doctor who denies the existence of a Supreme Being, and I will say that he has no right to practice the healing art. Our medical schools are doing a magnificent job of teaching the fundamentals of scientific medicine. However, I'm afraid that the concentration on basic science is so great the teaching of spiritual values is almost neglected.'

"Any truth," wrote Kuhlman, "no matter how valid, if emphasized to the *exclusion* of other truths of equal importance, is in practical error. My faith in the power of God is the same as that exercised by any physician or surgeon when he believes in the healing and the curing of his patient. He waits for nature (God) to heal gradually, while I believe that God has the ability to heal, not only through a gradual process, but should He so will, His is the ability and the power to heal instantly. He is Omnipotent, Omnipresent, and Omniscient: Therefore, He is not limited by time nor is He limited by man's ideologies, theologies, and preconceived ideas."

What were the chances of picking up a book on healing while I was writing a book on healing and finding in the first page a reference to a man from my hometown?

Other apparent confirmations, such as her description of the case of Eugene Usechek, soon followed.

Eugene was a nine-year-old boy who, in 1950, had gone to Kuhlman to be healed of a relatively rare bone disease. It was Perthe's hip, the same disease that had kept me in the hospital for two years and at home in bed for a year before that. I had never read another book in my life that even mentioned Perthe's disease.

The way Kuhlman described Eugene's case brought back a flood of memories, especially her description of how the disease was first diagnosed and how it first manifested itself. Kuhlman seemed to be describing, step by step, the way the disease had come upon me after my mother noticed me limping from my bedroom one morning. But for all the similarities, there was one big difference: Eugene was healed instantly of Perthe's, whereas my healing had taken three years.

On the day after Christmas 1949, Eugene's mother noticed him limping and asked if his leg hurt.

Kuhlman wrote:

When he said no, she didn't worry. Anyone who knows small boys knows how continually they roughhouse and engage in horseplay—so Eugene's mother naturally assumed that all that ailed her son's leg was a bruise.

But he continued to limp, and after several weeks, she grew concerned when it appeared to be getting definitely worse. She took him then, over his protestations ("But nothing hurts, Mom!"), to their family doctor who promptly came to the same conclusion as had Mrs. Usechek earlier: that it was doubtless just a bruise.

Two weeks later, however, Eugene came home from his school one day, complaining that his left heel hurt. His mother examined the foot carefully, but could find no sign of an injury.

For the next few days, Eugene complained more and more about the pain in his heel. His mother noticed that he seemed to be favoring it—at least he never let it touch the ground.

She took him again to the family doctor, who ordered X-rays. Two days later, with deep concern in his voice, the physician rendered the verdict: Eugene was a victim of Perthe's disease. To Mrs. Usechek's worried question, the doctor explained that this is a disease in which changes take place in the bone at the head of the femur (thigh bone) which result in a deformity. He urged her to make an immediate appointment with an eminent orthopedist at Children's Hospital.

Within a few days, Eugene and his mother were sitting in the specialist's office.

The physician examined the boy carefully, and then called in another orthopedist for consultation. They conferred for a few minutes together, and then told Mrs. Usechek that her son must be admitted at once to the hospital. They pointed out to her something that she had not noticed before—that the boy's left leg was underdeveloped compared to his right, and was already a good one and a half inches shorter.

During the ten days the child was in the hospital, more X-rays were taken; the diagnosis was confirmed beyond any shadow of a doubt, and he was placed in traction. This had no effect on the shortened limb, and he was placed in a cast from his chest to his toes, and released from the hospital.

This was in February, and four months later, in June, he returned to the hospital where the cast was removed and more X-rays taken. He was then placed in another cast, which was to remain on until August.

It was in late June that Mrs. Usechek first heard of the services being held in Carnegie Auditorium.

"A neighbor advised me to listen to the broadcast," she said, "and then send in my prayer request. The very next day I began to listen, and started to fast and pray for Eugene's healing."

On August 1 she took her son back for more X-rays. The cast was now removed, and a brace was substituted.

It had been bad enough to be in a cast during the blistering hot weather that summer, but the brace, also extending from the boy's hips to his toes and weighing 15 pounds, proved even more uncomfortable. Eugene, almost heart-breakingly patient during the whole period, never complaining, even attempting to play baseball with the "gang" while in his cast and on crutches, now pleaded with his mother: "Mommy, *please* can't I have the cast back instead of this brace?"

The pleas of her little son broke her mother's heart—particularly in view of the fact that he might well have to wear such a brace for the rest of his life, and that his leg, unless touched by God, would very probably grow progressively worse, continuing as it had already begun, to shrivel into complete uselessness and deformity.

On the last of August, she went alone to her first service at Carnegie Auditorium.

"I had only been to my own church and never seen a religious service like this," smiled Mrs. Usechek.

Confirmations

> I've decided that God doesn't have preferences in
> theology. We are the ones who try to put a fence around
> God, to bring Him down to our level. But it doesn't
> work. God is too big for us to confine.
> —Kathryn Kuhlman,
> *I Believe in Miracles*

MRS. USECHEK liked the service.

She felt something in that auditorium she had never felt before and she wanted to go back. So the next week she went again and took Eugene. But her son was not healed.

In early October 1950, Mrs. Usechek took Eugene again to Carnegie Auditorium.

"They were a little late getting to the service and could not find a seat, so they stood back against the far wall of the auditorium," wrote Kuhlman. "And suddenly it happened. Eugene's left leg began to twitch—the power of God was going through it."

Kuhlman said that when Mrs. Usechek stood her son up before her, she could see what had happened: The left leg had miraculously lengthened the lacking one and a half inches and was exactly the same as the right.

They walked home together, Mrs. Usechek carrying the brace.

From that day on, Eugene's leg remained perfect. His doctors were astonished at his healing and conceded that it was a miracle, according to Kuhlman, who wrote that three years later Mrs. Usechek received a letter dated March 1953 from the two orthopedists who had treated her son.

"They asked that she bring Eugene back to the hospital and offered to pay any expenses involved—so that he might help others without faith to believe and to prove to them that the healing power of God was real," Kuhlman wrote.

As I read that last sentence, I couldn't help think that it was meant for me.

In Perthe's hip, the bone wears away and disintegrates. In both Eugene's case and my own, the ball at the top of the femur that fits into the hip socket in the pelvis had deteriorated, leaving a rough, irregular surface of bone that caused excruciating pain when walking. In Eugene's case, referred pain from the hip went to his heel. In my case, it was my right knee that hurt.

Remissions do occur. But as far as I know, they occur over a long period of time—as in my own case. Complete bedrest was my doctor's prescription for me, bedrest that kept weight off the hip and allowed new bone to regenerate.

But again, it goes against the laws of biology for bone to regeneate instantly, as in the case of de Rudder at the statue of Our Lady of Lourdes at Ghent and in the healing of James McCutcheon by Kuhlman. Granted, there may be remission for Perthe's hip, but how can the ball that fits in the socket of the hip regenerate *instantly?*

When you're writing a book about spiritual things that can't be seen or touched or examined, you have to wonder if you're hitting the target as you shoot your arrows off into the darkness.

Born-again Christians are confident that for believers, God will provide confirmation in times of spiritual need, whether it be opening the Bible or a book to a passage that speaks directly to your problem, or whether it be something someone says to you.

Carol Wimber, John Wimber's wife, tells how, at one point early in his ministry, John was uncertain if he was on the right track. He was afraid of doing anything that was not explicitly outlined in the Bible. So early one morning, he cried out to God, "Lord, if this is you, please tell me."

A moment later the phone rang and a friend from Denver called. "John, I'm sorry to be calling you so early, but I have something really strange to tell you," he said. "I don't know what it means, but God wants me to say, 'It's me, John.'"

I guess that was the sort of confirmation I was looking for, although I didn't expect God to use a hotline for me, as he had for Wimber. Just a hint would do.

The book was taking great chunks of time away from my family. When I put Stacey to bed one night, she kissed me and then pressed a piece of paper into my hand. The paper read: "This is a contract to show that my dad will drop whatever he's doing when I need him, even if he's working on the book." She wouldn't let me leave her room until I signed it.

Was it all worth it? How could I justify writing a book on healing when it was hurting our family life? How could I dare to raise the mayor's hopes by sending him to a pair of *faith healers?*

The whole situation was just so strange, so unreal. It was a hard time for everyone. I would come home from the newspaper, say hello to Debbie, then head for my attic office to write until dinnertime. A quick bite to eat, then off to the attic again. Debbie would have to watch the baby all day and all evening without a break, trying to help Stacey with her nightly homework with Ian crawling up her leg. This was going on day after day, and the days seemed longer and longer.

One night, as I was sitting in the den alone, long after everyone else had gone to bed, I asked God for help in getting through this trying period. My prayer was, more than anything, a long, spiritual whine. "How about a little help?" went through my mind.

I got restless and wandered through the house, looking for something to read. I opened a drawer in the dry sink in the dining room and found a calendar my friend John Donovan had mailed from New York. Donovan had just finished a biography of Pat Robertson and was well aware of the psychological quicksand one has to avoid to finish writing a book. On each calendar page, he'd written an inspirational quotation or two. There were forty-four quotations, by everyone from Julian of Norwich to St. Teresa.

I had just spent a long day writing about Satan and the Beelzebub pericopes and researching Martin Luther's battles with the devil.

So what was the quote on top of the pile? It was a quote by *Martin Luther,* on *Satan,* dealing with *hard times:* "Our songs and psalms sorely vex and grieve the devil, whereas our passions and impatiences, our complainings and cryings 'Alas!' and 'Woe is me!' please him well."

The probability that by chance alone I would happen across quotes by Martin Luther on Satan and difficult times at the same moment I was personally involved with all three seemed astromically low.

Carl Jung, the famous Swiss psychologist, called such a "meaningful coincidence" of outer and inner events "synchronicity": A woman accidentally knocks a picture of her father off the mantel at the same time he falls from a ladder outside; a watch stops at 10:32 A.M., a year to the day before its owner dies at exactly the same time; a mother who has just lost a child opens a Bible to a passage that speaks directly to her situation and gives her comfort. All synchronistic events. Jung told of how he was counseling a young woman who had dreamed the night before of receiving a golden scarab, a costly piece of jewelry, as a gift. As she was talking, Jung heard a tapping at the window. When he opened it, a scarab beetle, of the same golden color of the jewelry in his patient's dream, flew into the room. Jung caught it and said to the woman, "Here is your scarab." The event so shocked the woman that Jung was able to achieve a breakthrough in her illness.

Most often, Jung said, such "meaningful coincidences" occur when individuals are about to enter periods of spiritual growth, crisis, or need.

M. Scott Peck, in *The Road Less Traveled*, calls synchronicity a form of grace, or God's love. Such things happen frequently to everyone, he says, but all too often, people fail to pay attention to meaningful coincidence because they are not aware that such things happen.

It was hard to think that the way Kuhlman's book had spoken to me was just "coincidental"—mind you, I had just asked God for confirmation minutes before I opened it, and in a very personal way the book seemed to indicate I was on the right track, doing what I was meant to be doing.

But was I out on a limb, believing that there was hope for Mayor Tullio?

Kuhlman seemed to have a word for me on that one, too.

She quoted an article from the *Pittsburgh Press*, written following a number of her miraculous healings. The thrust of the article was how doctors should stop telling "hopeless" patients that their cases are hopeless:

The *Pittsburgh Medical Bulletin*, official publication of the Allegheny Medical Society, cautioned physicians against trying to be arbiters of fate, because nobody can say when anyone is going to die. Even when all the medical evidence indicates there is no hope for a patient, the bulletin declared, the doctor must remember that the will of God, and little-understood mechanisms in the human body, may intercede on the patient's behalf. The physiologic activities of the human body may permit the continuation of life and a certain degree of comfort and well-being in some cases where pathologic examination and clinical evidence preclude the existence of hope.

I thought of what Mayor Tullio had said at the press conference when he announced his illness after doctors told him he would die in eighteen months:

"I'm going to beat this," he'd said. "I told my doctor, 'There's no such thing as an incurable disease.' He said, 'Yes, there is.' I said, 'No, there is no such thing, because God created this body and He can cure it.'"

It seemed as if Kuhlman wouldn't let me close her book until she said one last thing about faith, having diagnosed that that was a big problem for me. And she wanted to be sure I got the message this time:

You do not pray for faith; you seek the Lord, and faith will come. . . .

We become defeated when we fasten our eyes on circumstances, our own problems, our own weaknesses, our physical illnesses. The surest way in the world to be defeated is to focus our mind on ourselves. The storm will capsize our little boat, of that we can be sure. . . .

No person need ever be defeated on a single score; no person needs to lack faith. Look up . . . and see Jesus! He is your faith, He is our faith. It is not faith that you must seek, but Jesus.

The Giver of every good and perfect gift is the Author and Finisher of our faith!

"*God's precious gift,*" we'd named the baby.

"I want you to remember, when you have this baby, that *all good and perfect gifts come from above,*" Frances Hunter had said.

"*God's gift,*" the picture on the birthing room wall had read.

And now this quote, in the midst of my search for faith:

"*The Giver of every good and perfect gift* is the Author and Finisher of our faith!"

The Möbius had looped again.

CHAPTER	A Trip to the
20	Mayor's House

> It is common sense to take a method and try it: If it fails, admit it frankly and try another. But above all, try something.
>
> —Franklin D. Roosevelt,
> *address at Oglethorpe*
> *University, May 22, 1932*

"CLEAN ME!

"Clean me!

"Clean me!" somebody had written three times with a finger—it was a small finger—on the side of my old red 1977 Chevy pickup truck.

"Yo, Dad! I love you!" had been written under the admonitions, followed with a jaunty letter "S."

The whole family piled into the dusty truck, and seatbelts clicked all around.

We were off to see Mayor Tullio because we'd finally managed to set up a time for Dexter Manley to phone the mayor, who had asked us to come up to his house for the occasion.

"This should be interesting," I said as we slipped and slid on icy streets toward the southeastern section of town.

"What should?" Stacey asked.

"Oh, the mayor's gonna get a phone call from a famous football player," I said.

"What for?"

"Just to give him a little encouragement, to help him feel better."

Stacey rolled her eyes. "Is he a faith healer?"

"No, but his little girl was cured by one."

"I coulda guessed."

Debbie tussled Stacey's hair. "Still don't believe in all this?"

"Nope. It's all coincidence. Do *you* really believe in it, Dad?"

"A big part of me does," I said.

"Do you, Mom?"

"I believe God works through other people," Debbie said. "I believe if we pray for something, our prayers will be answered. Otherwise, why bother going to church?"

"Mom and I both think God helped us get Ian," I added.

"It was only six years you waited to have him. Still coulda been coincidence." She was nodding toward the reality outside the windshield to make her point.

"After six years?" I asked.

"Sure," Stacey said. "Other people wait six years to have a baby and when they finally get one they don't go around saying God did it. And anyway, if God is so powerful, why's He need faith healers' help to make somebody better?"

"I think when somebody prays for a sick person and lays hands on him, that demonstrates love," Debbie said. "God comes where love is."

"Healers call it a point of contact," I said, explaining as best I could that the laying on of hands is part and parcel of the doctrine of Christ: *They shall lay hands on the sick, and they shall recover.* (Mark 16:18) "When Jesus healed the leper, he touched him," I said. "When Jesus healed the deaf man, he touched him, too. Jesus touched most of the people he healed."

"That was Jesus and Jesus was God," Stacey said. "Why does God need reg'lar people to touch the sick?"

"I think the touch just helps people to have faith that they've been healed," Debbie said. "It's like a physical sign of a spiritual healing. It makes it easier to believe. Just like when you used to hurt yourself and Mommy kissed it to make it better. That let you know everything was going to be all right. It was a sign of love. People still need to be touched even when they're older, Stacey.

"Oh," Stacey said, somewhat satisfied, blowing out short little puffs of air and watching her breath become visible in the cold.

The thought kept trying to force itself into my mind that maybe this *divine healing* was just a flittering excursion into magical thinking.

It was one thing to believe myself that healing existed, but quite another to ask the mayors of Pennsylvania's second- and third-largest cities to take a chance on that belief. It was one thing to *believe* in healing, but it could be quite embarrassing to *act* on that belief in such a grandiose manner. I could just imagine what the guys in the city room would say if they found out I planned to drag the mayor off to see some faith healers.

But if I hadn't suggested to the mayor that he visit the Hunters, I knew I would always wonder if I could have helped him.

After all, how could magical thinking or the power of suggestion explain the healing of Dexter Manley's daughter? She was three months old when Fred Price laid hands on her, too young to have faith or to be subject to the power of suggestion. And what about the instantaneous healings of Lourdes and Kathryn Kuhlman? How can the power of suggestion, if that's all it is, cause *instant* regeneration?

It had to be worth a try.

Wasn't it better to do *something* than to do nothing at all?

My philosophy has always been, "Where there's hope there's LIFE— and to keep hope, get off your rear end and TRY SOMETHING!"

Many people say that if they ever have a stroke or head injury that leaves them in a coma, they'd want somebody to pull the plug on them.

Not me.

Debbie, dear wife, please take note: If I ever have a cerebral vascular accident that leaves me in a coma, I want you to pray, and I want you to try every conventional means of bringing me around you can.

Then when your conservative Republican neurologist gives you a sly wink and tells you, "I'm sorry, Mrs. Grazier, but your husband will always be a Brussels sprout, have you got plans for tonight?" I want you to go see a Democrat.

If the conventional methods of both parties fail, seek out the unconventional doctor with a mop of long, brilliant white hair parted in the center and worn over his ears in the 1960s hippie style. He'll be a thin man of medium height with high cheekbones who refuses to wear a white doctor costume. You'll know him by his dark-colored shirts and the way he keeps his top shirt button buttoned, with no tie. He should be wearing blue jeans and Docksider boat shoes (no socks) and an oversized brass belt buckle with a mother-of-pearl saber-toothed tiger on it. This buckle will indicate he favors heroic measures.

Call every research center you can (you'll find a list of these under our mattress, along with instructions on how to care for my tropical fish) and learn from these centers the latest techniques for coma arousal:

- sensory stimulation to reprogram the brain
- hyperbaric oxygen to revive idling neurons
- biofeedback to reinforce neural transmission lines
- neurodevelopmental training
- the Israeli double-portion coma arousal diet
- megavitamins
- orgasmic therapy

Wait! Reverse the order of that list!
Try it, Debbie! Try it all!

Bernie Siegel! Get Bernie Siegel, author of *Love, Medicine, and Miracles*. Take my limp hand and place it tenderly on his shiny bald head. Get him to tell me he loves me!

If the scientific approach fails, go a step further: Try parascience.

Fly me to Lourdes and have five strong men lower me into the Virgin Mary Spring Waters (Okay, *one* strong man will do.) If Lourdes doesn't do the trick, wheel my bed into every healing line you can find. Call Charles and Frances! Get Fred Price! For the intellectual approach, get Francis MacNutt, the Harvard grad with a Ph.D. in theology. Even try Oral Roberts, if God hasn't pulled *his* plug yet.

And if nothing works, have our marriage annulled so you can get on with your life. Have a fling or two, buy all the shoes you want, but please don't call Jimmie Johnson, that old college boyfriend of yours with the Dilly Dally ears and the spittle hanging on the corners of his mouth.

If we're no longer married, the state will pay for my nursing home and you won't be left destitute. Just come to see me at Christmastime and birthdays and pin Hallmark cards to my chest. Tell me how you and the kids are doing. Fluff my pillow, close my mouth for me, kiss me, then leave.

At other times of the year, pay a cute little nurse a few bucks to come in and give me a peck on the cheek every now and then. I'll think it's you.

But *don't give up* on me.

The bottom line is, *if you believe in God, give Him room to work.*

"What if all this faith healing stuff just raises the mayor's hopes and he dies anyway?" Stacey asked.

"Don't you think it would be better for him to have his hopes raised than to have no hope at all?" I said.

Stacey thought a minute. "I guess so." She fidgeted in her seat, as if she were still trying to find a warm spot for her bottom. "I just have one more question, Dad. . . ."

Oh, no, I thought.

"If people can make smoke rings with cigarette smoke, why can't they make breath rings with their breath when the air is cold?"

Lou and Grace came to the front door together to welcome us. The first thing the mayor did, wearing pajamas and a tan designer bathrobe, was point out the Christmas decorations. He'd put them up himself, despite his amyloidosis and lack of wind.

Before we even had our coats off, he took the hands of both our children and led them over to an electric train under the Christmas tree, and then from nowhere, more toys appeared. "Hey, lookit the reindeer, Dave! See the reindeer? Here, I'll wind it up for you. . . ."

"Hey Jack, Dave looks just like you," he said, down on his knees to look at the baby eye to eye and nose to nose. The mayor hadn't accidentally gotten Ian's name wrong. I figured he was trying to tell us in his own subtle way that the name "Ian" was hard to remember and was no proper name for a boy. Even my father called his grandson "Ion" for the first few weeks of his life, confusing him with an electrical particle.

With the mayor down on all fours playing with our children, the last thing in the world he looked like was a dying man. Then he stood up suddenly.

"Hey Stacey, want some Coke? Some pop? Jack, want a drink? Debbie, can I get you something? What's the baby need? Can I get the baby something? Hey Dave, you hungry?"

Once the mayor was sure everyone was fed and settled, he asked me to come into the kitchen and sit at the table with him.

"Turn on your tape recorder, I wantcha to get this for your book," the mayor said.

The mayor leaned back in his chair and smiled. "I talked to Dexter Manley already, you know."

"You did?"

"Yeah. I called him last night, but he was half asleep and he says, 'Give me a minute to wake up' so I says, 'Okay,' because I could tell he was really sleepy. I says, 'I watched you play many, many times on TV with the Washington Redskins and you were a very good player. I enjoy you. You're tough and mean, but you're also a good player.' That kind of perked Dexter up then, you know, so I told him I had amyloidosis and I just wanted to talk to him because I had read the article that was in *Sports Illustrated*. I said I enjoyed it very much, that I enjoyed it so much I sent it to Mayor Caliguiri, who has the same disease. I told him a little about amyloidosis, that it was a coincidence that both of us had amyloidosis and we were both Mediterranean extractions. There are only about two hundred cases in the United States, and we both have it."

The mayor was relaxed and enjoying himself. He still thrived on interviews, no matter what the topic.

"Dexter says, 'Well, I want to wish you the best of luck and I'm sure the Lord will touch you, I'm sure,' he says. So I says, 'I heard the Lord touched your daughter.' He says, 'Yes, she is doing very well.'"

The mayor said Dexter had wanted him to talk to Glinda, his wife, because she could give him the best testimony on how their daughter was healed.

"She's gonna be calling me here tonight, so it's good you came up," the mayor said. He reached out for the little black Dictaphone micro-recorder I'd set on the table and slid the recorder closer to him.

"I want to tell you now, like I told Dexter last night, what's been happening with me," he said, looking into the microphone of the recorder. "Let's get it on record for the book. Is this thing on?"

"It's on."

"Okay. I suspected I had something, because for a year I'd been suffering and never told anyone." He was talking as if the recorder were deaf. "I'd have a hard time breathing and I'd go to the doctors and they couldn't find out what it was. When I went to the Cleveland Clinic the doctor . . . told me I had amyloidosis, and it was 'primary'—an incurable form of the disease. This kind of shook me up, and I said, 'Well, I don't believe in such things as incurable diseases.' He said, 'What do you mean?' And I said, 'Well, you know God created my body and I think if He wants to he can cure it.' I said, 'You know, I happen to be Catholic and my wife's Protestant, but she is a very firm believer in the Bible and I've read about many of the miracles in the Bible.'

"Just a few days before I'd read about Shadrach, Meshach, and Abednego and how this king said he wanted these three guys to worship a statue, see, and when they didn't, he told them he'd throw them in the fiery furnace if they wouldn't. He made the furnace very, very hot and sure enough, the furnace was *so* hot it burnt the men who threw them in. But the king looked in and saw these three guys walking around in that furnace and he couldn't believe it and he knew that God did save them. So I said to the doctor, 'It's things like this in the Bible that make me say God can save me if he wants to.' "

"What did the doctor say?"

"He just said, '*Well.*' That was all he said. The next thing I asked him was how long I would have, to live, you know, if I had this disease. I'd never heard of it before. He says, 'Well, I'm a churchgoer too, but since you asked the question, I'm going to have to answer you as a doctor, scientifically. I'd say you've got eighteen months.

"He says, 'You *are* in good shape, you're in very good shape for a man of your age, seventy-one, and I can see what you mean about God and all, but I've got to answer you scientifically.' "

"But no one really knows how long anyone will live," I said.

"Yes, that's right, that's what he said too. *No one really knows.* I told the doctor I thought God was going to heal me, that God was going to touch me. He says, 'Well, I like your attitude, it's a good attitude to have, because so many people get down and out and they don't have room for God.' "

The mayor popped a chunk of cheese into his mouth and continued talking as he cut some more. "Naturally, I was kind of shook, you know. *Eighteen months.* My gosh. *Eighteen months!*"

Debbie and Grace were still talking on the sofa in the other room. I could hear them as plainly as if they were in the kitchen, because of the pass-through opening in the wall between the kitchen and the living room.

Now, most of those things you hear about reporters are true. I was trained by my first editor, for instance, to read typeface on papers lying the wrong way on someone else's desk. That editor gave me a stack of papers and told me to practice reading them with the print facing away from me. And when there are two conversations going on in one place at the same time, I usually listen to both of them. It's a reflex.

That was the case at the mayor's house. I was listening to both the mayor and Grace, because she was telling my wife how she and Lou met, a story I'd never heard.

A few months after Lou's first wife, Ceil, succumbed to a lingering cancer, friends talked the mayor into going on a ten-day Caribbean cruise—the mayor was still getting over the stress of losing his wife and a sister just a few months apart, as well as all the campaign rigors of an election year. (He had just been elected to his second term.) He hadn't had a vacation in over a year. So his friends cornered his eighteen-year-old daughter Marilyn and asked her if she'd try to take her father on the cruise with her. That did the trick, and the mayor agreed to go.

"I do believe this was all Providence, a gift of grace, that we met this way," Grace told Debbie, "because my parents had planned to go on that cruise, and then they backed out. They tried to talk me out of going, too, but I love ships and have loved them all my life, and really wanted to go. Finally a friend of my sister's ended up going with me, because *there was no way I was going to miss that cruise.*"

Grace recalled how the mayor was standing behind her and her sister's friend Josephine in the line waiting to board the ship. The mayor apologized to Grace for the boisterousness of his friends, who had had a little too much to drink while waiting for departure.

The next day Grace and Josephine were reclining on lounges on the prom deck when Lou sauntered by and said, "Good morning, girls. Are you enjoying the ship?" He told Grace later he wanted to talk with her again because he liked the way she smiled and how she had talked with him in line the night before.

Josephine, a finishing school graduate, looked at the mayor and said, "Are we supposed to know you?"

"That didn't faze him a bit," Grace told Debbie. "You know how Lou is. He just gave Josephine a look that said, 'Who are you? You're not the one I want to talk to, anyway.'

"I'm on this trip with some friends of mine. I'm the mayor of Erie. . . . I just lost my wife a while back . . ." the mayor told Josephine. "In about two minutes," said Grace, "Lou had told us his whole life story." One thing led to another, and that night Grace ended up at the captain's table with the mayor.

"He was very nice and we had a wonderful conversation," Grace said.

At least part of that conversation has been well publicized by the mayor in the ensuing years. At political functions, when the mayor tells the story of how he met Grace, he recalls how he asked her, "Would you like to dance?"

"Thank you, but I don't dance," said Grace.

As cigarettes were being passed around the table, the mayor asked Grace, "Would you like one?"

"Thank you, but I don't smoke," said Grace.

When the mayor offered to get her a drink, Grace said, "No, thank you, I don't drink."

The mayor finally said to Grace, "Listen, I have two more questions to ask you."

A devout Catholic, the mayor asked Grace what her denomination was.

"Protestant," she said.

"That figures," the mayor said. "Do you mind if I ask you how you're registered to vote?"

"Republican," said Grace.

"I figured that as well," said the mayor, and then proceeded to eat all the olives on the table.

"So what do you think I did then, Jack?" the mayor said.

My eyes focused again on the man sitting across the table from me. "Huh? Oh, you mean about announcing your illness?"

"Well, yeah, that's what I was talkin' about, wasn't it? Weren't you listenin'? So anyways, I saw how the Pittsburgh media blasted Mayor Caliguiri for not announcing that he had his illness, so when I saw that editorial the Pittsburgh paper wrote, saying he was trying to keep everything a secret, I made up my mind I was going to let my public know everything, and that's when I gave my press conference. Even Bill Knupp from WICU-TV said to me, he said, 'Lou, why don't you just chuck it all and go home and enjoy yourself?' I said, 'Well, Bill, I'm not that type of a personality. I have to be doing something. I have to be active. I like to be around people. I like to do things. I said if I went home every day and did nothing, I could fade away, and so is it better to fade away at home or fade away at City Hall doing the things I enjoy? That was my whole theory, and I've had such a *good* theory and what amazes most people— even the bishop said to me last night—he says, 'The way you've handled this whole thing, everyone *admires* you, the way you've handled it.' You want some more cheese? Have some more cheese."

"Thanks. Remember when I called you up the night of your press conference? I was really impressed."

"Yeah, *everyone* was. So that's my story and I was relating that to Manley, Dexter Manley, and he said, 'I wish you the best,' but you know, he was kinda sleepy, so I didn't go into as much detail as I did here, but I told him. He said, 'That's the spirit to have.' He said, 'We had a lot of confidence in the Spirit, the Holy Spirit, in our daughter and we are very happy the Lord has healed her.' So Dexter tells me the Lord can heal. And I tell him I know that."

The mayor popped another piece of cheese in his mouth. "Did you ever get a copy of the *Pittsburgh Press* with that article on me in it? Here, I saved this copy for you. This tells you a lot of stuff. I think you should have this and put some of this stuff in your book. Here, right here, here's the page, here's the story."

"That *is* a good picture of you, Mayor."

"Yeah, it is, isn't it? That is a good picture. So. It's all here. All you need. That and the Associated press story. That should give you most of the information."

"Hey, mayor," I said, "I'm not here just to do a story, I don't want you to think that. I did want to connect you up with Glinda Manley, because I want you to hear what she has to say. There *is* a part of me that is a reporter, but that's not why I'm here. I'm not here tonight to get a story out of you."

"I know that. And I don't want a story or publicity when we're in Coraopolis. But later on you can talk about Mayor Caliguiri and me and this and that, you can tell our story in your book. Your book can help the people who come along after us."

"Well," I said, "There is a part of me, the *reporter* part of me, that is standing back and watching this whole thing."

"Sure. Why not? The guys who wrote the gospels were reporting, weren't they? Besides, I *am* an interesting story, with this amyloidosis thing and healing and my attitude and everything."

"You've been interesting for the past twenty years, Mayor."

"Yeah, but this is a little different. I didn't know I was going to end up this way. Ha. So you gotta write all these stories down about me. Like the time you jumped out of the box at me. That was cute! You gonna write about that? That was such a cute story. You gotta write that story!"

"Don't worry, I'll put that one in the book."

.   .   .

In the living room, I could hear Grace telling Debbie how she was a born-again, died-in-the-wool Pentecostal . . . how being raised in the Pentecostal church, living in very small towns, there was much that Grace hadn't been exposed to . . . and how she knew Lou Tullio wouldn't be one of those friends you meet on a cruise, write to for a while, and then just forget about. "Once you meet Lou Tullio, there's no way you're going to forget him," I heard her say.

CHAPTER	Encouraging Words
21	

Providence seldom vouchsafes to mortals any more than just that degree of encouragement which suffices to keep them at a reasonably full exertion of their powers.

—Nathanial Hawthorne,
The Scarlet Letter

I WAS TELLING the mayor how I made fifty bucks when Debbie gave birth to Stacey.

When my wife was just a few months pregnant, she'd had what she called a "daydream"—she described it as a picture of a ladybug that flashed into her mind while she was awake, driving the car.

"We're going to have a little girl," she'd said afterward, "That's what it means. There's no doubt in my mind."

Debbie doesn't go around having these daydreams often. But when she does, I pay attention to them because there's this *earth-mother*, intuitive part of her that you sense probably goes way back through the centuries and is usually right on the money. So I went to work the next day and bet a friend at work ten bucks that my wife and I were going to have a girl, not a boy. I then went around betting with everybody else I could find. Fifty bucks in all.

About six months later, we had Stacey and I collected.

At the mayor's house that night, we were all sitting around the kitchen table, waiting for Glinda Manley to call.

"Tell the mayor about the daydream you had the other day," I said to Debbie.

Debbie blushed. "Well, I had been thinking a lot about you, Mayor, and one day—I wasn't sleeping, it wasn't a dream, it was just sort of a daydream—I saw you in the distance, but couldn't quite recognize you.

All of a sudden your body came much closer and you had this *glow* in your chest and it grew bigger and bigger and it was in the shape of a *light*, a lantern, you know, and it just grew larger and larger and *larger* and finally it just filled the whole chest cavity and it *rose up* through your head and it disappeared. That was it. And then the vision was gone."

Grace nodded. "I believe God gave you that, Debbie, because you know, in Scripture, light is always significant."

"Gee, that's something," the mayor said. "That's a good story. Maybe it means I'm being healed right now, huh?"

I looked at the mayor and asked myself what in the world my wife and I were doing, sitting in his kitchen, telling him these things.

Debbie had told Frances Hunter about her daydream a few days previously. "That was an open vision," Frances said. "As you draw closer to God, more and more, things like that will happen to you." Frances said it sounded like a predictive dream, a dream of healing, but it probably also indicated the mayor's spirit was becoming "filled with Jesus," perhaps through the spiritual lessons he was learning through his affliction. She reminded Debbie that Christ said, "I am the Light . . ."

"Want some more Coke?" the mayor asked.

Grace told us about a woman at her church, a Mrs. Sullivan, who "prays for the sick a lot."

"Her husband is dead now, but they were evangelists, something like the Hunters," Grace said. "She told me she had a dream the other night and she knew it was from the Lord. She dreamed that Lou and I were at her house visiting and she said she had made all these eggs and all the stuff he likes, you know, sausage and all that, and then she said in her dream, 'Oh, my goodness, he's not allowed to eat this!' And she said I came in and looked and I had this big smile and I said, 'Oh, yes he can!' So she filled this big plate and he was eating it and able to eat what he wanted. You see, there was a confirmation of your vision, Debbie."

Debbie nodded.

"I believe God confirms His words in different ways," Grace said, "and it's wonderful to be open to the Holy Spirit so He can speak to you like that. It's a marvelous thing. We may not always understand in every detail, but eventually we will, when it all comes together. We'll eventually understand and see it all."

"Anybody want some more cheese?" the mayor asked.

At about 8:00 P.M. the phone rang. "That's Glinda," the mayor said. "Jack, why dontcha get on the other phone, too?"

I picked up the receiver and we all said hello.

"I read that article about your daughter and it was so, so nice, and your husband told me last night that she is wonderful now," the mayor told Glinda.

"Thank God she doesn't have what she was born with anymore. She's just *fine*."

"How old is your daughter now, Glinda?"

"She's now a year and a half, and she is the only person in the history of this disease in the world where the disease has mended itself. And you *know* doctors don't believe in *miracles*, they believe in *medicine*."

The mayor explained to Glinda his "God made our bodies, he can cure them, no disease is incurable" philosophy.

"God gave us our health," Glinda said. "When Jesus died on that cross with those whip marks on his back he took those lashes, which represented every illness and sickness and death-causing disease that there was in the world or was to be in the world, and when he died with those stripes on his back, *so died the diseases*. That's Scripture."

"No, I didn't know that part, I never heard it that way, I know he had the lashes, but I'd never heard it that way," the mayor said.

"I was looking for my little pamphlet that has all these certain Scriptures just for healing to send it to you. . . ."

"Oh, you don't have to do that because you've been so nice already."

"It says, '*with these stripes* you are *healed* through my death.'"

"I didn't know that," the mayor said. "I didn't know it was done from the—"

"I didn't either, until I needed to know it. Then I read the Bible and realized that everything that happened in the crucifixion was for a reason, right down to the whipping—I mean cancer, the disease that you have, what my daughter had—I mean *everything* that can afflict us."

"Say, let me tell you about a little dream Jack's wife, Debbie, had the other night," the mayor said. "Debbie happened to be thinking of me, see, and she got a vision and she didn't know what it really was and it started getting brighter and brighter and brighter, by my heart, see, and everything else, and it was me she saw, as if in the future I was healed."

There was a long silence on the other end of the line while Glinda tried to digest that.

Meanwhile, the rest of us, sitting with the mayor, had to laugh at his "condensed version" of the story.

Throughout his twenty-three years in office, people have often underestimated the mayor's intelligence because of the way his words come tumbling out in such a helter-skelter fashion. But anyone who knows him knows that's because the mayor's brain usually is twenty paces ahead of his mouth and fifty paces ahead of those he's talking to. Those who know him well, from presidents on down, say Tullio's one of the most cunning, intelligent men they've ever met.

"Let me tell you something that you can keep in mind when you have hands laid on you, Mayor, so you have a good understanding of what it's about," Glinda said. "Sometimes, when you have hands laid on you, it's like a *lighting bolt* that goes through your head, through your body, and *knocks you out.* I went up to New York this summer to see the same man, Reverend Price, who healed my daughter last summer. I wanted some healing and he laid hands on me. I said to Dexter afterward, 'Well, *my goodness,* no wonder our daughter is healed, that power is *unreal.* It literally knocked me out. I came to, and I was on the floor, and *I don't know how I got there.* It is the most beautiful feeling.

"But what I want you to keep in mind is, like you say, these people aren't healing you, it is the Lord's power, and He is just channeling it through these people."

The mayor put his hand over the mouthpiece and nodded at me, smiling. Glinda seemed to be getting through to him.

"One key thing to know, Mayor, is that throughout your healing, even after you've been healed and everything, Satan is going to work on your mind from now on and he'll be tellin' you that you're not healed. Because, you know, all of these diseases are what Satan gives us—"

"Oh, I know—"

"And so he is always trying to capture us with them. He feels we're *his* people, our flesh is *his* flesh, that this is *Satan's world,* and so he is going to constantly bom*bard* you the more you get closer to God and the more you get closer to *claiming* that you are healed. You've got to tell Satan, 'You are *not* going to claim any parts of my body, you are *not* going to claim me, I am going to LIVE, I am going to *be healed* in the name of Jesus Christ, *back away, Satan.*' I mean, sometimes you've gotta just *get mad* and look in the mirror and say, 'Satan, *get outta here, you are not claiming me!*' I mean, sometimes Satan will throw those things at you, those darts and spirits just to confuse you, because once you believe in your healing, you'll feel so wonderful and Satan will want to get at you. As soon as you know you're healed, Satan is gonna work on you."

The mayor, listening attentively, kept nodding his head as Glinda spoke.

"Mayor, every time that happens, *every time* you get a negative thought in your mind, a discouraging thought, you say at that exact moment: 'Lord, thank you for healing me,' no matter if you're not 100 percent believing it when you're saying it. Just say, 'Thank you, Lord, for healing me, praise your name! Thank you, Lord for healing me!' Keep the joy in your heart because as long as you've got joy and happiness in your heart, Satan *cannot win the war.*"

"That's right," the mayor said. "I agree with that."

"He might get you down once in a while, he might win a battle or two, but if you keep the joy, he can't win the war. You just keep praising the Lord in your heart, and be happy, and say, 'Satan, I have been healed since I was born, I am a healed person because I am a child of God, I am not to be sick, I am not to have illnesses and diseases, and Satan, *you are not going to take . . . this . . . health . . . from . . . me!'* You keep saying it, Mayor. I don't care what those doctors tell you."

The mayor put his hand over the mouthpiece again. "She's sayin' some pretty good things . . ."

"The doctors told me when the bone started growing in my daughter's leg that the disease could not allow for that to happen. The doctors told me—I think Satan wanted to fill me with doubt—'Well, Mrs. Manley, we're now pretty sure that your daughter now has neurofibromatosis,' what the Elephant Man had, and that as an adolescent, she'd probably go blind and break out in tumors everywhere. Do you believe that?"

"No. That is, I saw that in the article, it's hard to believe—"

"I'm telling you, Mayor, keep your faith, keep your happiness, and if you walk into that doctor's office toMORrow and he says something that may be a little discouraging, *don't let it get you down, Mayor.* Do like I said. Just say, 'Thank you, Jesus, for healing me.'"

"I will," the mayor said. "And I'm going to send you a clipping that appeared in the *Pittsburgh Press.* It's a beautiful article and I'll send it with a letter and some memorabilia of the city of Erie."

"Just let me know how it goes, and I'm going to be praying for you and praying for your faith and your happiness and your health."

"Okay, and I'll write you a nice letter, and say hello to Dexter for me."

"I will and God bless you, and . . . is it Grace? Is that your wife's name?"

"Yes. Grace."

"Tell her I love her. *Mayor Tullio, you're going to be fine. I'm claiming you.*"

Grace Tullio's reaction to Glinda's phone call was, "God bless her. I couldn't have said it better myself."

Not only had Grace been raised a Pentecostal and thus was familiar with healing and the other gifts of the Holy Spirit as taught in her church, but also her father had been a trustee for the Oral Roberts evangelistic organization.

Grace said she knew Oral Roberts personally, through her father, and went to many of his healing campaigns. She said that Oral's son Richard also was a friend of her family. She told us an Erie minister had recently visited Richard Roberts in Buffalo with a group of other ministers from all over the country.

"When he was introduced to the Erie minister, Richard Roberts said, 'Lou Tullio's still the mayor there, isn't he? He's got some kind of strange illness, hasn't he?' Lou had given him the key to the city at some time or other."

Grace said Richard Roberts told the Erie minister, the pastor of a Baptist church, "My father, Oral, and I are praying for your mayor."

"Richard then asked all the ministers to pray for Lou," Grace said, "and afterward Richard Roberts said he had a Word of Knowledge that God was going to heal him, that he had started healing him already."

The mayor had gone to bed. Not long after Glinda hung up, he suddenly became very tired. We could see the fatigue sweep over his features like a wave as we sat there with him. It was like somebody had flipped a switch and all the life went out of him.

Ian ran down the long hall after him and followed him into the bedroom, proving the adage: Give a child a long hall and he'll run all the way down it.

As we drove home that night, I told Debbie how strange it was to find out Grace's father had been a trustee for Oral Roberts, one of the two giants of the 1940s healing revival.

"Oral Roberts is weird," Stacey said. "He's the one who gets death threats from God, right?"

I raised my eyebrows at Debbie, surprised that Stacey would have heard about Oral Roberts. "Do *you* believe the guy is sane?" she asked me.

"I haven't the foggiest," I said.

She looked at Debbie, who just shrugged her shoulders. That seemed to please Stacey, the fact that her parents hadn't gone so far off the deep end that they'd vouch for Oral Roberts. She rested her head on her mother's shoulder.

I told Debbie I thought it was odd how I was drawn into writing a book on healing, then how the mayor and Grace were drawn into the book, and how way back when, Grace's father was personal friends with one of the premier faith healers of all time—and here we were, about to take her husband to faith healers in Coraopolis.

"It all sounds like coincidence to me," Stacey said, her head popping up from Debbie's shoulder.

The Happy Hunters

Thou hast turned for me my mourning into dancing:
thou has loosened my sackcloth, and girded me with
    gladness;
To the end that my soul may praise thee and not be
    silent.
O Lord my God, I will give thanks unto thee for ever.
                      —Psalm 30:11,12

THE HEALERS who were to lay hands on the mayors are spiritual descendants of Kathryn Kuhlman, having been slain in the Spirit for the first time through her touch.

Charles and Frances Hunter had heard all about the divine healings that took place at Kuhlman's "miracle" services, but they had never attended one until early 1971, when they found themselves in Pittsburgh, standing outside the First Presbyterian Church with about two thousand people who had just been locked out for lack of room inside.

"We were probably about ten or fifteen feet away from the door when it closed," Charles told me. "We just stood there waiting, hoping it would open again, and as we waited, there was a man standing next to us who had a little girl about nine or ten years old draped over his shoulder. She looked like she was almost *dead*—she had bad color and cancerous knots as big as hens' eggs all over her body. We just prayed, 'God, if we can't get in, let *her* in some way.'"

The Hunters stepped back to let the girl's family in ahead of them, but then heard an usher say, "Charles and Frances Hunter, will you step this way, please?"

"We could hardly believe our ears," said Frances. "But immediately we stepped out and followed the usher to a seat in the second row. Apparently God wanted to be sure we could see everything clearly."

They saw things they had never seen before—divine healings of all kinds—including the healing of the little girl with cancer.

"We heard Kathryn Kuhlman say, 'There is a child here with cancerous lumps all over her body. *That child is being healed by Jesus right this minute!*' And then we saw this little girl who had been next to us outside, the little girl with cancer, go running down the aisle and up onto that stage. She had good color and no lumps on her body. It was an astounding miracle," Charles said.

The Hunters watched in amazement when, as people went up onto the stage to give testimony to their healings, Kuhlman simply placed her hands on them and they all fell backward, slain in the Spirit, fallen "under the Power."

"We had heard of this before, but I felt it must be for weaklings," recalled Frances. "Either that, or she pushed them over. But when I saw Kathryn Kuhlman for the first time, I realized she wasn't big enough to push anybody over, and yet here I was, sitting in the second row and watching while as many as six or eight people all fell to the floor at the same time. I couldn't understand it, but I still wondered if there wasn't some kind of a trick connected with it. I thought she had some kind of little electric buzzer in her hands that knocked people over."

Kuhlman lined up twenty-five Catholic nuns and told them to hold hands. She touched the nun at the end of the line closest to her and all the nuns fell over except one. "It was awesome to see," said Charles, "but it was no trick. Sometimes Frances and I will do that now—we line people up in a row, get them to hold hands, and Frances touches the hand at one end of the row and I'll touch the hand at the other end, and the whole row goes down. The power of God just flows through the people and knocks them over."

At one point in her service, Kuhlman left the podium after announcing that the power of God was so strong He didn't need her there. "She said she was going to do something she normally didn't do," Frances said. "She said she was going to walk down the center aisle, and she asked that no one touch her, and she also asked that no one come out of their seats until she called them.

Frances had just discovered she had a cataract on her left eye and needed an operation. Kuhlman looked in her direction and then stared at her. "I looked directly at Kathryn, and saw she was pointing her long, slender finger, and at the end of that finger was me!" Frances said. "I decided I was bigger than she was, so I stepped out. She just laid those soft hands on my temples ever so gently and asked God to bless me, and bless me He did, because would you like to guess where I was? Zzoop! Down under the power of God—and in my best dress besides, knowing I had to speak at a luncheon that day! I could have cared less. I felt as if I was in heaven. The Spirit of God breathed on me and I felt light as a feather as I went down."

Frances was not physically healed—an operation was needed to remove the cataract—but something inside her *had* changed. "It was right after that when Charles and I both got the Baptism of the Holy Spirit," she said. "I think everyone ought to go under the power of God at least once in his life. It does something that nothing else does. I have never been the same since that day."

Kuhlman didn't lay hands on Charles until a few months later, at a service in Houston where Charles was ushering for her. The woman with the long, skinny fingers had called out a word of knowledge about a healing, and Charles took the man who said he had been healed to the stage. "When I brought him up, she laid hands on him, but the person didn't receive the power. Then she reached over and touched me, and I went under the power," Charles said.

Frances Hunter was born in 1916 in a one-room log cabin in Saratoga, Illinois, which has a population of about sixteen people today. She attended high school in St. Louis, where she learned to type up to 125 words per minute. Widowed before she was thirty-five, she raised her two young children, Tom and Joan, by herself.

After her first husband died, she started a secretarial service in a closet-sized office in the Sunnyland Shopping Center south of Miami. The service grew into a printing business at a new location and became one of the most successful printing companies in Florida.

Between her mid-thirties and mid-forties, she fell away from religion after going into business with an all-female print shop staff she calls "the wildest bunch of sinners you ever saw." Then in May of 1965, Frances discovered she had slowly been losing the vision in her left eye and found that she had a cataract. The discovery sent her "screaming to God for help."

She went to her Bible—the dusty old one she hadn't read since a previous operation a few years back—and read the Twenty-third Psalm.

Suddenly, while reading, she understood the *real* meaning of the words. "They were telling me that God loves each of us personally. 'Frances Gardner, I love *you!*' my Bible said."

With her life spread out before her in a conversion experience, Frances promised God that when she got out of the hospital she would spend "the rest of my life seeing what I can do for Jesus Christ and not what he can do for me."

Charles Hunter was born in Palo Pinto, near Fort Worth, Texas, in 1920. His parents taught him what they'd learned from Scripture, and he grew to love the stories in the Bible and Bible story books. He grew up and worked for an oil company and a large consulting engineering firm, then served in the U.S. Air Force, and later established his own accounting business.

In 1968, Jeanne, his first wife, developed cancer. Charles found himself at the altar of his church, praying, "Take all of my life and make me spiritually what You want me to be." He also prayed, "Take all of Jeanne's life spiritually and make her the person You want her to be."

"I continued praying," he says, "and a new thought came into my mind: 'even if you have to take her life physically.' I meant every word. When I said it, I turned loose of Charles Hunter."

Cancer took his wife's life later that year.

About four months later, Charles says, God gave him his first set of instructions, speaking to him in his mind: "Go into my Word and listen to no man, and let *Me* tell you what I want you to know."

"As I picked up my Bible," Charles says, "I simply said to God, 'Tell me what you want me to know and I'll do anything you say!'"

By the end of 1969, Charles had moved away from the "spiritually dried-up prune" he thought he had become, and after spending two thousand hours reading Scripture and meditating upon God's word, "I no longer wanted anything except to follow Jesus."

Charles met Frances in October 1969, while she was a speaker at a Christian college in Houston. After a romance by mail, they were married on January 1, 1970, at 12:01 A.M., in the first minute of the new year.

Since then, the trademark for the "Happy Hunters" has become two linked hearts, symbolizing their unity as husband and wife in flesh and spirit.

The home base of the Hunters is 201 McClellan Road, Kingwood, Texas. But rarely are they home.

Between 1984 and January 1989, they had healing crusades (they call them Healing Explosions) in over thirty-four American cities from coast to coast, including New Orleans; Virginia Beach, Virginia; Jacksonville, Florida; Chicago; Lakeland, Florida; St. Louis; Minneapolis; Fargo, North Dakota; and Anaheim, California. They also had Healing Explosions in twenty-two cities in countries such as Finland, Colombia, the Philippines, Brazil, San Salvador, Guatemala, Taiwan, Argentina, Uruguay, Chile, Paraguay, Hong Kong, Sweden, and Japan.

Only the cities with Healing Explosions are included in this list, which doesn't include smaller services like the ones my wife and I attended in Jamestown, where only about a hundred people attended. Somehow, the Hunters find time amid their "Explosion" schedule to work in other cities, such as Buffalo, Cleveland, and Jamestown, for smaller services along the way.

At their Explosions, the Hunters draw crowds of from 4,000 to 50,000—50,000, at a stadium in Belém, Brazil, was their largest crowd ever.

More than 168,000 persons attended the first twenty-one Healing Explosions in the United States between July 4, 1985, and October 1987.

For the places the Hunters miss, they produce their books (thirty-three of them, over nine million copies sold) and their videos on healing the sick, both of which have been translated into languages understood by 80 percent of the world's population—English, Spanish, French, German, Portuguese, Mandarin and Cantonese Chinese, Korean, the Indian languages of Tamil and Hindi, Romanian, Swahili, and Japanese, as well as Swedish, Dutch, Finnish, and the Slavic languages.

Their goal is to have each and every person hear the word of God before Jesus comes back. They want to get the believer "out doing the work of Jesus."

Most people expect the Hunters, considering their age, to get tired. But they don't. "God renews their youth," says Frances' secretary, Barbara Schneider. "I've known them for about ten years, and to me they seem younger now than when I first met them."

The Hunters themselves say they never thought they'd be doing so much traveling. One day, says Frances, she had a little chat with God about it. "I said, 'God, why would You pick such old people to do all this work? Charles and I are 138 years old together.' And God said, *'Because you're dumb enough to do what I tell you.'* "

There's a lesson there, she says: "Some people have faith that is so simple they can step out and do what God tells them to do and not worry about it. I think that's a special gift from God."

In the late 1970s, the Hunters were planning a multimillion-dollar "total living center" on eighty-five acres of property on the San Jacinto River near Houston. The idea was to provide a retreatlike atmosphere for spiritual growth. They built a fifteen-hundred-seat church auditorium "Portomod" dome of bright blue weatherproof fabric, as well as an office building. They also built—"generated" would be a better word—a "steeple of light" made up of four powerful beams of light from xenon lamps, the rays of which blended into one in the sky at their City of Light property. The Federal Aviation Administration had to approve the "steeple," which ended up being visible for miles, because of its proximity to Intercontinental Airport.

"The military of the United States developed these lights to light up a mountain in warfare," Charles says. "They're powerful, powerful things, but they don't require a lot of electricity, so we decided we would put them out by our dome and shoot them up into the air ten miles high to draw people into our place. We had quite a traffic jam when we first switched them on."

The beams were turned off in 1984 because of maintenance costs.

From 1981 to 1983, the Hunters had a school of ministry on their property, where they conducted classes on supernatural healing. During this time they filmed their fourteen-hour videotapes on healing. They also started a church in 1981, called the City of Light, as a base for a school of ministry. The church membership ran about 300, and the school of ministry classes averaged 100.

Long-term plans included a dove-shaped lake; a convention and teaching center; a four-thousand-seat auditorium under another Portomod; a bookstore; a hospice; a recreational-vehicle park; a mobile-home park; a tent park; a chalet village; and a boat launch leading into the river.

But their plans changed. Their traveling ministry, which they started in the early 1980s, became so successful that they were forced to drop their previous ministries. Also, somewhere along the line the Hunters began to feel that they were starting to place too much emphasis on the material aspects of their ministry. "I think we just got carried away with it all," Charles admits. They began to feel that God did not want them building structures and taking care of property.

"We were frantically trying to do it all—the video school, the church—and then God said, 'Drop those extra weights!'" Frances remembers. "Now, this is hard, because lots of people think, 'If they closed, the school or the church, it must have been a failure.' But when we were obedient to God to close these things . . . that's when the Healing Explosions began."

By the mid-1980s, the eighty-five acres on which the auditorium and the Hunter Ministries offices sit went up for sale for $2.5 million.

But the Hunters' decision to change direction was not viewed as a failure. As one Houston pastor said, referring to the Hunters, "People in the ministry have no trouble *starting* things. We're all innovative and entrepreneurial. The hardest thing we in the ministry have to do is to *stop* something God has told us to stop."

The Hunter office building in Houston is quite humble. It's just a metal building with blown-in insulation. "This is a working office building, and that's all," Barbara Schneider says.

The Hunters live in Kingwood, an affluent Houston suburb, on a 1.4-acre lot in a contemporary home appraised in 1987 at $236,900. The home was paid for out of Charles's C.P.A. earnings.

Their ministry pays the Hunters a salary of $1,000 a month each plus a housing allowance. "With thirty-three books out and over ten million sold, we could be millionaires," says Charles. "But sixteen years ago, we signed all that over to the ministry."

Charles says that in 1987, that ministry was bringing in a little more than $2 million annually.

"I can assure you every penny they get from the ministry and their book sales is pumped right back into the ministry," says Barbara Schneider, who notes that in 1988 the Hunters' staff totaled fifty people.

The Hunters, like John Wimber and Francis MacNutt, believe every Christian can heal the sick, and in their Healing Explosions and their books they emphasize the spiritual authority of the Christian believer.

"God is taking the spotlight off the 'star' and putting it on the believer," Frances Hunter says. "Our motto is: If Charles and Frances can do it, you can do it, too, because Jesus said, 'Those who believe shall lay hands on the sick and they shall recover.' The Bible does not leave any doubt. It does not say *some* of you or just a *few* of you who believe; it says that all those who believe will lay hands on the sick and the sick *will* recover."

The Hunters believe that as thousands of Christians around the world get off their pews and act to heal the sick, unbelievers will be won to the Lord as they see miracles. They see their Healing Explosions as a way of laying out the red carpet for the Second Coming by evangelizing the masses through the miraculous, just as Jesus produced believers through his own signs and miraculous healings.

It is Jesus who still performs those cures today through the *believing touch*, the Hunters maintain, and it is Jesus who will bring music and dancing and laughter into our lives if we will let him, they say.

In a sense, the Hunters have picked up where Kathryn Kuhlman left off when she died in 1976. But the Hunters emphasize that Kuhlman was a one-woman show, a "star."

Their mission in life, they say, is to impart the healing gifts of the Holy Spirit to as many people as possible, to fill auditoriums, arenas, and stadiums with the light of not just one star, but many.

"Jesus told us before he left this earth 2,000 years ago that *every* believer would lay hands on the sick and they would be healed," says Frances. "It used to be that this had been done by only a very few people who seemingly were specially chosen to do miracles. We still tend to speak of the great healing ministries of people like Kathryn Kuhlman as though they were something unusual and very special. But that isn't what Jesus said would happen. He simply said *all believers* would do these works and miracles so that people would believe in him and thereby receive eternal life."

"We're all stars," says Frances. "The universe is filled with stars, and we all get our light from Jesus."

But the Hunters' ministry is like Kuhlman's in at least one respect. As did Kathryn Kuhlman, the Hunters share their stage with physicians who conduct quick external exams of people who claim to be healed.

One of these, Dr. Roy LeRoy, a chiropractor from Minneapolis, says that at one Hunter crusade he saw a man cured of Parkinson's disease. "I never saw that happen in my office," he notes.

Dr. LeRoy's wife, Norma Jean, claims to have documentation for the healing of her numerous spinal problems by the Hunters in 1973.

Debbie and I sat next to her on the couch on the Regis Philbin *Morning Show*. The producers had asked her to appear on the show with my family and the Hunters.

A woman in her sixties, she told Debbie and me in the makeup room how she'd had two auto accidents which had injured both her lower back and her neck. She couldn't bend over after several operations to fuse the vertebrae in her back, and she was forced to wear a cervical collar. Then her hair began falling out, probably due to the medication she was taking. She had to have a tool that looked like oversized barbecue tongs made so she could pick things up off the floor without bending over. On top of everything else, she had kidney problems and a thyroid disorder.

Then she told us how, when she went to one of the Hunters' services, she was singled out by Charles Hunter, who had been told by an usher that she was in severe pain.

"I still felt that it was emotion that caused people to fall backward, and I had good control of my emotions," Norma Jean said. "I was afraid that if I fell back I would hurt my back again, so I wasn't going to go down. But Charles touched me softly and asked Jesus to touch me and heal my back. . . . I felt a power go into my head, and the next thing I knew, I found myself flat on the floor."

First, Debbie and I were called out of the green room to tell our story to the audience, Norma Jean joined us afterward, when the camera broke away for a commercial. Ian sat quietly on Debbie's lap, playing with the chain that only minutes before had bisected her face.

"Let me just move on to Norma Jean, because we're *al*most out of time," Philbin said when we were back on the air. "As I understand it, you had spinal problems, right?"

The camera moved in on Norma Jean's face. "Yes, I did, six spine operations. Every disk in my lower back was removed, and two in the neck, and—"

"You were confined to a bed?"

"I had a hospital bed at home with an electric button to get me up and another to let me down, and I couldn't take a bath alone or get dressed alone or anything, and my husband had to take me—"

"And today you walked right across this floor and joined us!"

"Yes, but the thing is, I was bald-headed, my skin had all flaked off. . . . Charles prayed for me—"

"And your hair grew back?"

"Yes . . ."

Philbin pointed at Charles: "*Well, how come his hair didn't?*"

Charles and everybody on the stage and in the audience laughed, and Frances and Ian both clapped their hands in delight.

"We'll be talking with Dr. Joyce Brothers about successful marriages on Monday and also the Mommas and the Poppas—" Philbin began, but he was interrupted by his co-host, Kathie Lee Gifford: "I think Charles and Frances would like to point out that for every truth there is a counterfeit in life. There are a lot of people out there doing this sort of thing, people that you should be very careful of."

"Yes," said Charles, "But the counterfeit won't last. The *real* will."

Philbin swept a hand toward Norma Jean as the *Morning Show*'s theme music began to play and the credits began rolling by on the screen: "Norma Jean LeRoy had all those wires in her body, the doctor said you would *never* bend over, you were bedridden, and *there she goes, folks,* right over there!"

Norma Jean stood up, bent over, and touched her toes.

The audience burst into applause.

After the show, people who said they had never believed in such things came up and shook our hands and then went over to the Hunters to ask them if sometime they would pray for them.

Whatever the Hunters' human failings may be, false pride and taking themselves too seriously aren't two of them. Frances, for instance, tells the story of a mishap that occurred when she wanted to make a big impression as a featured speaker at the Christian Booksellers Convention in 1970. "Many an unknown author has been 'made' by an opportunity such as this," she says. After she finished speaking, a number of booksellers came up onto the platform—made out of folding tables—to shake her hand. "All of a sudden . . . the platform very slowly, but oh, so very surely, began to collapse, and there I was on a sliding board, falling toward the bottom with a woman sliding down the incline right on top of me."

Frances found herself at the bottom of a pile of people. Her notes had gone flying along with her wig and eyeglasses, and her legs were askew in a most unladylike position. The president of a publishing company whom Frances had wanted to impress rushed over and looked down at her. Frances grabbed her wig, put it on sideways with the bangs hanging over her ear and a hunk of her own hair hanging down over her face, and came up shouting, "Well, praise the Lord *anyway!*"

Charles Hunter doesn't put himself on a very lofty pedestal either. When Regis Philbin kidded him in front of a TV audience of thirteen million people about losing his hair, he laughed as loud as anyone.

Both Hunters are completely, utterly uninhibited. When they tried to teach my family to speak in tongues in the green room at the Philbin show, neither one of them could have cared less about how many actresses or presidential press secretaries were looking at them askance.

They don't feel at all self-conscious about speaking in tongues or talking about warrior angels and demons—or about divine sounds that go boom in the night.

Frances tells of how, in Belém, Brazil, amid the crowd of 50,000 that filled the stadium and the surrounding field, "Charles began to minister the Baptism of the Spirit, and there came a point where we lost the entire service. The power of God literally exploded with a crack that you could hear all over the stadium—it was a cracking sound like lightning hitting a building. And before you knew it, somebody lifted a wheelchair up over his head and passed it up to the stage, then another wheelchair, then a stretcher, then came crutches . . ."

One young boy who had been paralyzed from the waist down as a result of an automobile accident was instantly healed, Frances says. "As the power of God touched him, he got up and ran all the way around the outside of the stadium."

She said one of the leaders of the thirteen-million-member Brazilian Assemblies of God which sponsored the Explosion wept and sent her a message saying, "I have never seen anything like this in my life—none of us ever saw anything like this in our lives."

I hadn't heard of anything like it in my life, either, at least as far as the "cracking sound" went. The description gave me the same misgivings as did Frances's "warrior angel." When I mentioned to Frances's secretary, Barbara Schneider, that it was hard to believe such a thing could happen, she said she had no doubt that it did. "Frances's son-in-law, Pastor Bob Barker, was with them when it happened, and he described the same thing. I wish I could have been there myself. You can talk to Bob. He'll tell you about it."

Schneider said that from what she'd been told, the sound was like the noise that might come from a discharge of power from some huge battery. "When you've got fifty thousand people all clapping and praying in tongues and believing one thing in unison, God's power is there, and it's ready to be released," she said.

Indeed.

Then again, I thought, we all believe basically what we've experienced, and before I'd experienced being slain in the Spirit, I wouldn't have believed that phenomenon could occur either. And when was the last time I'd been with fifty thousand people praying and speaking in tongues to see what *could* happen?"

Unearthly lights in people's bedrooms, God speaking to people, God incarnating in human form, the virgin birth, saintly levitation, divine healing, warrior angels—all of it was unbelievable if viewed from a rationalist point of view.

By now I knew the Hunters well enough to trust that they sincerely believed in all they said and did. Lying for pride or profit or ego did not seem to be within their capability. And anyway, what would be the need for lies about divine cracking noises?

I made a decision to suspend my disbelief and to take their description of the "Holy Spirit Thunder" on faith, at least until I could ask Bob Barker about it.

"Frances Hunter said she definitely felt that you are going to be cured, Mayor," I told Mayor Tullio on the phone a few days before we were to meet with the Hunters in Coraopolis.

"She did?"

"Yes. When I told her more about your heart problem, she just said, 'You tell him I said that's easy to fix,' and then she laughed."

I told the mayor that Frances felt she was being "led by the Spirit" to lay hands on him; that she had told me, "I just don't go somewhere immediately when people ask me to. I pray about it, and if I feel I'm being led, I go. If I don't, I say, 'Maybe some other time.'"

"What exactly did she say about me? What else exactly?" Tullio asked.

"She just said, 'We're really excited about this because we *know* that Jesus has something special in mind for your mayor. We're just *believing* for a miracle in his life.'"

"Gee, you know, sometimes I feel like I've already been healed what with that lantern-thing in my chest that Debbie saw. Sometimes I think the Holy Spirit is already touchin' me. But it can't hurt to be touched again, and I hope something happens that is really going to be wonderful."

The Twenty-third Chapter

Thou preparest a table before me in the presence of mine enemies: thou anointest my head with oil; my cup runneth over.

—Psalm 23:5

[*All are gathered in a fifth floor suite of the Royce Hotel in Coraopolis. At left is a queen-size bed covered with a blue bedspread.*

A heavy-looking dark pine dresser-vanity is at center, in the background. At right is a white Formica-topped round table, surrounded by seven chrome-legged chairs and one beige upholstered lounge chair.

Seated in the upholstered chair is the author's wife, Debbie. To her left is Grace Tullio, then Lou Tullio, Frances Hunter, Charles Hunter, Richard Caliguiri, Jeanne Caliguiri, and the author.

A chrome hanging light shines a bright spot onto the center of the table. The light reflects a silvery sheen off the Hunter-written, Hunter-published books scattered on the tabletop. An October 1987 issue of Charisma, *with the Hunters smiling on the cover, tops the pile.*

A black Dictaphone microcassette recorder sits in plain sight on a lamp table, recording the conversation.]

FRANCES [*She has just finished telling Joppa Wiese's story. She leans forward, looks at Caliguiri, and stops smiling.*]: When did you have the first symptoms, and what were they?

CALIGUIRI: Oh, I guess I began to get some indication of some problems back in 1986. It's funny . . . they started on Sunday mornings when I'd walk to the corner to get a newspaper. On the way back I'd start feeling uncomfortable, and get these pains in my chest. I went to a local hospital in Pittsburgh to have it checked out. On a treadmill. Stress tests.

I passed them all. And the doctors were sort of puzzled because of that. Jeanne even bought me a Nordic track for exercise—

JEANNE [*Breaking in*]: For Christmas.

CALIGUIRI: But in March 1987 I was out on the golf course for the first time that year, and was walking up the hill after I had hooked a golf ball very badly into the woods. Thank God I hooked the ball and it didn't go as far up the hill as it might have. Because I had to walk up the hill to get the ball, and as I walked up to it, for the first time in my life I almost passed out. Everything just got blurry, and I made it back to the car just in time to almost collapse. I called my golf buddies over and mentioned to them that I was, uh, dizzy, and ready to pass out. And they laid me down in the clubhouse. Within a matter of minutes, I was feeling fine. But I knew there was something wrong, since that had never happened to me before.

FRANCES: How old are you?

CALIGUIRI: Fifty-six

FRANCES: You're just a kid. [*Laughter*]

CALIGUIRI [*Wryly*]: I wish I were.

CHARLES: He is a kid. Frances and I are 138 years old, put together. [*Laughter*]

CALIGUIRI [*Speaking slowly, deliberately*]: I've always felt young. Age never meant anything to me. I think age and numbers are relative. But I went to the hospital again and they started me on the treadmill and all the tests. This time I didn't pass the tests. Fortunately, Shadyside did an exhaustive study and testing on me and diagnosed amyloid. You may or may not know, it is a rare disease. Only about two hundred people in the whole country have it. Nobody knows how you get it. Nobody knows at this point. There is no cure for it. There are, uh, certain things that Lou and I can take to slow the process down, and maybe arrest it temporarily. But the prognosis is not very good. What they said to Jeanne and I, after they told me what I had, is that I'd have about eighteen months . . . uh . . . to live—

FRANCES [*Breaking in*]: Do you know, I'm almost laughing? Do you know what Jean Knox Hayes was healed of? [*She looks at Charles.*]

CHARLES: Was that the same thing?

FRANCES: We were on the plane this afternoon with a girl who we have not seen in years but we have been in contact with because she was pregnant, was going to deliver a baby. The baby inherited the same thing, and there was a touch-and-go period for about two months where nobody was going to live. Everybody prayed, everybody prayed, everybody prayed, and everybody prayed, and then every day you'd call and they'd say, "Well, we didn't think she was going to live through the night tonight," because she was in the very acute stages of it. And she was here today, up here, on a singing engagement at a church here.

GRACE: You've heard of this disease before?

FRANCES: Yes, yes. I didn't realize till all of a sudden you were talking to me and said "amyloids." When you said that, something really lit up in me and I thought, "Now, is that what Jean Knox Hayes had?" She is the *total* picture of health today. We left her less than two hours ago on the plane and her baby was also *totally healed*.

CHARLES [*Leaning forward*]: I just have one picture in my mind of one little . . . skeleton of a baby, and then, while we're getting our luggage, the next picture is *robust* and *healthy*.

FRANCES: There's not a sign of the disease in either one of them.

CALIGUIRI: That's unusual. Amyloid is not supposed to be hereditary at all.

FRANCES: But you see, the thing that I think is so interesting is that it came through the power of prayer. And these prayers were from people who were not actually there. These are people from all over the United States who were praying for her and her kidneys and her baby.

CALIGUIRI: Well, amyloid, what it does, is attack the organs of the body. Amyloidosis is an accumulation of protein inside you. With Lou and I, it's attacked our hearts, and where it got me the most is the small part of my heart where there's a buildup of protein, and what my heart does, is now it has a hard time pushing the blood back out into the system so that when I exert myself, if I were out to dig a ditch, run, or do anything like that, uh, the heart can't pump enough blood to your system and that's why you get dizzy and pass out.

FRANCES: Now, is that the same for you, Lou?

TULLIO: Yes.

DEBBIE: If it attacks the organs of the body, that's probably why it attacked her baby, because she was pregnant at the time, and the disease probably perceived the baby as being a body organ.

AUTHOR: Uh, what organ produces the protein? Does it come from the blood or the spleen or what?

CALIGUIRI AND JEANNE: They don't know.

CALIGUIRI: But it goes through our systems and goes to our hearts.

TULLIO: And in my case, also my liver.

CHARLES [*Softly*]: We've seen people eaten up by cancer—

CALIGUIRI [*Emphatically*]: It's not at all like cancer. You can take certain pills—Lou and I both are on similar medicine called colchicine, which is administered to people who have the gout, but it also helps people with our disease. But in our case, it will only slow down the process. And there are other things like prednisone, which is the closest we can come to chemo.

FRANCES: I would assume that it also affects your immune system.

CHARLES: Any disease, if you can't fight it, must be affecting your immune system.

CALIGUIRI: I guess so. But it has not kept me from work one day. My only regret is that I can't do all the things I used to. For example, I walked in fifty parades this year. Mayors are famous for walking in parades. Pittsburghers like to have parades. The only time I have not been at work is when I am in the hospital for a checkup at the Mayo Clinic. I've been there twice and will go there for a third time . . . .

CHARLES: Does it clog the arteries or affect the blood system?

TULLIO [*Somewhat impatiently, chomping at the bit to be healed*]: Let me explain it to you the way it was explained to me. There is primary and secondary, see, and we both have the primary incurable disease. What it does is form a starchy thing around your heart. That's what they don't know how to get rid of, and when it forms a starchy thing, only about 60 percent of the blood is going in and because of that, when only 60 percent goes in, 40 comes out. So really, it's because of the starchy thing around there, it destroys those muscles.

AUTHOR: It must reduce the size of the chambers.

TULLIO: Yeah, see, my heart was like this the last time [*forms a circle with his hands*] . . . now it's shrunk a little bit [*forms a smaller circle*]. So the doctors said there's three steps to a trend. Three steps. My heart tested weak. It started weak. Then it got weaker the next time I was tested. If the next time I get tested, it stays the same, then there's no trend. If it gets stronger, there's no trend. If the next time, when I go up there at the end of February, if it's weaker, then I'm in a trend, which is . . . probably . . . could be fatal.

CALIGUIRI: See, the heart, as we all know, is a muscle, and what's happening is our hearts are being destroyed by these amyloids.

CHARLES: Now you know that healing is a natural thing, and God put it in the Bible; He said, "Dick and Lou, above all things I want you to prosper in health even as your soul prospers." He wants you to be in health and prosper in everything you do. Marriage is prosperity. Mayors, leadership is prosperity. Prosperity is—money is part of it, sometimes. God wants you to be healthy and prosper. Because of that, he has designed it so that His power, flowing from individuals, can heal. And it's all released just like you took a syringe needle, and have it pricked in, and when you say, "In Jesus' name, I command thus and so," the medication, God's power, goes into the body and you get a shot of the Holy Ghost. Basically, oversimplified, that's what happens.

FRANCES: It's the *sovereign power of God* . . . all that we have learned, all the things we know, it is still *the sovereign power* that does the healing and one of the most important things we always feel, before a person receives healing, is to know that you've been born again. Whether you're a Catholic, a Methodist, an agnostic, I don't care. So could I just ask us all to hold hands and we'll all say a prayer? A lot of people say, "born again?" The words don't mean anything but having a relationship

with God. All I know is that this is the most important thing of all. So let's
hold hands and pray . . . .

*   *   *

Up until this point, sitting at the table, the overhead light glaring
down, I felt like an actor in a play seated at a table with the other
characters.

But at the same time, I was the audience, sitting at a distance,
watching the players say their lines.

Participating and observing. Asking questions and listening. Noting
the quotes that stood out.

It was something I coudn't help—I always carried the Annoying
Observer with me.

I was the mayor's friend of twenty years. I'd jumped out of a box
for him.

I wanted to see him get well, to see Grace freed of her burden of
worry.

Still, part of me—the Annoying Observer, the reporter—was aloof,
watching, doubting, and tending the tape recorder. I decided and hoped
that if this was all God's will, that God certainly must have known my
nature if He had somehow chosen for me to be there.

Finally, though, when Frances said, "Let's pray" and asked us all to
join hands, the touch of Jeanne Caliguiri's hand brought me completely
into myself.

While we prayed, the Observer and I were one. I was surprised at how
firmly I was holding this sad stranger's hand; how warm it was; how
strongly I felt her pain.

I remembered the touch of another hand, in the night, in the
children's hospital years ago.

It was the same hand. The same need. We are all one. Desperate,
groping, searching for each other in the darkness, seeking help.

"So let's pray, " Frances said. She prayed, and we repeated her words,
our heads bowed, holding hands in an unbroken circle around the
table—the two mayors, best friends, slowly dying of the same rare disease;
their strong, frightened wives; the elderly, joyous husband-and-wife
faith-healing team from Texas; and the bemused reporter and his
faith-filled wife.

We all repeated after Frances:

"Father . . . I want to know I'm saved. . . . I ask you to forgive the
sins of my life. . . . I ask you to wash me in the precious blood of
Jesus. . . . And now, Lord Jesus, I open the door to my heart and invite
you to come in and take over my life . . . and make me the kind of person
you want me to be. . . . Now, Father, I thank You . . . because I
believe my sins are forgiven. . . . And Jesus, I thank you, because you

have come into my heart . . . in a brand-new way. . . . Thank you that I'm born again . . . and I know it. . . . Hallelujah!"

"Hallelujah!"

I have never been comfortable with the word "Hallelujah."

But as we finished, there seemed to be a Presence at the table. When we clasped hands to close the circle, it was as if the "whole" suddenly became bigger than the sum of its parts, as if the actors were, in a sense, creating the Playwright Who had created them.

"There's so much power in this room," said Frances. "There's an *anointing* here. Can't you just feel it?"

'Where two or three are gathered together in my name, there am I in the midst of them," I couldn't help but think.

*   *   *

FRANCES [*Laughs*]: Thank you Jesus. Thank you *Jesus*.

CHARLES [*Reaching out toward the mayors and making pouring motions with both hands*]: If you were not born again, that was jes' like two big bottles got filled up with the Spirit of Jesus.

FRANCES: Amen, amen, amen. Hallelujah! Well, who wants to be first? Or will we do you both at the same time?

CHARLES: Before we do this, let me share two other things. We don't want to keep you here, but we love to talk about what God can do because we're seeing Him do so much. [*He picks up from the tabletop a copy of* To Heal the Sick *by Charles and Frances Hunter, and he opens the book while he's talking.*] We have one long chapter in here that scares people unless they understand it, but it is a simple, normal thing. You see, when Jesus dealt with disease, he dealt with certain incurables— insanity, deafness, epilepsy, leprosy—and in the cases which had been set down in the Bible he cast out devils that were causing these diseases. Now, that doesn't mean the person who had the devils and the diseases was bad. It just means that a demon power from the devil has the supernatural ability to implant in his body the *cause* of incurable diseases. The Bible says you can't fight these unseen evil spirits with things of the flesh. Frances and I take the position that very likely all incurable diseases are caused by an attack of the devil, who somehow opens the door for the factors or the chemicals or whatever cause illness to begin to work. Sure, doctors can point to the causes of disease—tobacco smoke or whatever—but what is it that makes smoke hurt some people and not everybody? Cancer can get a minister of the gospel just as well as it can an atheist, but in either case, cancer can be ushered into the body by a demon spirit. Very simply, you heal sickness by casting out the devil. You must bind the strong-armed man, Satan, by the power of God's spirit in Jesus' name. . . .

AUTHOR [*Fidgeting in his chair*]: For someone like me, and probably for someone like the mayors, this talk of demons and devils . . . seems strange and foreign . . . but I guess if you believe in the positive, there must be a negative. Yin and yang, that sort of thing. . . .

FRANCES: Oh yes. Satan got thrown right out of heaven like a bolt of lightning, the Bible says. And you see, demonic spirits do attack your bodies.

DEBBIE: An important thing to mention is that often the devil will make you think you are not cured and he will put doubts in your mind. . . .

GRACE: But the Bible says resist the devil, and he will flee from you—

FRANCES [*Interrupting*]: Go back to the beginning of that verse, though. It says, "But lift yourself to God . . ."

GRACE: Yes, lift yourself to God. First. That's very good to remember.

DEBBIE [*Debbie recaps the* Sports Illustrated *article on the healing of Dexter Manley's daughter. She relates Glinda's advice to the mayor about Satan—even picking up Glinda's speech patterns and inflections.*]: . . . So Glinda told the mayor, "Through your belief and love of Jesus you'll be cured, but you have to remember that the devil is going to *come in,* and he's gonna make you have *doubts,* but you just cast those doubts right out because I just know that you're gonna be cured!"

AUTHOR [*Turns to Frances*]: As I listen to this I can hear a little voice saying, "Ha! You really believe all this?" I can feel myself being pulled back and forth, back and forth. . . .

CHARLES: The devil *totally* operates with doubt, and Jesus *totally* operates with peace and certainty. There's no doubt when you're in Jesus.

CALIGUIRI: But we're trained to deal in logic . . . and . . . and . . .

TULLIO [*Mumbles something to Frances, then speaks louder for the whole table to hear*]: . . . and I'd like to get going with this because we have to drive all the way back to Erie tonight, and that's a three-hour drive, and I—

FRANCES: Oh, bless your heart!

CHARLES: So all we're gonna do, we're gonna give y'all a shot of the Holy Ghost penicillin.

FRANCES: And we're gonna *believe.*

GRACE: Amen!

CHARLES: Or maybe it's the Holy Ghost prednisone. Whatever it takes for this. We're gonna call on God for a creative miracle for this thing you have—it's gotta have something to do with your immune system—and that doesn't mean you got AIDS, either. It just means your immune system isn't functioning as it should. But when we pray, we'll come against each one of these things, but if we leave something out, you just tell us and we'll command that thing to leave your bodies.

FRANCES: Anything the Lord might drop into our heads, we'll just add to our prayers to make sure. . . .

CHARLES: *I don't want you to forget this:* Do stay on your medication. Let the doctors tell you what to do and what not to do. Lou has been watchin' some of our videotapes we sent him. You keep doing that, Lou, you read everything you can and build your *faith* and *faith* and *faith* and *faith*. Just plug the tapes into your VCR and watch 'em as you want to. [*Looking at Caliguiri*] We'd love to send you a set, too. They'll keep you right close to God and keep you Spirit-filled.

CALIGUIRI: Thank you.

CHARLES: As far as Frances and I go, we're just ordinary people. It doesn't matter who does the praying, but we happen to be here.

FRANCES: We're as ordinary as any people in the *whole world!*

AUTHOR [*Turning to Caliguiri*]: Everything that Charles and Frances have said, as strange as it may seem, I've heard from many others all across the country. To me, that gives what they're saying credibility. It means that there must be some sort of universal principle that—

CALIGUIRI: I'm a firm believer. Not only in my religion, but that you can help yourself. And I have been trying to convince myself that I am going to get better in my own way . . . and I've been trying to . . . *get this out of me*, uh, by just concentrating, because I've read books on how people have gotten better just through their own . . . tenacity . . . and positive thinking.

CHARLES: That's true, but when my wife died of cancer many years ago, my pastor came in, and I had *The Power of Positive Thinking* and some of those books around, and he said, "These are wonderful books, you should always have positive thinking, but positive thinking will just take you up to a certain point, then drop you." You can think your way out of sickness and do a lot to maintain health with a positive attitude, but in the end, it's God's power that creates miracles. Now, you know, God wants miracles to be a witness to his power, and people have almost lost healing because they don't tell anybody about the miracles that have happened to them, so—

FRANCES: After you go back to your doctor and verify it . . . .

CHARLES: So don't hesitate to tell your city or your neighbors or friends or whoever.

DEBBIE: Jack was so paranoid about getting up and speaking in front of people that in college, when he had to give a speech or a talk, I used to literally have to stand behind him and push him through the classroom door. Now here we are, telling this story to you after getting on live television in front of thirteen million people and telling our story.

CHARLES: We're not saying you have to get on television and say, "Hallelujah, I jes' got healed by a couple faith healers!" We just want you to acknowledge your divine healing when you get it, if only to your friends.

CALIGUIRI: We'd be delighted to. Lou and I had to tell the world about our problem; we'd be more than happy to tell the would about our cure.

FRANCES: You give the glory to God! Give the glory to God!

GRACE: Amen.

FRANCES: Well, let's stand up because I work better on my feet when I lay hands on the sick. Hallelujah! Thank you Jesus!

[*All stand and move away from the table. Frances and Charles lead the way across the room and motion for the others to follow, who do so somewhat hesitatingly. Except for Tullio. He beats the Hunters across the room.*]

FRANCES: I really felt as we were talking that faith was just rising up within everybody here. [*Turns toward Tullio*] And I think it's beautiful what Mayor Tullio just said to me. He just got himself all primed up to get us over here to lay hands on him, and now we're gonna give him a *double whammy!*

[*All stand in a circle around Tullio and Caliguiri. The two mayors stand inside the circle with their heads bowed. Everyone else reaches out to touch their arms or backs or shoulders. Jeanne Caliguiri's eyes appear to be rimmed with tears.*]

CHARLES: Now we're all baptized in the Spirit . . . we're all a part of this circle and the Body of Christ. And when we're in faith, we don't close our eyes, 'cause you can't see that way. The more natural you are, when you pray to Jesus, the better you are.

[*Frances and Charles begin to pray—in tongues. Both mayors look up quickly, and just as quickly put their heads back down. Then Frances starts praying in English.*]

FRANCES [*Whispers*]: Thank you, Jesus. Thank you, Jesus. [*Louder*] We just want to *praise* you. And right now, by the Spirit of God, in *Jesus' name*, you foul, stinking devil that has attacked his body, I command you to *come out* in the name of Jesus, you foul spirit that causes these amyloids to be made and produced in his body. I command you to come out. I curse the *seed* and I curse the *root* of this disease and I command them to *die* in the name of Jesus. I command his immune system to be raised . . . so he'll be able to throw off anything and everything that might attack him in this area. I speak a new heart in here [*she places her hand on Tullio's chest*] in the name of Jesus. I command all of that . . . what did you call it? . . . *starch* that's covering his heart to *totally* disappear. Anything that's clogging those arteries or blood vessels, I command it to *go in the name of Jesus!* Father, we just give you the *praise,* we give you the *glory,* we command every part of this body that has been touched by this disease to be totally healed in the name of Jesus.

CHARLES: Hallelujah!

FRANCES: And we call into being those things which are not, as though they were. We give you the praise, Father, and we give you the glory in the name of Jesus. Thank you, Jesus.

THE TWO MAYORS: Thank you Jesus.

CHARLES: Thank you Jesus.

AUTHOR AND DEBBIE: Thank you Jesus.

FRANCES: My goodness, when I lay my hand on him . . . I mean, there is tremendous heat going into his heart! Thank you Jesus!

[*Everyone repeats "Thank You Jesus" again. Although both mayors have been touched by the Hunters, they do not fall over.*]

FRANCES: There you go. When you say, "Thank you Jesus" it means, "I got it!" And "I'm proud!" And "I'll be healed!" Thank you Jesus. Thank you Jesus. Thank you Jesus!

CHARLES: Jes' relax and let it go through you.

FRANCES: There is this *tremendous* heat. Thank you Jesus. Thank you Jesus, for a brand-new heart. Amen!

CHARLES: This 'un will last you until Jesus gets back. Hallelujah.

GRACE: Thank you, Lord.

[*The mayors lift up their heads. But the prayers are not over.*]

FRANCES [*To both mayors, as if they're little boys*]: You come here! Let me hug you! Hallelujah! Thank you Jesus!

[*Everyone laughs.*]

CHARLES: Jesus, we thank you for taking dominion over this heart and over this whole system and over this whole blood system and the whole chemical system and nerve system in Jesus' name. Now, devil, we bind you by the power of the Spirit of God. You miserable devil and darkness bearer, we command you to leave him and never come back, in Jesus' name. And we take authority over the seed, the core, the root of all this. We command death to this disease in Jesus' name. We command the Spirit of Life to come back into this heart and all the other parts here. We command that, uh, that the covering over this heart, the starch to be totally healed, the protein to be absolutely brought back to normal and to stay there in Jesus' name. Now, that part of the body, which assimilates the protein, we command you to be healed. We command you to be normal in both of our brothers in Jesus' name. We command a new heart and new parts around there. We command all these vessels to be opened up perfectly. We command the Roto-Rooter of Jesus to open up all these vessels perfectly. We command the muscles to these hearts to pump normally, we command that never again shall there be any dizziness or anything else, that this is totally . . . healed . . . by the power . . . of God. And Father, we thank you in Jesus' name. Everybody say, "Thank you, Jesus."

ALL: Thank you, Jesus.

TULLIO: Could you just do one thing? Say again to stop the protein that is causin' this—

FRANCES: Amen. In the name of *Jesus*, I command the *cause* of this to be *stopped* in the name of *Jesus*. Let's just lay hands on both of them again. Father, in the name of Jesus, we speak *total* healing to both of these people, both of these bodies—

GRACE: Yes!

FRANCES: And we'll just give you the praise and we'll give you the glory in Jesus' name, amen, amen, *amen*. Hallelujah! Father, let us *turn Pittsburgh upside down* because that city will have seen God heal its mayor. And Father, Erie's not as big, but it's just as important.

TULLIO [*Smiles the Tullio smile, looking toward the ceiling*]: It's the third-largest city in Pennsylvania. [*Nods toward Caliguiri, then looks up again, still smiling*] He's the second-largest city. But we're the third.

CHAPTER 24	His Glory in the Thunder

The voice of the Lord is upon the waters: the God of
Glory thundereth, the Lord is upon many waters.
—Psalm 29:3

WE HEARD no thunder in the Hunters' room at the Royce Hotel.

Ever since I'd heard about the "divine noise" at the Healing Explosion in Brazil, I'd been curious about that phenomenon. No other healers I'd interviewed or read about had experienced anything like it.

But D. Scott Rogo, in his book *Miracles*, does cite examples of strange lights in the sky seen at large gatherings—like those seen on March 29, 1972, at an open-air healing Mass in the courtyard of Arroyo Hondo College in the Dominican Republic.

The 5:00 P.M. meeting of about a thousand people had been headed by Sra. Luciana Pelaez de Suero, a forty-year-old Catholic charismatic leader and healer well known in her country:

The priest saying Mass opened the ceremony by beseeching the crowd to pray for healings. At the very moment Sra. de Suero fell into a trance during the communion service, a huge glowing disk appeared in the sky. The disk resembled the moon, but was yellow and seemed to pulsate. Since the moon appeared in the sky at the same time, there can be no doubt that the disk was an independent object. It had emerged from behind a large dark cloud, behind which it sank and ultimately disappeared.

Rogo speculates that the disk could have been related to a "cloud of fire" seen in Ireland in 1859 at an open-air revival meeting attended by six hundred to a thousand people. In this case, a strange, radiant cloud suddenly appeared in the sky and floated above the congregation, hovering for a time and then slowly drifting away, filling everyone with awe.

Similar lights were seen in Wales in 1904 and 1905, during which time a religious revival movement was spreading across the country. One of the most popular evangelists of the Welsh revival was Mary Jones, a thirty-five-year-old housewife who had been converted in 1904. During her very first sermon in her hometown of Egryn in North Wales, lights like fireballs were seen above her church. The lights, bobbing and moving in the sky, often appeared near or above other churches at which she spoke, and were seen by hundreds of witnesses, including many British journalists. The lights continued to appear in the towns that Mary Jones had left, making it seem as if somehow they were associated with the crowds that had gathered for the revival, not just with Jones herself.

Rogo theorizes that "Miracles may potentially occur when large crowds of people who share a common religious background and a similar world view come together to worship. Their combined faith and emotion may somehow become psychokinetically linked to the world around them. . . . Religious revivals—especially energetic and emotional ones —may be especially susceptible to the production of signs and wonders."

Bob Barker, pastor of the Greater Life Christian Center in Dallas, was only too happy to tell me about the strange noise he heard at the July 1987 Healing Explosion in Brazil.

On the day Barker and his wife, Joan, arrived in Belém with his in-laws the Happy Hunters, the temperature was in the nineties, and the humidity caused by the nearby falls of the Tocantins River made it seem all the hotter. Barker wondered if many people would brave the heat for this meeting.

But in Brazil, he said, people are hungry for the Word. And after seeing the Hunters' billboards all over the city asking, "Do you need a healing miracle in your life?" the Brazilians were also hungry for signs and wondrous cures. More than thirty-five thousand people arrived at the stadium hours early to sit in the heat and wait for the Hunters and their miracles.

Soon the stadium was overflowing with a sea of expectant faces and laughing, shouting, singing, crying people waiting to see if God still works miracles. Even the areas underneath the stands were packed with those who couldn't find seats or space to stand in the field.

Encircling the stadium was a wall about fifteen feet high. Against the outside of that wall people had stacked boxes, crates, cartons, and whatever else they could find. Then they climbed the piles to get to the top of the wall and over.

Those in wheelchairs and on stretchers had been placed on the field in front of the stands so they could see the stage. All around the field they were lined in rows two or three deep. Soon, though, those who could walk were standing in front of the crippled, and from the stage, their twisted bodies were lost from sight.

The people kept coming. They poured into the stadium on foot, in wheelchairs, on stretchers—and even on makeshift stretchers of brightly colored lawn furniture. Some were dressed in suits, some in rags, some even in nightclothes. By the time the sun went down and the field lights came on, crowd estimates were running as high as sixty-two thousand.

Once the gates were locked, some people carried their sick children up the piles of junk and dropped them over the wall to waiting hands below, in hopes they would be healed.

"So there we are. It's dark, the lights are on, and the people are pressing against the stage," Barker recalled. "We've got a line of ushers around the stage trying to keep everyone back. We'd had the singing, and Charles and Frances were introduced. The ovation was simply ear-pounding. It was deafening. It was beyond words. Charles and Frances then spoke, through an interpreter, to the people about leading a holy Christian life and led them in the sinners' prayer."

Following a brief teaching on the "miracle-working power of God," the Hunters ministered salvation to the audience and called for the Baptism of the Holy Spirit. (They asked those present to "praise God in His language" and not their own—to speak in tongues. Most of the sixty-thousand people in the stadium raised their hands to the sky and tried to do so, after the Hunters tried to teach them the basics.)

"Soon everybody in the crowd was speaking in tongues," said Barker, "and that's when it happened, when this big clap of what sounded like thunder occurred. At that point the miracle power of God broke out all over the people. It was like a crack of thunder overhead—not like distant thunder at all, but thunder right overhead."

Maybe it *was* thunder, I offered. Normal, natural, unsupernatural thunder of the type caused by the sudden expansion of air in the path of the electrical discharge of lightning.

"But the sky was clear," said Barker. "There were a few wispy clouds overhead, but nothing like the kind that produce lightning and thunder."

But lightning—and the thunder that accompanies it—*can* come from a cloudless sky. On July 27, 1988, a bolt of lightning from a clear sky struck one of eight youngsters who were playing softball in San Antonio, Texas. The bolt critically injured Hugo Arauz, thirteen, melting his sneakers on the way through his body. The National Weather Service said there was a strong thunderstorm about four miles away at the time. "Lightning can travel for long distances even though the cloud may seem far away from you," said meteorologist Cristy Mitchell afterward.

Lighting is always followed by thunder, of course—but Barker said there was no lightning before the sound was heard at the stadium.

"Everyone said, 'Did you hear that?' " he told me. "It was a situation where everyone who heard it started looking around and asking, 'Where did that come from?' "

There's plenty of biblical precedent for what those onstage heard, Barker reminded me. He cited the Book of Exodus, where God promises Moses that the Israelites shall hear Him "talk" to Moses from a dense cloud, "so that when the people hear Me speaking with you, they may have faith in you also." And true to His Word, God spoke to Moses with the voice of thunder, which frightened the bejabbers out of the Israelites.

And when Jesus died on the cross, there was a sound like thunder as the earth shook and terrified those who were present.

In Brazil, however, when the thunder was heard, there was no fear. "People were too caught up in the Spirit to be afraid," Barker said.

I asked him whether the sound couldn't have been the sonic boom from a jet passing overhead.

"There are any number of things it could have been, and the world will try to explain it away," he said. "But I saw no jets overhead. There were no explosions. To the best of my knowledge, it was nothing from the natural world. And I've given a lot of thought to this—when you know your in-laws are going to be relating these things to the world, you better have a good understanding of them, because you're going to be challenged."

But really. Couldn't it have been a sonic boom?

"It all depends on what God you serve as to whether you believe or not," he said.

"The power of God in that stadium was something none of us had ever experienced before," Frances told me later. "It was so strong it was almost frightening."

Frances took the sound as a signal that God was ready to begin healing. A few seconds after it was heard, the Holy Spirit swept through the sea of faces like a wave, she said, and suddenly an empty wheelchair was held aloft in the air and passed hand to hand over the heads in the crowd to the stage. "Then came another empty wheelchair . . . then another . . . then came a stretcher with no one on it, then came crutches, a back brace, another empty wheelchair. . . ."

More than six thousand trained healing team members were going through the crowd, touching people and praying for them and ministering signs and wonders. Often, four or five team members would lay hands on a single person at once and pray. But as in the Kuhlman services, many were healed who weren't physically touched at all.

Soon after the "thunder," Frances heard somebody scream, "She was blind and now she can see!" In one part of the stadium, people began dancing around a woman who said she had just regained her sight. In another area, two children who had been deaf were reportedly healed. Their parents brought them to the stage.

Then a scream rose from the audience at the end of the field. The Hunters' interpreter said the crowd was yelling, "Watch for the orange shirt!"

"We had no idea what that meant. But we looked until we finally located a person with an orange shirt running with about a hundred people following after him," Frances said.

"We didn't know what had happened," Barker said. "In a crowd like that, somebody might have snatched a purse or whatever. Pretty soon the guy with the orange shirt had two hundred or three hundred people chasing him. Come to find out this young man had been paralyzed from the waist down in a car accident. The pastor on the platform with us knew him personally and said there was no way he could have been walking."

Barker later sent me a videotape that showed the boy. A handsome youth, he looked to be about thirteen years old. Tears streamed down his face and he laughed as one person after another in the huge crowd hugged him. At one point he started jumping high off the ground, and two pastors he was talking to started jumping up and down with him.

Frances told me that after running nearly a quarter of a mile around the track, the boy had run up to the stage, hugged her and Charles, and said, through their interpreter, "I'm not even a Christian, and God healed me! Please, I want to be a Christian!"

Everything on the tape was just as Bob Barker and Frances Hunter had described it, although the cameraman had missed the Hunters administering the Baptism of the Holy Spirit and thus the thunderlike sound afterward everyone thought they had heard.

Empty wheelchairs were indeed passed over the heads of the tumult, along with walking sticks and crutches and canes.

One young man was shown flailing his walking stick in the air and shouting for joy after he reportedly had been healed of a malformed leg that had left him unable to walk. He sent the stick on its way to the stage with great joy.

"Whatever we bind on earth is bound in heaven!" Frances shouted into the microphone. The video showed her words being interpreted for the multitude. "Whatever we loose on earth is loosed in heaven also!" she shouted.

*   *   *

I thought about Barker's statement, *"It all depends on what God you serve as to whether you believe or not."*

He seemed to be allowing for two interpretations of reality: The thunder of the Holy Spirit could have been supernatural, or it could have been something like a sonic boom.

But even in the second case, how fortuitous it was that a jet might have created the boom at exactly the moment needed to galvanize into belief those at the gathering of sixty thousand. If the sound *was* from an airplane, who's to say that God had not synchronistically looped the Grand Möbius back on itself to provide for the jet to be overhead at that moment?

I recalled the story of the pastor who prayed for his car's windshield to be cleared when the wipers stopped working—it wasn't rain, it was the overspray from the windshield wipers of the car in front of him. Nonetheless, his prayers had been answered.

And the birth of our baby. Doctors could indeed provide valid natural explanations for his birth, but again, what force started those natural mechanisms working after all those years?

And Moses turning the river to blood, causing the fish to die and the water to become so polluted that the Egyptians couldn't drink it. That could be explained as a sudden proliferation of microorganisms or red algae that deprived the water of oxygen.

And the "plague of frogs" that came out of the river into the palace of the Egyptians and into their beds and kneading bowls—the *Rana lasciviatus*, the horny green frog, just getting into the mood for breeding season, no doubt.

And the rest of the ten plagues in the Book of Exodus—the gnats, the flies, the pestilence, the boils, the hail, the locusts, the darkened sky, and the deaths of the Egyptian babies—there are natural explanations for all these events. But what made them happen just when they were needed most?

When Moses spoke to his people, and the Lord spoke to them as thunder from a dense cloud, maybe God *was* speaking through normal, everyday thunder of your "It always rains when we plan a picnic" variety. But a meteorological experience had been transformed into a phenomenological one just the same.

Just once I'd like to make a point in an argument with my wife and have it backed up by a clap of thunder. I wouldn't much care if the thunder came from a cloud or from the divine vocal cords of the Almighty. The effect on her would be the same.

"That dust ball stuck to my sock under the bed was NOT seven inches long. WOMAN, DO NOT EXAGGERATE . . ."

Ker . . . BLAAAMMMM!!!!

(The most I'd ever been able to manage along those lines was to get the toilet to flush on cue in the rest room of WABC-TV just before the Regis Philbin show. But then again, maybe that wasn't bad for a beginner.)

So what if the Hunters' "divine thunder" was of natural origin?

Those at the stadium believed it to be a sign from God; it gave them the confidence to inspire healing.

For them, it *was* divine, *because of the God they serve.*

                              *   *   *

For weeks after Grace Tullio's husband was diagnosed with amyloidosis, the television and newspapers had almost daily made the disease part of his last name: "Mayor Louis J. Tullio-who-has-amyloidosis-a-rare-and-fatal-illness, today told the City Council . . ."

Every day for months, friends and people Grace didn't know would offer their condolences, as if her husband had already died. Not for a minute was she able to forget that unless God somehow intervened, she would soon lose the great love of her life.

It also had to be unnerving to watch her husband handle the situation—he was going around town with a Polaroid camera, having his photo taken with individuals he considered to be his friends.

"It's not ego," one city worker told me. It's because he genuinely likes people and he wants them to have something to remember him by. How many people would even think to do something like that?"

Grace attended all the social functions required by her position as the mayor's first lady and kept smiling all the while friends and strangers offered their condolences.

There were a lot of functions to attend. When one local college would decide to have a testimonial dinner for the mayor while he still could appreciate it, the next would follow suit because it didn't want to be shown up by the first. Then the third would schedule still another dinner because *it* didn't want to be shown up by the first two.

Meanwhile, the heavy schedule of going to dinners and parties being held in his honor all over town was draining the mayor's strength and making him even sicker.

The mayor himself scheduled a huge party at the Hilton Hotel for the news media, a thinly disguised farewell party at which he gave out personally autographed pictures of himself so his media friends wouldn't forget him.

I remember how, as the mayor passed out *in memoriam* photos of himself in the reception line, Grace stood by his side and kept smiling. Just once did she appear to reach up and wipe a tear from her eye.

"I believe God is going to heal Lou," Grace told me a few days after our visit to the Hunters. "I believe God's hand is on him and that God has laid it upon many people's hearts to pray for him. I believe he *will* be healed. I think healing is in his body right now. And I believe faith is the substance of things hoped for. It is the evidence of things unseen.

"I can't look at the circumstances. I've got to look at Jesus. No matter what.

"People ask me what I'll do if God doesn't heal my husband. Well, the Lord gives, and the Lord takes away. The Lord is *sovereign* above all things. God in His wisdom knows when our work is finished. It may be that Lou's work here is done—God sees through time, and He knows all things. I'll accept God's will, *that's* what I'll do."

Another icebreaker, crashing through the vast expanse of icy doubt that freezes faith in most men. What is it that lets women be this way?

Searchlights of Science

Beyond the bright searchlights of science,
Out of sight of the windows of sense.
Old riddles still bid us defiance,
Old questions of Why and of Whence.
                              —William Cecil
                              Dampier-Whetham,
                              The Recent Development
                              of Physical Science
                              (1904)

WEEKS had passed since we'd gone to Coraopolis.

One night, when we were almost ready for bed, my wife reminded me to put the dogs out. Because Pooh was blind, I had to carry her down the back porch steps to the frozen ground—otherwise she'd walk headfirst into the milkbox.

When I brought Pooh inside, Stacey took one look at her and said, "Yeeck. Look, Dad, her eye's all crusty!"

I lifted the old dog onto the kitchen countertop and stood her, dripping and trembling with melting snow, under the fluorescent light. As her nails clicked onto the plastic surface, she began to pant nervously. She associated Formica with veterinarians. Her legs splayed out from under her and knocked a small dish of old tea bags into the sink, sending her facefirst into the fleshy fronds of a potted aloe plant.

She looked pathetic. As I steadied her I could feel the knobby bones of her spine under her fur, as well as lumps of calcium deposits along her ribs. She was losing weight, the way old people do.

She was 119 years old, in dog years. I felt sorry for all the times I had shoved her out of the way with my foot over the past few months as I bustled about doing Important Human Things Requiring Impatience, especially after we'd had the baby. I remembered the look in her big brown eyes that said she couldn't understand why no one loved her anymore.

But she still loved us, even though she couldn't see or hear us. As I stroked her under her chin to calm her, she licked my hand, as she had since she was a puppy. For a few seconds, after I took the hand away, she licked the air, trying to find me.

The eye, which had been afflicted with cataracts for years, was full of pus, obviously infected. The eyelid seemed to be pulling away from it.

All illness comes from the devil, Glinda, Grace, the Hunters, and millions of Pentecostals kept saying.

I could understand why two Catholic big-city Democratic mayors would be attractive targets, but why would Satan want to mess with a poor old *French poodle*?

And what about plants? Are we supposed to believe the devil invented Dutch elm disease to make trees miserable?

Is there somewhere a flatworm afflicted with a lingering illness given it by the planaria-hating Lord of the Pond Waters?

Does an amoeba cry out in its high-pitched little voice, "Why me, Lord?" when tiny foul stinking spirits gobble up its molecules?

Does *all* death and illness come from Satan?

"Yes," my born-again friends said. "Satan hates ALL life, because it comes from God."

There's a force that builds up, and a force that breaks down, was one thought that came to me.

Physicists call the force that builds the "strong force." It is the force responsible for binding together all the protons and neutrons in the nucleus of an atom.

The force that breaks down is called the "weak force." and it disintegrates nuclei.

These are two of the four forces that physicists have been trying to unite somehow in their search for a unified-field theory, a comprehensive mathematical theory that would unite and make sense of all known forces in the universe—the Theory That Would Finally Resolve All That Humiliating Ambiguity.

As I looked at the bloodshot eye of my dog and pondered these forces, I thought of what physicist Robert Jastrow said: When the world's great physicists finally manage to climb the mountain of truth in their search for the meaning of the universe, they will find on the top a band of theologians who have been waiting for them for centuries.

Or, I wondered, was it the other way, as Thomas Henry Huxley had said:

"The cradle of every science is surrounded by dead theologians, as that of Hercules was with strangled serpents."

I found in a kitchen drawer the small tube of eye ointment the baby doctor had given us for the baby's just-healed sty; I slathered a glob of it into my poor dog's bad eye and went to bed, wondering if a healer had ever laid hands on a dog.

The healer Oskar Estabany did lay hands on animals, as a matter of fact.

Back in the early 1960s, Dr. Bernard Grad of McGill University conducted controlled experiments with Estabany, a retired Hungarian military officer who claimed to be a healer. Grad asked Estabany to lay hands not on dogs, but on mice.

In one of the experiments, Grad surgically wounded a number of mice by removing patches of skin from their backs. He then divided the mice into two groups. The mice in one group were touched by Estabany's hands or fingers for about ten minutes daily. The other group was deprived of the healer's touch. In the group of mice left untouched, the wounds took as long as fourteen days to heal. The group of mice treated by Estabany healed in as few as seven days.

But other scientists had reported that rodents handled by people seemed to grow faster and withstand stress better than unhandled animals. So Grad devised another experiment to contend with this factor. He took three hundred surgically wounded mice and divided them into three groups. One group was treated by Estabany; a second by a skeptical medical student; and the third, the control group, was left untreated.

Estabany and the student were not allowed to touch the mice. They *were* allowed to touch the cages, but for the most part they held their hands over both the cages and the mice in them without touching anything.

The experiment showed that the mice attended by Estabany healed more quickly than the control mice. The mice treated by the skeptical student healed more slowly than either the control group or Estabany's group. This suggested to Grad that the negative attitude of the student seemed to hinder healing and regeneration, while the positive attitude of the healer accelerated it.

In still another experiment, Grad fed several mice iodine-deficient diets, which caused goiters to develop. Estabany was asked to "heal" them merely by concentrating on the animals and holding their cages. Half of the mice were treated by Estabany for several weeks—five sessions per week, fifteen minutes per session. The other half were not treated by him. At the end of the testing period, Grad found that the goiters of the mice treated by Estabany had grown much slower than those of the control group.

These experiments are described in the *International Journal of*

Parapsychology, Spring 1961. They are viewed as significant because mice do not respond to suggestion or the placebo effect and don't have faith in the laying on of hands—as far as anyone can tell.

Shortly after midnight on July 15, 1986, Jessica Hagenbuch, fifteen, of Waterford, Pennsylvania, suffered a serious head injury in an auto accident. She was not expected to live.

Surgeons removed a massive clot from the base of her brain, but still, Jessica's future looked bleak. A nurse explained to her parents that the swelling of Jessica's brain would probably kill her. The nurse recommended against resuscitation should brain death occur. "I remember that nurse saying how important it was to let a person die with dignity," Jessica's mother, Patricia, told me. "She said that perhaps it would be a blessing for Jessica to die, because what quality of life would she have if she lived?

"But at one point, I was in Jessica's room with her when suddenly— it's hard to describe it—it was as if God gave me a confidence that she wasn't going to die. That she was going to live. I could feel His loving presence with me."

Within a matter of hours, groups of friends, relatives, and fellow church members from Wesley United Methodist Church began to stream through the hospital's intensive-care unit to visit Jessica. Patricia Hagenbuch said that within forty-eight hours, "literally hundreds" of people had been in Jessica's room, standing around the bed, praying for her. Some prayed aloud, some silently, and several laid hands on Jessica as they prayed. Their prayers continued and multiplied through prayer groups in the days after they left her bedside.

Other friends formed prayer groups in England, Africa, and throughout the United States to pray for Jessica. It was a geometrical progression of friend to friends, church to churches, and prayer group to prayer groups, so that eventually the Pennsylvania teenager had over a thousand people all over the globe praying for her regularly. (The Hagenbuchs had done lay missionary work, and their contacts were widespread.)

Jessica remained in a coma for two and a half weeks and then suddenly began to improve dramatically, her progress jumping in leaps and bounds that amazed the medical staff.

Shortly before Thanksgiving, 1986, Jessica was released from the hospital, just four months after her accident.

"She recovered at least three or four times more quickly than anyone had thought possible," her mother told me. "Her therapist said she had never worked with anybody who improved that quickly."

By the summer of 1988, Jessica was preparing, at seventeen, to enter eleventh grade. She had lost only one year of school. She has some difficulty with muscle groups on her left side, but that is disappearing rapidly. Her speech is completely normal. She plans to go on to college.

This is a teenager who was supposed to die, who was supposed to have no "quality of life."

"When we took her in for her six-month checkup, Jessica's physical therapist just looked at her, shook his head, and said, 'You know, Jessica, you are a miracle!'" her mother told me.

"I know it was the prayers that did it," she said.

Does God really heal people through prayer?

Cardiologist Randy Byrd attempted to answer this question in a study that began in 1983 and concluded in 1985 at San Francisco General Hospital.

"We've got loads and loads of anecdotal experiences like the one you just told me," said Byrd, referring to Jessica's story, when I interviewed him. "But when I reviewed the literature, I realized that prior to our study there was no scientific literature on the effect of prayer. The unique thing about our study is that one like it has never been done, as far as I know."

In the study, Byrd split a number of patients who had had heart attacks, heart failure, or other cardiac problems into two groups. One group consisted of 192 patients who were prayed for; the other group was composed of 201 patients who were not prayed for. The prayers were said over a ten-month period. The rest of the three years was spent in preparation and evaluation.

Using a computer to develop impartial selections, patients in a coronary intensive-care unit were assigned either to a group prayed for by prayer groups or to a group unremembered by prayers. All the participating patients, as well as the doctors and nurses, did not know which group the patients were in.

First names, diagnoses, and prognoses of patients were given to prayer groups throughout the country. The members of the prayer groups individually petitioned God daily for improvement and prevention of complications in the patients throughout their hospital stays, which lasted from a few days to a few weeks.

The group remembered by intercessory prayer showed a dramatic difference in complications compared to the control group.

None of those prayed for had to be placed on breathing devices, while twelve of those not prayed for needed respirators.

The prayed-for group was five times less likely than the unremembered group to develop infections requiring antibiotics. That same group was three times less likely to develop a lung condition that lead to heart failure.

In the prayed-for group, only 4 percent suffered congestive heart failure during the course of the study, versus 10 percent in the control group; 3 percent of those prayed for required diuretics versus 8 percent in the control group; 2 percent of those prayed for suffered cardiac arrest versus 7 percent in the control group; 2 percent of those prayed for suffered pneumonia versus 7 percent in the control group; 2 percent of those prayed for required antibiotics, versus 9 percent in the control group.

Fewer patients in the prayed-for group died, although Byrd did not consider this statistically significant.

The complete results of the study were published in the July 1988 issue of the *Southern Medical Journal*.

"The study confirms what most people believe about prayer in general," Byrd told me. "That is, as you pray for people, it will make a difference. The study shows that yes, all those prayers being said for people do indeed have an effect, it's just sometimes difficult to see the effect in a short-term setting."

This study also demonstrated two other important points: first, that distance between the patient and those praying has no effect; and second, that the "faith factor," positive thinking, or the placebo effect are not responsible for the effects of prayer.

In other words, the power of prayer comes from without, rather than within.

What did the medical community think of Byrd's study?

"Well, it was published, so it passed peer review," he told me. "That's a fairly significant step, indicating it met the general criteria for a scientific evaluation."

Dr. Rex Gardner of Sunderland District Hospital in Great Britain—who has lectured on healing in this country at Fuller Seminary—is another physician who has been impressed by the apparent power of prayer.

An article in the October 1986 issue of *Omni* magazine describes how Gardner tracked seven cases in which prayer seemed to play a part in healing. One case involved a parishioner in Monkwearmouth, England, who suffered from a large, ulcerated varicose vein in her leg. Her entire church prayed for her, and the ulcer healed the day after the prayer meeting. A doctor had warned that even if her leg were somehow healed, skin grafting would be required. Gardner himself had examined the leg both before and after the healing.

Another case concerned a little boy who was slowly dying of a lung infection. Long-term antibiotics were ineffective, and the child was getting worse. His doctors at the Royal Victoria Infirmary in Newcastle upon Tyne gave up all hope, but his mother took him to a prayer service, and to his doctor's amazement, the child recovered almost immediately.

Gardner admits that spontaneous remissions occur all the time, and doesn't claim these cures as proofs of miraculous healings. But he did say in the article that the term "miraculous" is "permissible as a convenient shorthand for an otherwise almost inexplicable healing that occurs after prayer to God."

Another experiment on healing prayer was conducted in the 1970s by Francis MacNutt, then one of the first Catholic priests to bring healing into the Charismatic Renewal Movement and author of the book *Healing*, the first comprehensive Catholic book on the subject, of which more than a million copies have been sold. MacNutt has left the priesthood, but he and his wife, Judith, still have an active healing ministry.

MacNutt told me how, in a study involving twenty-four patients at Toledo's St. Vincent Medical Center who were prayed for over a two-day period, twenty improved dramatically. The cases ranged from a nun with severe osteoarthritis in both knees to a man with lupus to a woman with Lou Gehrig's disease to a burn victim.

In explaining how healing works, MacNutt says that Jesus died to free us from sin and sickness and that when Jesus saw a sick person, he became angry. God resents illness, says MacNutt. "Many patients in hospitals, when they are thinking about God, go back to the garden of Gethsemane and their prayer is often '*thy* will be done,' and that seems to have a special reference to sickness in their minds. But it is very important to notice that Jesus was not talking about sickness. It was something else altogether. He was talking about going to the cross and suffering, but nowhere in the New Testament does it speak about the sickness of Jesus."

The suffering that Jesus is referring to, MacNutt says, should come to Christians in the form of persecution from without, not sickness from within.

"He promises suffering, but nowhere does he promise sickness as part of the Christian's life. Every time we meet sickness in the New Testament, every time we meet someone who is sick, Jesus reacts toward that person as though that were not his will, that his will is to *heal* the person."

The odd thing, says MacNutt, is that people have a kind of "double-think" when it comes to illness and God's will. "We bring patients to the hospital believing that the Christian thing to do is to get them well and that God will work through the hospital doctors . . . under the assumption that it is God's will to work for the healing of the sick. But then somehow, on the spiritual plane, this is all transposed, and the person prays, 'Not my will, but thine,' as though it is God's will that they remain sick."

Concerning his own experiments with prayer, MacNutt notes that "several people said that when they first came into the room where we were praying for healing, they experienced a love in the room such as they had never experienced in their entire lives. Something happened in a moment of time on a very deep order where they sensed the love of the Christian community, and in that sense, the very personal love of Jesus."

"Healing seems to go in stages," he says. "The first stage is diminished pain. But even when the pain disappears, it doesn't necessarily mean that the person is healed. The next stage seems to be that there's a greater mobility in the affected part if that part cannot move. The third stage is that if there is a structural problem, real swelling of the joints or whatever, that is the last thing to be healed, and that usually takes a greater period of time."

Healing does not have to be a noisy phenomenon, either, he says. "I've found there is a kind of stereotype of what it means to pray for physical healing . . . like it has to be loud or emphatic or dramatic . . . [but] most of the time, when we are praying with a few people, it's rather quiet, and we're just ministering the love of Jesus Christ. We don't have to fake anything, we don't have to shout, we can just be who we are, dealing with the sick as they are."

Philip Stiff, M.D., chief of staff at St. Vincent from 1975 to 1979, said after the MacNutt experiment at his facility that he was impressed at how prayer was able to bring about "results that we in medicine haven't been able to get.

"Twenty out of twenty-four is a highly significant figure . . . I'm inclined—after seeing what's gone on and seeing the statistics—to say that we certainly should include prayer in our . . . regimen of care for our patients."

Len Kholos, managing editor at the *Erie Daily Times* when I wrote this book, is an avuncular guy in his sixties. I used to kid him about his impending seven-eighths life crisis until he had a near-fatal heart attack.

He had taken an interest in healing, perhaps because he'd had his own close encounter with mortality. But when I told him about the experiment involving prayer for cardiac patients, he became upset.

"I can't *believe* that God would participate in a blind study, helping only the group that someone thought to pray for," he said. "That dis-*gusts* me."

I was back in his office when he told me that as a Jew, he didn't believe in petitionary prayer anyway. He said that even when he was lying in bed in the hospital's cardiac intensive care unit, certain he was about to die, he hadn't prayed to God to save him. But he did tell his mother, "Mom, I don't want to die."

His eyes filled with tears. "She's been dead for years, but I still talk to her, in my mind, every day. I talked to my mother, but I didn't pray to God or ask him to heal me. Not once."

I told him about the communion of saints, how Catholics believe those already with God can pray to God for those still living, and half-seriously raised the possibility that his mother had done his praying for him.

He just raised an eyebrow.

Later, he wrote a few lines on prayer which I told him I'd like to use in the book.

"Supplication Conflicts with the Concept of a Perfect God," he titled the following essay:

Proposition: A San Francisco cardiologist used two groups of patients in a blind study.

Let's stipulate, for the sake of argument, that the samples were scientifically appropriate, that the cardiologist was comparing statistically equivalent groups and that his numerical conclusions are accurate. If we accept the premise that God heeded the prayers for some, and thus improved their health to some degree, and if we also stipulate . . . since there is no evidence to the contrary . . . that those who were not helped were as worthy and deserving of life as those who were, are we not maligning God? The premise would present an imperfect creator. I would pray that this not be true.

I believe that God created the world and all that is in it and that he is omnipresent and omniscient. I do not believe he can be bribed, cajoled, or conned.

He will not heal a stricken person, deliver someone from a dangerous situation, help one side or the other win a ballgame or a war, or make it rain—unless it is the right thing to do.

What is the purpose of prayer? Is it to tell an omniscient God what is right? Is it to tell an omnipresent God that someone needs his help? Is it to tell him that the supplicant is worthy? Putting it in the human perspective, we would be insulting his intelligence.

When we praise God and then ask for a favor which we have not earned, whether it be for help in improving our lifestyle or to continue living, we are trying to con him.

I believe in praising God as a means of expressing my devotion . . . and perhaps fear . . . to my creator. I may call out to others to "render praise unto Him to Whom all praise is due," but that is to serve Him, not to feed his non existent ego. I want to add my voice, to help make all his creatures aware of and grateful to their creator.

I live what, within my frame of reference, is a moral life; but I do not do it with the hope of any specific reward. Sure, I hope it will impress Him, even move Him to look with favor upon me when a need arises; but this is not a tit-for-tat arrangement. I do good because it makes me feel good.

Does God pay special attention to me? I don't know if it's special, or that He pays me any more mind than the run-of-the-mill sinner; but I know that he inspires me to do my best.

But he doesn't give me any special advice; if he did, I wouldn't have lost so much on the stock market or written so many dumb sentences over the years.

I am highly skeptical when self-styled prophets such as Oral Roberts and Pat Robertson claim that God spoke to them, and gave them specific instructions, particularly when those divine words result in their personal profit. God can't be conned, but an unfortunately large segment of the public can be.

When God passes a miracle . . . or what appears to us to be a miracle . . . clinical evidence not withstanding, it has nothing to do with prayers. He doesn't make deals. He does what is right in specific circumstances for reasons we may not understand.

Nor does he limit His mercy to those of us who believe in Him. Those who claim that only believers will be redeemed impugn His perfection. I don't think that God would be that vain.

Having said all this, I will still concede that if it makes us feel better to pray for help when we get into trouble, why not?

I agreed that God doesn't make deals but had come to believe that a prayer-dialogue with God *can* produce results. As I thought of Kholos' question, "What is the purpose of prayer?" a response was forming in my mind.

It had to do with the creative power of prayer, our own creative power, and the contradictions of the Möbius.

But it would take a few more sessions sitting in the outgoing water of the bathtub before I was ready to try to express it.

CHAPTER 26

A Matter of the Mind?

Say you are well, or all is well with you,
And God shall hear your words and make them true.
—Ella Wheeler Wilcox,
Speech

So there's Tullio, in the huddle. The quarterback nods to him and calls the play one more time.

The ball's in motion. Tullio goes out, the quarterback passes the ball to him. Tullio leaps! He reaches out! And the ball slips through his fingers.

Back in the huddle: "That's impossible what I just did," Tullio says. "I don't do that. I've never dropped the ball like that in my life. C'mon. Let's do that play again!"

He gives the quarterback a wink and manages to convince him to let him try again, "just one more time."

THE MAYOR had a quart of water in his lungs and had lost forty pounds, and he no longer looked like an ex-football player.

But he still had the same old attitude:

"Me die? *Impossible.* I've never done it before in my life! I'm going to beat this! I like a challenge. There's no such thing as an incurable disease. C'mon. One more time!"

To what extent is divine healing caused by the mind's own ability to heal? I wondered. To what extent could healing come from within? From where does the mind draw its creative force, and why? Whence comes the mind-force that heals? I decided to explore these questions for the mayor's sake.

In *Love, Medicine, and Miracles*, the book Caliguiri was trying to use as a blueprint for healing, Dr. Bernie Siegel defines three classifications of patients based on their attitudes.

Siegel says about 15 to 20 percent of all patients consciously or subconsciously wish to die, and on some level they welcome serious illness as a way to escape their problems through death and disease. Their method of coping with illness is to die with it.

The second group of patients, a majority of about 60 to 70 percent, are like landlubber guests on a sailboat. They'll do what they're told—haul in a line, give a winch a halfhearted crank—but they would never think of taking a turn at the tiller themselves. People in this group do what they're told, "but it never occurs to them to question the doctor's decisions or strike out on their own," Siegel says.

Then, he says, there is a third group—the 15 to 20 percent who are exceptional. Exceptional patients refuse to be victims. They question their doctors. They do what they think is right for themselves. They want to know every detail of their X-ray reports, their blood tests, and their biopsies.

They say, like Tullio did, "I'm going to beat this. There's no such thing as an incurable disease."

Siegel says that to test for an exceptional, hope-filled, positive-thinking patient, he simply asks, "Do you want to live to be a hundred?"

If the patient says "yes" without hesitating, he is obviously filled with a love of life and the will to live and thus is exceptional.

I had no doubt that if Tullio were asked that question, he would not only answer in the affirmative, but would probably also say he wanted to run for another term of office.

Norman Cousins, author of *Anatomy of an Illness*, is the template of the 1980s for the patient who wishes to pattern himself as exceptional.

In 1964, Cousins contracted a serious collagen disease, a disease of the connective tissue, which is the fibrous substance that binds the cells together. Nodules appeared all over his body and he had difficulty moving his neck, arms, hands, fingers, and legs, or even rolling over in bed. Ankylosing spondylitis was making the connective tissue in his spine degenerate.

Physicians gave him a one-in-five-hundred chance of full recovery.

"It seemed clear to me that if I was to be that one in five hundred I had better be something more than a passive observer," Cousins wrote, describing how he analyzed his situation and then decided that stress and negative emotions had weakened his immune system.

He concluded that if negative emotions could wreak havoc with the body, then positive emotions and a good outlook should have a healing effect. "Is it possible that love, hope, faith, laughter, confidence, and the will to live have therapeutic value? Do chemical changes occur only on the downside?" he wondered.

He decided to take responsibility for his own therapy in partnership with his doctor. With his doctor's blessings, Cousins took himself off aspirin, which his research indicated might aggravate a collagen disease. He started taking massive doses of vitamin C, which is known to have an anti-inflammatory effect. He checked out of the hospital and into a motel, where he could get much-needed sleep. He watched Marx Brothers movies and read books of humor, hoping that positive emotions and laughter would heal his body.

In the course of a few months, against all odds, Cousins reversed the course of his illness.

He never accepted the verdict his doctors had handed him. And because he didn't buy into the reality that doctors had conjured up for him, he was free to create his own. He wasn't trapped in the cycle of fear, depression, panic, and all the other negative emotions that can make a doctor's diagnosis a self-fulfilling prophecy.

One conclusion he came away with is that the will to live "is not a theoretical abstraction, but a physiologic reality with therapeutic characteristics."

Cousins also noted that a highly developed sense of purpose is a powerful curative force in the human spirit.

This, too, made me think of Mayor Tullio.

In a speech at Gannon University in October 1987, after he had been diagnosed as having amyloidosis, Tullio had said, "If I were to go back and begin again, I would do exactly what I have done—serve people as a teacher, a coach, an administrator, and a mayor. . . . Since graduating from Holy Cross College, I have held positions which were people-oriented, and to me, that is the reason for being put on earth—to help others, to have an influence on their lives, and hopefully, to make their lives better. It has been said many times by many different people that 'Service is the rent you pay for your space on earth.' Well, believe me, I personally have enjoyed paying my rent."

"Not every illness can be overcome," Cousins wrote. "But many people allow illness to disfigure their lives more than they should. They cave in needlessly. They ignore and weaken whatever powers they may have for standing erect."

"*I want to finish my term,*" Tullio had said. "*I'd rather be carried out of City Hall than carried out of my home.*"

Consider the story of "Mr. Wright," whose case was documented by his physician, Bruno Klopfer, in 1957.

Wright had cancer of the lymph nodes. Tumors the size of oranges were scattered in his neck, chest, armpits, abdomen, and groin. His liver and spleen were greatly enlarged, and each day one or two quarts of milky fluid had to be drained from his chest. He had been given little time to live—two weeks at most.

But Wright had heard of a new miracle drug called Krebiozen, which he persuaded Klopfer to administer to him.

He received his first shot on a Friday. By Monday, his tumors had shrunk to half their original size. The tumors "had melted like snowballs on a hot stove," Klopfer later wrote in a psychology journal.

When Klopfer arrived at the hospital after the weekend, he had expected to find Wright dead or dying. But instead, his patient was up and walking, chatting with the nurses and other patients.

Within ten days of his first Krebiozen injection, Wright was discharged, almost all signs of his disease vanished.

He was cured.

But within two months, Krebiozen began getting bad press. The testing clinics were saying the drug didn't work at all. Wright read the reports, lost faith in the drug, and after two months of almost perfect health, relapsed to his original state and became gloomy and morose.

By now, Klopfer suspected it was the patient who had cured himself and not the drug. To test this theory, he told Wright that he would soon receive a new, improved double-strength Krebiozen which hadn't deteriorated in the bottles, as the earlier batches had. To build up anticipation, Klopfer delayed giving his patient the new injections for a couple days, and finally, with great ceremony and flourish, he administered the new, double-strength cancer killer—which was actually sterile water.

Wright's second recovery from his near-terminal state was even more dramatic than the first, Klopfer wrote. His orange-sized tumors vanished and the water in his chest disappeared. He became the picture of health, and remained symptom-free for over two months while his sterile-water injections were continued.

But then Wright read about a final report by the American Medical Association which said, unequivocally, that nationwide tests had shown Krebiozen was a worthless drug.

A few days later, Wright was again admitted to the hospital, laden with tumors. "His faith was now gone, his last hope vanished, and he succumbed in less than two days," wrote Klopfer.

And then there is the case of Dan Turner, described by the *Los Angeles Times* in the fall of 1987 as one of the longest-living AIDS patients on record.

Turner was diagnosed with the disease in February 1982, when he was thirty-four years old. He was one of the first two patients diagnosed with the illness at San Francisco General Hospital before the disease was even called AIDS. The only thing doctors knew at the time was that Turner had Kaposi's sarcoma, a rare cancer that manifested itself as five painless spots above his right ankle that looked like cigarette burns.

Turner told the *Los Angeles Times* that he felt the fact he had not been given an absolute death sentence may have contributed to his ability to survive. Also, he said, a close call with mortality seven years before had taught him a valuable lesson.

He had been plagued with a case of hepatitis that had not let up. The symptoms were dragging on far longer than normal. At the time, he was working on his M.F.A. in drama, serving an internship with playwright Tennessee Williams. Turner noted that despite the fact that Williams was aging and had health problems of his own, Williams worked with zest, arising at 4:00 A.M. every day to write.

Turner said that from observing Williams, "I learned I'd been perpetuating my illness through this negative mind trip I'd been on. From then on, when my mind said, 'You can't do it,' I'd say, 'But that's just your mind.'

Drawing from that experience, Turner took charge of his AIDS from the beginning. He quit his job and prescribed for himself much-needed rest. He also prescribed a lot of grains, vegetables, and chicken; he took vitamin C supplements and used acupuncture as an adjunct to his chemotherapy.

The *Times* article described how Turner went to a holistic doctor who urged him to vent his feelings about his illness in any fashion he could—art, activism, conversation. "The sure sign of someone who's going to kick the bucket early is someone who turns inward, keeps the fear to themselves," Turner told the *Times*.

The doctor suggested that Turner visualize his lesions and then draw pictures of them. Turner did so, and portrayed his cancer as ineffectual-looking little lesions rather than huge, monstrous ones, indicating that he was in control of the cancer rather than the other way around.

Turner drew his cancer as a cross-hatched blob, looking like shredded wheat. He visualized the little tips of the cross-hatching as continually falling off, reducing the size of his lesions.

Apparently the visualization technique worked. The lesions disappeared. Dr. Jay A. Levy, a professor of medicine at the University of California Medical Center in San Francisco, said that Turner's cancer simply "dried up."

Levy also found that Turner had a subset of lymphocytes in his blood that seemed to act as suppressor cells, keeping the AIDS virus at bay. When Levy removed the suppressor cells from Turner's blood in the laboratory, the AIDS virus replicated itself and multiplied. When he reintroduced the suppressor cells, replication stopped.

Did Turner's positive attitude have something to do with the presence of these suppressor cells in his blood, or did it allow them to work more effectively? That is one question science might answer. But the fact that Turner had never been "prophesied" into a self-fulfilling death sentence certainly must have helped, Turner and his doctors believe.

Usually AIDS victims live an average of eighteen months after diagnosis. But in the long-term-survivor study launched at the Centers for Disease Control in Atlanta, Turner and over twenty-five other AIDS victims who have far outlived that average time were being studied in 1988 to determine why they survive.

Michael Callen, a New York City singer-songwriter, was another of these survivors. Callen railed against those who claimed to be able to predict when a man must die:

In his guide *Surviving and Thriving with AIDS*, Callen cited New York City Department of Health statistics that of a group of a hundred gay men with AIDS, thirteen were still alive four years after diagnosis. Callen said that to a large extent AIDS deaths may be the result of a self-fulfilling medical prophecy. People who have AIDS *must* die, as everyone knows; if they don't, then doctors simply say the patient must never have had AIDS at all.

"I don't think anybody should pretend that the mortality rate is not 80 percent after three years," he told the *Los Angeles Times*. "But I get really crazy when they don't mention the 20 percent survival beyond three years."

"The unthinking repetition of the notion that everyone dies from AIDS denies the reality," he said. "But just as important, it denies the possibility of survival. It's hard to say which is the greater crime."

"The human mind can discipline the body, can set goals for itself, can somehow comprehend its own potentiality, and move resolutely forward," wrote Norman Cousins in *Anatomy of an Illness*, and in the 1980s, a legion of doctors and researchers began to agree with him.

A whole new field called psychoneuroimmunology—PNI—was developed in the 1980s to explore how the mind and body interact; how positive and negative emotions affect the body; and how the nervous system, the endocrine system, and the immune system interact to promote health and healing—or how they fail, and allow illness to occur.

There *is* a relationship among the mind (psycho), the brain (neuro), and the body's immune system (immunology), researchers have found.

They discovered that prolonged stress, for example, can lead to a wide range of illnesses, including high blood pressure, heart disease, arthritis, ulcers, migraine headaches, urinary tract problems, digestive disorders, and complications of pregnancy and allergies. And they began testing everything from biofeedback to visualization to tender, loving care and prayer to see what helps patients and what doesn't.

It was demonstrated in the lab that a sense of control can keep excessive stress hormones such as catecholamines from flooding the body and causing artery damage, cholesterol buildup, and heart disease. On the other hand, a sense of helplessness can release these hormones and depress the immune system. Researchers found that hostile, cynical, or inwardly angry people are prone to heart and artery disease. Depression depresses the immune system, leading to a lowered ability to resist infections, allergies, autoimmune diseases, or even cancer.

Finally, it seems, researchers were discovering why, as was written in the Bible thousands of years ago, "A cheerful heart doeth good like medicine."

Dr. Herbert Benson, a noted cardiologist at Harvard Medical School, has made a study of what he calls the "relaxation response," which is a natural ability of the body to enter a stress-free state characterized by lowered heart rate, lowered blood pressure, and lowered respiration as well as slower brain waves and an overall reduction of metabolism.

To induce the relaxation response, Dr. Benson says, only four steps are needed: finding a quiet environment; consciously relaxing the major muscle groups; focusing for ten to twenty minutes on a mental device such as the word "one" or a brief prayer; and assuming a passive attitude toward intrusive thoughts.

The relaxation response alone can help reduce stress, lower blood pressure, and enhance physical and mental well-being, but when coupled with what Dr. Benson calls the "faith factor"—the person's deepest beliefs—it can do even more, he says. In the May 1984 issue of *Prevention* magazine, Dr. Benson said, "If you truly believe in your personal philosophy or religious faith, if you are committed mind and soul to your worldview—you may well be capable of achieving remarkable feats of mind and body that many only speculate about."

Practicing the faith factor is simple. Dr. Benson told a twelve-year-old boy with severe congenital migraines, for example, to say and meditate on the Jesus Prayer twice a day. A devout Roman Catholic, the boy meditated on the phrase "Lord Jesus Christ, have mercy on me" as directed, and within two weeks the intensity of the headaches lessened. The boy found that after two to three months, he could head off his headaches when he felt the first twinges of discomfort by reciting this prayer for ten to twenty minutes, and as a result he has been enjoying a relatively pain-free life for the first time.

Another patient, a sixty-nine-year-old woman with chest pains, meditated on "Jesus saves" while she elicited the relaxation response, and eliminated the angina attacks she'd been having three or four times daily.

The pains had prevented her from leading a normal life. After a time she was able to decrease greatly the nitroglycerin she was taking for the pain, increase her activity levels, and become virtually pain-free.

In another instance, Dr. Benson cites the case of a retired Greek Orthodox shopkeeper suffering from rapid heartbeat. Meditating on the phrase *Kyrie eleison,* or "Lord have mercy," slowed down this man's heartbeat and brought it under control after all medication had failed.

At the University of Massachusetts Medical Center, physicians had success using meditation techniques such as Dr. Benson's, coupled with imaging to supplement traditional medical care in treating gastrointestinal disorders, high blood pressure, chronic headaches, cancer, and complications of coronary bypass surgery.

Still another technique being used in the 1980s was biofeedback.

At the Menninger Foundation in Topeka, Kansas, clinicians used biofeedback to help twenty-eight hundred patients monitor their own body temperature, heart rate, and blood pressure. The machines gave audible and visual signals whenever the body physiology varied. As the patients became more and more relaxed during meditation or relaxation sessions, the beeping from the machine would become slower and slower, the beeps farther and farther apart as the patients reduced their heart rate. The same signals were given for lowered blood pressure and body temperature.

Using these signals, patients learned to control their internal processes, reporting success in everything from lowering blood pressure to alleviating back and neck pain and alleviating migraines.

All of these techniques—visualization, the faith factor, biofeedback, and other mind-body mechanisms—should be used only to supplement modern medicine, not replace it, physicians of the "New Age" stressed.

The developer of the "relaxation response" was asked the following question by Dr. Timothy Johnson on ABC-TV's *Nightline* program in the fall of 1987:

Is there such a thing as false hope?

"Indeed there is," answered Dr. Benson. ". . . But what we can actually do is make the best of modern medicine and combine that with what's scientifically proven as to what the mind can do for the body. Our job as physicians is to . . . make better use of what the mind can do for the body, but do it in the context of modern medicine with its proven course of cures."

On the same show, Bernie Siegel added, "If you develop an illness, and your life is threatened, and someone gives you hope—it's not false. How many patients have been killed by false 'no hope'? *That* worries me."

I made a videotape of that show and gave it to the mayor, along with a copy of *Love, Medicine, and Miracles.* I knew somebody else had already given him a copy of *Anatomy of an Illness.*

None of the material did much good, though.

"I'm too busy workin' at City Hall to have time to sit down and go through all that stuff," Tullio told me.

A Cheerful Heart

For his heart was in his work, and the heart giveth grace
unto every Art.

> —Henry Wadsworth
> Longfellow, *The Building
> of the Ship*

IT WAS 1967, the year of "urban unrest" and race riots, the year blacks
got tired of being the crack in the Liberty Bell.

They were starting to burn the city down. First-term Erie mayor Lou
Tullio wasn't having any part of *that*, even though the buildings torched
were in slum areas. Maybe East 18th Street wasn't the nicest street in the
city, but it was part of *his* city. He took it very personally.

A crowd of angry young blacks—several hundred of them, aged from
thirteen to thirty—had gathered around him. The mayor grabbed the
microphone and waved his arm in a wide sweep toward the city outside
the walls of the neighborhood center.

"Why're you doing all this damage? Why? I mean, hey, I taught most
of you fellas, didn't I?"

Tullio *had* taught most of them at Academy High School. A few heads
nodded grudgingly, but most of the men stood with their chins tucked
down into their necks, glaring at their mayor from slits of eyes. As soon as
the mayor stopped to get a breath, the crowd started buzzing angrily.
Then one young man started shouting, "BOO, LOU!"

Then everybody joined in:

"BOO, LOU!

"BOO, LOU!

"BOO, LOU!"

The police chief was standing shoulder to shoulder with Tullio, noting
the locations of all the exits.

The crowd was getting louder. "Hey, I taught mosta you guys!" Tullio repeated. "Didja hear me?

"Didja hear me Willie?

"And you, Fred!

"Benny!

"Ike!

"I taught you! You know me!"

The angry black faces were pressing closer. The young lords, the leaders of the black packs, were pushing toward the mayor. Some were rubbing their knuckles.

But Tullio wasn't afraid. He had never backed away from a fight in his life. And besides, people liked him. Everybody liked him. Everybody he had ever met in his life liked him. Even these angry black fellas liked him. They just didn't know it.

"I know you fellas and you know me," Tullio said. "And what's the one thing about me? Tell me. The one thing?"

No answer.

"It's this," Tullio said, shouting to be heard over the crowd. "The one thing about me is this: I always tell the truth!"

He paused for emphasis, and looked straight into the eyes of a tall Angry Young Lord of the ghetto. "I always . . . tell . . . the truth!" he said, and went on with:

"I don't make promises I can't keep!

"You can trust me down the line!

"I tell it like it is!"

He smiles. The Tullio smile. The sincere smile. The winning smile. The "How can you not like me when I smile like this?" smile.

And loudly, he proclaims:

"I always call a spade a spade!!!"

Suddenly, there is silence. The young men look at each other and draw the corners of their mouths down while pushing their eyebrows up.

Man have guts.

Or he be crazy.

Or both.

The silence just hangs there. Tullio looks puzzled, turns to the chief, and says in a loud stage whisper, "Whatid I say? Whatid I say?"

"Just keep talkin'!" the chief says. His eyes look like his mind is screaming, "Where did I park our car? I can't remember where I parked our car!"

Tullio looks out at the crowd and keeps smiling his Tullio smile. He still doesn't know what he did, but he trusts it was the Tullio magic, whatever it was.

Lookit 'em listen. I always tell the truth! They still know me!

Someone in the crowd starts to laugh. Tullio says to the chief, out of the corner of his mouth, still smiling, "Lookit, I got em' now!"

"Look, now, fellas . . ." Tullio said to the crowd, "I think if we all work together . . . your concerns are my concerns, you know me, and I know you. . . . You come down and see me at City Hall any time you got a problem," he said, establishing the open-door policy he kept for twenty-three years.

The crowd became quiet and attentive. It was as if somebody had just pricked a balloon, suddenly making all the tension vanish. Tullio had gotten their attention.

The incident marked the beginning of the end of the city's unrest. The new mayor had shown he had guts. He had gotten involved. He was accessible.

"You guys come down and see me!" he kept saying.

Not long after, the slums would be razed and replaced by new housing, paid for by federal Model Cities Program funds Tullio would bring into the city. A new community center would be built. Streets would be widened and more streetlights installed. Tullio would work with the school district to establish recreation and educational programs for youths in the area. The neighborhood would be cleaned up and revitalized.

Fred Rush, one of the angry young men in the crowd, would later became an administrator for the city of Erie. Years later, telling me the story, he'd look back on the incident, laugh, and say, "That's the mayor for you. Sometimes it's better to be lucky than right."

It's the middle of February 1988, about twenty years later. The mayor has just returned home from a long vacation. He's very tan, the furnace is cranked up, it's a sunny day, and he's just gotten back from California. So he's wearing his summer pajamas—shorts and a short-sleeved top, unbuttoned, to keep the California mood.

The pajamas are that ambiguous pajama color. Not blue nor green nor yellow. Just faded.

He's got a small gold cross hanging around his neck. There is no Christ on the cross, because Christ has risen and lives. Always one to cover all bases, he's wearing on the same chain a medal with the face of Jesus on it. They both hang over the scar he got from a quadruple bypass a few years back.

It's 3:30 P.M. He's following doctors' orders, cutting his workday short, battling his amyloidosis. He's sitting on the side of the bed talking on the telephone, helping somebody with a political campaign—an Erie County judge seeking the Democratic nod for the Pennsylvania Superior Court race.

Grace leads me into the bedroom, motions to an upholstered wing-back chair, and says, "Please sit down, Jack. Lou will be done soon."

The mayor winks at me and keeps talking.

Piled around the chair is a vacation's worth of unopened mail—magazines, letters, fliers, coupon books, and numerous Pentecostal Evangels, with their testimonies of healing miracles.

I look around the room. King-sized bed. Dark walnut Mediterranean furniture. Gold shag rug. A row of louvered closet doors with clothes and their hangers hooked over the doorknobs—three white shirts and one of Grace's fancy blue gowns with rows of little sequined beads on the front. The mayor's slippers to the right of the bed, next to two used black socks. And rising up from behind the bed's headboard, going from wall to wall, floor to ceiling, are pale gold draperies. They make the bedroom look decidedly majestic—with the emperor sitting on the side of the bed, not in his new clothes, but in his old pajamas and seeing to the business at hand, caring for his charges.

LOUIS (TEUTONIC): *"renowned in battle." Variations and diminutives: Aloysius, Clovis, Lewes, Lewis, Ludovick, Ludvig, Luigi, Luis, Lew, Lou, Louie, Lou the Tool, as we used to call him in our high-school days.*

Lou the Tool sitting on the bed in his PJs, his black trousers tossed over the stool at the foot of the bed, doing politics on the phone. How many Annoying Observers have seen the emperor like this?

In a few minutes he'll be off the phone and telling me more about his ghetto experience.

He hangs up. He shows me some of the get-well letters he's received, then says, "Ya gotta put funny things in that book, that's what sells books, I want ya to make a lot of money." Then he tells me his East 18th Street story, pretty much the same way Rush had described it.

"Can you believe it?" the mayor says. "There we are in the middle of a race riot practically, and I tell 'em I always call a spade a spade! And I say to the chief, 'What happened? Why'd they get so quiet?'"

Then, before Grace can stop him, he says, almost as one word, "Then-a-course there was that time we had the problems with all those prostitutes and I got all my police captains together in front of the TV cameras and promised the public we'd lick the situation."

"Oh, Lou—"

"Now, Grace, Jack can use that if he wants to. . . ."

Grace offers me some chocolates from a heart-shaped Valentine's Day candy box.

"You can't have any, Lou," she says.

"Dr. Grace—she's watchin' me like a hawk. Hey, Grace, since I can't have candy, would ya get me a glass of ice water, please? Hey, Jack, lookit this . . ." He walks over to his dresser. On the top is a picture frame, done in clear plastic script saying, "I (heart) you," with a picture of Grace and the mayor in a big red heart, their arms around each other. "Pretty nice, eh? I like that. I got it for my wife for Valentine's Day."

"He's just got to start taking it easy," Grace says, handing him the ice water. He's killing himself. He's starting to retain water again. . . ."

"Yeah, the water's buildin' up."

"Lou, if you don't—"

"Now listen, Grace, listen. I told you. Leave the politics to me. I gotta help people with their campaigns."

"But you can't—"

"Listen, I'm not goin' to parties, I'm not makin' the rounds any-more. . . . I'm just makin' a couple phone calls. . . ."

"But people can organize their own—"

"Listen. There's only one organizer in this town, and that's Lou Tullio."

"Oh, Lou, play that song for Jack," Grace says, handing him a tape and a small cassette recorder.

"Oh, yeah, you gotta hear this song this woman wrote for me. It's beautiful. You'll love it."

I knew what was coming. I'd written the headline for the story about it: "TULLIO LAUDED IN SONG." A woman had written a song for the mayor. The song was composed by Sarah Tanner and sung by Julie Moore, both of Erie. "It's kind of a 'thank you' song for Lou," Tanner had said. "I wrote it for the people of Erie. The people who want to thank the mayor for a job well done."

What she didn't say is that it was a song to help him fight his amyloidosis.

The mayor pops the cassette into the machine.

"Listen. You'll love it."

Drumrolls, trumpets, voice: *"You can stand up and be counted as a friend/For we're proud to say we know you/ And on you we can depend.*

"Through the years you always stood strong and tall/And you've tried to do what's best for us all."

The mayor is beaming. His index finger on his right hand is jumping peripatetically, conducting the voice on the recorder. His still-muscular legs are dangling over the bed, his feet keeping time on the carpet, and he's singing along, with a huge smile on his face. The emperor looks positively cute, like a big little boy.

(Chorus) (The mayor breaks into song himself) "Lou-ooo, we love you-ooooo!!!"

"Isn't that great? The lady who wrote it didn't even know me."

"That was so sweet of her," says Grace.

"Listen," the mayor says.

"Let's all stand up and be counted as your friend/We'll support you through the years and never let this friendship end. For we know you'll always stand strong and tall/and you'll always be a winner to us all.

"It's a good song, isn't it? She's got a good voice, doesn't she?" the mayor says.

(Chorus) "Lou-OOOO (the mayor's voice cracks) we love you-OOO. . . ." And there the mayor sits, singing and grinning, in his pajamas, at three in the afternoon, following doctors' orders, his wife, Grace, by his side, both battling his amyloidosis, listening to his song as it ends with the melody from "The Battle Hymn of the Republic."

Louis: victorious in battle?

The phone rings.

Grace picks it up. "Oh, Dr. Anderson, I'm so glad you called. He's only lost one and a half pounds of water after that shot. Shouldn't he have lost more? . . . Yes, he's here . . . he's in bed, behaving himself. Just a minute, I'll put him on."

"Louis—it's Dr. Anderson."

The Bible's on the nightstand. The mail's unopened on the floor. Grace and I leave the room.

Two days later, at my office, the phone rings. It's almost noon. "What kind of sandwich do you want?" the mayor asks, on the other end of the line. "Fish or chicken?"

"Uh, fish, I guess."

"You're still coming down here to see all those letters, right?"

"Sure. But you don't have to get me a sandwich."

"No problem," the mayor says, and hangs up.

He'd told me he'd received over two thousand get-well letters from all across the country, once people learned of his illness from the *Time,* Associated Press, and *USA Today* stories.

"You gotta see these letters," he said. "People really care about me. I didn't realize how many people thought I've been a good mayor all these years after all."

When I got to his office, he sat me down at a huge walnut conference table and dumped a few stacks of letters in front of me, then brought the fish sandwich. "You want something to drink with that? A glass of water, maybe?"

One letter writer, William T. Shea, told how he had read the

Associated Press's "two mayors" stories in both the Poughkeepsie, New York, and Worcester, Massachusetts, papers. He wanted his letter published in the newspaper as a letter to the editor.

"For your readers, I might tell of Lou in the years he was away from your fine city of Erie," Shea wrote. "Extremely popular at Holy Cross College, Lou saved a classmate from drowning and received a gold watch for his heroism. After graduation, he developed a milk business in this city, which was quite a feat, coming from a distant area. With his own hands, he cut down trees, brought them to a sawmill, and with the boards, he built a small roadside ice cream stand for the summer.

"He sold his milk company and went into the service as a Navy lieutenant, in a remote base called Gamadota in Milne Bay, Papua, New Guinea. He was the principal administrator of our group called "Navy Coastal Pilots." A small group, the Navy trained us to be Marine coastal pilots for New Guinea and the Admiralty Islands. Later, those of us who became licensed became harbor pilots in the Philippines. In the Philippines, Lou administered a social service-recreational program for some 100,000 men in the area.

"Back home [to Worcester] from the war, Lou coached high school and ran an ice cream parlor business, which was successful. He also managed to get a master's degree from Boston University.

"He has dozens of friends in the Worcester area. As one of his Holy Cross classmates, I also knew him through my five months in New Guinea, a year in the Philippines, and later, both of us running businesses on Main Street in Worcester. I know and admire his upbeat attitude on life. Lou is fun. Lou is generous to a fault. There are go-getters in this world and he certainly qualifies for that description— but his greatest asset is that he is a 'go-giver.'

"When Lou leaves office, people in Erie will say, 'Nothing is ever like it used to be.'"

My favorite letters were from the kids:

"Dear Mayor Tullio, I hope you start to feel a little better. We are praying for you. I think you are doing a good job as mayor. My mom does, too. And happy Ground Hog's Day, even though it's over.

"Your, Friend, Ian, grade 5."

"Dear Mayor Tullio, I like you. We have been praying for you. You are a good man. Have you had a good job? I am reading second-grade books. I have read over 200 library books this year. I want to read 400 library books this year.

"Justin, grade 1."

"Dear Mayor Tullio, I hope you get better because we have been praying for you. We wanted to cheer you up by giving you a card. I hope it worked. I hope you'll stay the way you are except for your disease to go away. See you sometime, maybe.

"Sincerely, Joey Caldwell."

"Aren't they nice?" the mayor said. "And look at those drawings they made on those. Those kids took a lot of time for me. They're pretty good artists, don't you think?"

He plopped down three more boxes of letters on the conference room table. "Here, you can go through these too."

The top letter on the pile, from a former U.S. president, caught my eye:

"I am sorry to learn that you have been ill. I want you to know that Rosalynn and I are thinking of you, and we send you our love and prayers.

"With best warm wishes,

"Sincerely, Jimmy Carter."

I thought of the photo in Tullio's office showing the mayor giving Rosalynn a peck on the cheek as the Carters arrived at the Erie airport a few years back.

(I wondered if the mayor knew that Jimmy Carter's sister Ruth Stapleton Carter had had a healing ministry. In her book *In His Footsteps*, she tells of her first experience with healing, which involved a deaf woman. "Lord, I know that you can heal this woman's ears. Please heal her now," she said, after a friend had goaded her into it. Much to her surprise, the woman regained her hearing. Later Ruth Carter would write, "God has provided various tools for returning our bodies to wholeness. He will choose mud, medicine, or the word of faith, depending on what we need and are able to accept.")

The next letter was from former Speaker of the House Thomas P. "Tip" O'Neill, Jr.

"Your concern and support for me during my recent illness is greatly appreciated. I regret to learn of your illness as well. I suppose at best we have two things in common: regular visits to the doctors and the love and support of our family and good friends. Again, you are to be commended for the excellent service you give the good folk in Erie. I am proud to hear how well you're managing. May God keep you in His care."

Also tucked into the stacks of letters was one from President Ronald Reagan, congratulating Tullio for being named Pennsylvania's Government Leader of the Year by the Pennsylvania Chamber of Business and Industry.

"This recognition is truly well deserved," the president said. "Your twenty-two years of public service to the citizens of Erie testify volumes about your dedication and your leadership . . . you have my best wishes for continued success. God bless you."

The mayor received letters from other mayors, judges, and government officials from all over the world. He also got a few letters from finger straighteners like me, suggesting he try everything from megadoses of vitamin C to ancient Chinese herbal formulas. After reading a number of these, I began to wonder how much of a pain in the rear end people like me could be to a man in his situation.

Before I left the mayor's office that day, I read two more letters. One, from the evangelist Leighton Ford of Charlotte, North Carolina, said, "I still remember our time in Erie years ago and especially the ride you gave me from the airport when all the lights turned green at a signal from your escort's radar. I have used that many times as an illustration of miracles —that God can make all the lights turn green when He is coming through on a special mission—as the mayor of Erie did!"

The last thing I read was a card showing a sun that could have been rising, or setting, over an ocean. It carried these lines:

"God grant me the Serenity to accept the things I cannot change . . . Courage to change the things I can, and Wisdom to know the difference."

Mysterious Ways

Gentle Jesus meek and mild,
Look upon a little child . . .
—Charles Wesley,
Gentle Jesus

I T'S 6:30 A.M., and Zona stops by my desk on his way to McDonald's for his preworkday coffee. He's got this funny-looking powder-blue cap on with a tiny little visor.

"What is *that?*" I ask him, pointing to the thing on his head as if it's a dead animal.

"This is an Irish motorman's hat," he says. "I want people to think I'm Irish like you. Then I can go around borrowing money and not paying it back."

He reminds me that I've owed him a dollar for a week, but I tell him I'm willing to forget about it if he is.

He shakes his head. "Got a story for me today?"

"I'll think of something."

Zona nods, smiles, makes an obscene gesture, and strolls off down the hall.

It's a springtime Friday morning, and the sun is shining. It's tough to get my mind on work, and I don't have the faintest idea of what I'm going to write about. Then I think about Eric Danowski, the Harborcreek baby who had the two liver transplants. From what his mother, Debbie, had told me the day before, the little guy was going down fast.

"We really appreciate it when you write about our baby, Jack," she'd said. "It means a lot to know the people in our hometown are thinking about him and praying for him. I hope they keep praying. Our baby needs all the prayers he can get."

"*Hey, how about an update on Danowski?*" I yell to Dick Deckert, the gray-haired, long-suffering assistant city editor.

"Okay," he says. "How long?"

"Fifteen inches," I say, telling him how long the story will be so he can plan for it on the local page.

And so the day begins. I start typing, but my eyes burn and I have to get up a couple of times and walk around before I can finish the story.

God, I'm getting soft.

Sniffling as I type and having to get up. That's all I need. To start crying in the middle of the city room.

I look around at the other reporters cracking their gum and jiggling their legs as they type, staring into their cathode ray tubes, and I remind myself who and what I am. I'm a reporter, not a doctor or some nun, and I work in a newsroom, not in some hospital with people who can afford to care.

I can always depend on my co-workers for an insult to bring me back to the real world, so I walk up and stand in front of a desk.

"Hey, how's it goin'?"

"Get away from me," my fellow reporter says with a snarl.

A perfect, effortless backhand. He didn't even look up from his paper.

I head out the city room door and walk down the hall, where I can be alone for a few minutes.

Eric Danowski is not *my* baby. He's not Ian Christian Grazier. *Quit getting the two entangled.*

What happens to Eric doesn't involve me. And I can't let it. Thousands of babies all over the country are dying and having transplants and doing poorly all the time. I can't cry for all of them. The newspaper might as well start an *organ transplant beat,* we're getting so many of these stories—babies getting sick, being flown off to hospitals for new livers, kidneys, hearts, bone marrow transplants. Then the fund-raisers back home start and dewy-eyed people come to the paper asking us to help them raise $150,000 or else the kids' parents will lose their homes. The cost of the new technology that's keeping these children alive has never been matched to blue-collar pocketbooks.

How can the newspaper not get involved in raising money to save a dying baby? But then again, how can we do it for everybody? There are so many dying babies and sick children and desperate cases—it seems that everybody knows someone in a coma these days—if we covered all these stories, we wouldn't have space for any other news. Cripes, we could put out a weekly tabloid on dying babies and all the fund-raisers being held for them. Where does it all stop?

Yet here I was, covering the Dying-Baby Beat.

Hello. Grazier here. You say your baby's got ameleodic biphasial

*sclerosis of the left quadrant of the right kidney? Phase six? Yes, I'm
your man!*

It doesn't—can't—involve *me*.

Got to pull back.

Remember, Jack, you're an Annoying, Obnoxious OBSERVER!

I've often said that the only reason we all come in to work at the paper
is that we have no insensitive clods at home to keep us company. I'm
starting to identify too much with the nice people of the world. Complete
strangers to boot. That's dangerous for a journalist. It's a cruel world, and
you can't get all sappy about it.

But still. That poor sick little baby . . .

Who knows? Maybe I can cover the news and help the little guy at the
same time. His face looked so much like Ian's, when they showed him on
TV news. They showed Eric laughing, eyes crinkled and smiling; Eric,
eyes big and round, looking up at his mother; Eric, eyes and skin
jaundiced, lying in bed on his side, his abdomen distended as he gasped
for breath.

I think of the experiments at San Francisco General Hospital that
showed that heart patients remembered in prayer fared better than those
who were not prayed for. The prayed-for group was five times less likely
than the "unremembered group" to develop infections requiring antibiotics and three times less likely to develop a lung condition leading to
heart failure.

Maybe if enough people pray for Eric, maybe that *could* bring him
around.

A half hour later, I file the following:

Debbie Danowski is asking for your prayers to help her baby live.

Ten-month-old Eric is now afflicted with a life-threatening virus.

He underwent a second liver transplant at Children's Hospital in Pittsburgh
about three weeks ago, having suffered from a hereditary disease called Alpha
1-Anitrypsin Deficiency, which meant he needed a new liver to survive. The
second transplant was necessary after the first liver failed.

The new liver is functioning beautifully, his mother said Thursday. But the
liver is no longer the doctors' main concern.

"He came back from X-ray today with his lungs showing completely white on
the film where they should have been dark," she said. She explained that the
whiteness indicated an adenovirus (any number of DNA viruses that cause eye
and respiratory disease) infection that had spread from the right lung to the left.
Inside Eric's lungs, doctors say, is a thin, gluelike mucus coating caused by the
virus. The baby is slowly smothering.

Eric has been placed back on a respirator to help him breathe. Doctors are also
using the machine in an attempt to break up and suction some of the mucus. So
far, that has not been working. "When they put in the tube, nothing comes out,"
Debbie said.

"The doctors said they can't promise me anything," she said. "They can't promise he'll get better. I've never been so scared in my entire life." Her son is now listed in critical condition.

Eric had been put on Cyclosporin, a drug that prevents the body from rejecting transplanted organs. In Eric's case, the drug was a two-edged sword. It may have kept his body from rejecting his new liver, but it weakened his immune system to the point where it could not fight the virus that started in his right lung. The baby has been taken off Cyclosporin in hopes his immune system can make a comeback and fight off the virus. The danger, said Debbie, is that the virus will spread to Eric's new liver. Doctors have told her if that happens, the organ will be destroyed.

So far, Debbie has spent forty-six straight days at Children's Hospital. Social workers have told her that for her own sake, she and her husband, Scott, should stay in a motel, but she won't leave her baby's side. "I'm afraid to do that for fear of what might happen while I'm gone," she said.

If Eric is to die, doctors have told Debbie it will probably be a slow death, taking about three weeks. If he is to live, the next three or four days should tell.

"Doctors just can't promise he'll pull through," Debbie said. "I'd gladly stay with him in ICU for another six or seven months, or however long it took, just so he could go home with me."

She gives thanks to God for bringing Eric this far, but admits that sometimes she has her doubts. "My baby's been so sick, he's had such major operations, he's such a skinny little guy—and now this virus. Meanwhile, I see other kids leaving the floor just a few days after their transplants. Why my baby? Why does it have to be my baby?

"We still have hope that Eric will pull through, but sometimes I wonder if God hears our prayers. He knows how sick Eric is. He knows he's suffering. We've been praying to Him—why won't He heal him? I lost my own mother when I was seventeen, and sometimes I ask myself, 'Why is this happening again?'"

In the next breath, though, Debbie says, "I take a look around the unit, at all the other deformed babies who are sicker than Eric, and I thank God he's as good as he is. Eric still has his mental faculties. It's such a relief and a blessing to know that on the neurological side, he's just fine. When he comes to, he puts his two fingers up to my face—he likes to do that so I can kiss them—and he pulls on Scott's mustache. I thank God for that, I can tell you.

"I just keep praying I can take him home with me."

She said that for all of you who read this, she asks for your prayers, too.

"Hey, Dick, what did you think of that story?" I ask the assistant city editor.

He shakes his head. "To tell you the truth, I didn't read it. I don't think it will make it in today. We've been cut back half a page."

I know Deckert pretty well and begin lobbying for the story. "You believe in the power of prayer, don't you?"

"Sure."

"Well, wouldn't it be nice to get forty thousand people praying for this baby?"

"Of course it would, Jack, but we don't have any room."

"Can't you pull something off local page? A rape? A dismemberment?" Deckert shrugs. "Lobby Zona."

"Oh, sure, Dick. I'm supposed to tell my city editor, "Hey Zona, we've got to get this story in so people can pray for a dying baby!"

Deckert has been staring at his page dummies the whole time, jotting down story slugs and inch counts. But now he looks up and squints at me over the top of his glasses. "That *is* the reason for the story. Don't be ashamed to tell him that."

I sigh and stroll casually back to Tony. He's just printed out a chart on the Macintosh's laser printer. I come up behind him and ask what he's doing.

"Graphic," he says.

What that means is, "I'm printing a graphic to use on page one, and I'm busy, so if it's not important, *leave me alone.*"

The chart he's just printed shows how the fluorocarbons from hair spray cans are depleting the ozone layer, and how if something isn't done, by the year 2000 there will be no ozone to protect us from the sun's harmful ultraviolet rays. That means our children will end up looking like bacon strips. An Associated Press story that goes with the chart says that depletion of the earth's ozone layer could threaten the world's food supply because increased untraviolet rays could kill the ocean's plankton —"the grass of the sea"—at the bottom of the globe's food chain, which could eventually become a chain of death that could lead, link by link, to all mankind.

The graphic comes out of the laser printer and Zona sprays it—with a can of *hair spray*—to fix the ink so it doesn't smudge.

"Got a minute?" I ask.

"This is going to be a pain-in-the-butt conversation, I can tell," Zona says.

"How can you tell?"

"You're using that tone that says, 'Hey, Tony, get ready for a pain-in-the-butt conversation.'"

"You believe in prayer?" I ask him.

"I knew this was going to be a pain-in-the-butt conversation."

"Do you? Do you believe?"

"Yes."

"Okay. I do, too. Especially since I've been working on the book."

"God, I'll be glad when you're done with this book."

"Here's the deal. The real reason for doing the story on Eric is, it looks like he's not going to make it, and if prayer really does work, it would be nice to get people praying for him. I've told you about the scientific studies that show prayer works. If ten thousand readers prayed for Eric, maybe that would bring him around."

Zona puts his elbows on the table and leans forward. "If Mary Beth Kennedy needed prayers for her day school, would you put a story in the paper asking people to pray for her? Or how about running stories asking people to pray for everybody who's starving in Africa?"

"Cripes, Tony, this is different. It's a little baby's life."

Zona sighs. "Look, I hate to take a hard-hearted approach. I believe in prayer, too. But I just don't have the space for this story."

He leans forward again. "You know, there are other ways to do this. Prayer chains. Call Dave Alexander's wife and before you know it she'll be on the phone and have a ton of people praying for that little sucker. She'll have hundreds of people praying by the end of the day. That's what I did for Gregg's wife after she had that traffic accident. I called Dave Alexander's wife and got a prayer chain going. And I've gotta believe those people praying for her helped her pull through."

He settles back in his chair again. "Look, what you do is, you call Debbie Danowski and explain to her our space situation. Then get going calling some of these prayer chains and parishes. Meanwhile, I can't afford to have you known as our resident freak. It's okay that you're working on this book, but I can't have it interfering with your work here. Your credibility—you've got to keep your perspective."

"What do you mean, 'resident freak'? Has anybody in the front office said anything?"

"They just indicated to me with a raised eyebrow that I should make sure you don't go off the deep end. Don't get me wrong. They believe very strongly out there, too. But we have our credibility to maintain here at the paper. We cover the news. We don't pray for it."

He stands up and sighs again. End of conversation. "We'll have to wait till Monday to run this. If he dies by then, I'll feel terrible. But I'll have to deal with that then. I can't handle it now. In the meantime, don't worry. I'll smack you on the face every once in a while when you need it to bring you out of it."

Later I hear Zona discussing editorial space problems with Managing Editor Len Kholos. Zona's agitated. Maybe our pain-in-the-butt conversation got through to him after all.

At times like these, I do what I always do: I go for a cup of coffee. Then, usually by the time I get back to my desk, I find that everything has somehow resolved itself.

As I walk back into the city room, Deckert calls me over and says, "You say here that Debbie Danowski has been at the hospital forty-six straight days. I thought she went home in between once or twice."

"You're reading my story? Does this mean there's space for it after all?"

Deckert smiles ever so slightly and looks back into his terminal screen. "God works in mysterious ways, Jack," he says.

When the story finally does come out that day, it's got a nice little box around it, smack in the center of the local page.

I grab Zona by the shoulder as he's hurrying off to a meeting.

"You're not such a hard case after all, are you?' I ask him.

"What do you mean?"

"That story got in today."

Zona shrugs and throws his hands up at his sides. "I didn't have anything to do with it. Stories fell down, stories got moved, space opened up. It worked. What can I say?"

Later I ask Deckert what really happened.

"I told you: God works in mysterious ways."

A few days after our plea for prayers is published, I receive a packet of photos in the mail from Debbie Danowski. The pictures, taken a week and a half before, show a smiling baby ready to leave the intensive-care unit and go to a regular floor. The photos of little Eric hugging his teddy bear are all the more poignant because of the sudden turn for the worse he'd taken after they were mailed.

"What's the matter with you?" Zona says, stopping by my desk. He's wearing a navy blue Greek fisherman's hat today. When Zona starts rotating his hat collection, you know spring has sprung.

I don't tell him I am feuding with God. I just say, "Take a look at these photos."

He nods and shuffles through them. "I came to work one morning and the first thing I saw on my desk was a color photo of two girls killed by a train that day. Screwed me up for weeks," he says.

"Eric Danowski is dying," I tell him. "So much for prayer. Doctors don't think he'll make it to his first birthday on Saturday after all."

At least, I assumed he was dying because I hadn't heard from his mother.

"Kind of makes you wonder how many 'miracles' are just wishful thinking imposed on coincidence, doesn't it?" I ask Zona.

He hands the photos back. "Oh, I don't doubt that prayer works and there are miracles, but we're in trouble when we think we see them happening everywhere."

"Yeah, but, hey, Tony—if God's going to answer any prayers, why not prayers for some poor, innocent little kid?"

"Why should God favor a baby over someone else? Would you want to have God choose to save Eric over your wife, if she were sick?"

I see his point.

I tell Zona a story about a local pastor and his wife who had been unable to have a child of their own. They prayed for a baby. Within a few days they were connected up with a teenage mother who wanted to give up her child. And the next day, in a trash dumpster, they found boxes of brand-new baby clothes. They took that as confirmation of a miracle, praise the Lord.

A couple of days later, the couple received a phone call saying the mother had changed her mind and didn't want to give up her baby after all.

So much for *that* miracle.

"Maybe the real miracle occurred when the mother came to her senses at the last minute before putting her own baby up for adoption," Zona says. "Who can say what God intended? Maybe the baby clothes were put there to assure the pastor and his wife that God's still got their case on file. Or maybe they were put there to remind them that we can't impose our version of reality on Him."

I thought about that and concluded that logic and thinking can take you only so far before you hit a wall. There are just too many *counterfactuals* to consider—an infinite number of alternate motivations for an infinite God. I was finally beginning to feel rather stupid. How many times did I have to be reminded that we just have to do our best, pray, and take the rest on faith?

Zona went back up to the city desk, and I looked into my computer screen and said a silent prayer, apologizing to God for my anger and my impudence. I told Him I'd understand if He wanted to take care of Eric in His way rather than mine.

No more than an hour later, I received a call from Debbie Danowski, saying how she had meant to call me sooner, but she had been too busy planning for Eric's birthday party.

"His *birthday party?*"

"You won't believe it," she said, "but the day after your story ran, Eric did a 180-degree turnaround. All his doctors are shocked."

"The Friday that story was published was our darkest day," Debbie said. "Eric's lungs had gotten much worse, and his liver was failing. Doctors thought that either the virus had spread to the liver, or the liver was being rejected. Nurses kept trying to suction his lungs. Nothing worked. They all thought it was hopeless, and the doctors told me not to expect him to live."

I knew she wasn't exaggerating. I had talked to hospital spokesmen that day who had said the same thing.

Debbie said that the next morning she prayed that God would strengthen her for whatever she would have to face that day. But when she walked into the intensive-care unit, she was met by smiling nurses and doctors.

They told her excitedly that chest X-rays showed Eric's lungs were clearing. His fever had disappeared overnight, and his vital signs had strengthened. And his liver functions were picking up.

On Saturday, April 2, the day before Easter, Eric had his first birthday. At 4:40 P.M. that day, a doctor gave him his best present: "As of now, I would say that Eric has beaten the virus," he told his parents.

"I'm going around telling everybody he's my little Easter miracle," Debbie told me when she called me at work that Saturday night.

I had volunteered to work every Saturday night for nine months so I'd have Saturday days, Sundays, and Mondays to work on the book. (Monday would be my day off for working Saturday nights.) That was one Saturday night I was glad to be there.

The following Monday Eric was taken off the respirator. Three days after Easter he was moved out of the intensive-care unit and onto a regular floor, at least two weeks sooner than his doctors thought would have been possible.

"The way my husband and I look at it, heaven was totally bombarded with prayers that Friday when your story ran," Debbie said. "Eric's condition completely reversed itself overnight, even though doctors had said nothing more could be done. It gives me goose bumps just to think about it."

She said that one doctor told her, "Mrs. Danowski, somebody had a hand in this Who was much more powerful than we are."

"Now Eric's playing pattycake," Debbie said. "For months I had been praying, 'Please don't let me lose him.' But that Friday night I finally stopped trying to impose my will on the Lord. I stopped trying to have God bless *my* decision, and left the decision for Him to make. I just prayed, 'Lord, let Your will be done, but just help me to accept whatever happens, let me keep my grip on things.'

"Saturday I prayed, 'Lord, whatever it will be when I walk into ICU, please let me handle it.' And when I walked in there, I couldn't believe it. His blood gases were better. His X-rays were better. And his fever was gone. From the point where I turned it all over to God, both Eric's condition and my attitude changed."

There was one more thing she mentioned: "This little Chinese priest, I don't know his name . . . he would come into ICU every morning and lay hands on Eric. He'd pray the Twenty-third Psalm, and encourage me to put my hands on the baby and pray with him.

"Then we'd both be touching Eric, and praying the Twenty-third Psalm together."

I wrote a story for Easter Sunday's paper that carried the headline, "EASTER 'MIRACLE BABY' WINNING FIGHT FOR LIFE." As I typed, I savored every word, and I ended with:

Debbie knows Eric's grasp on life is still tenuous.

But over the head of his bed is this saying from the Book of Isaiah:

"See, I have not forgotten you, for I have carved you into the palm of my hand."

Eric's mother believes God means that, and no matter what happens now, Christ is risen, and he is with her baby.

Naturally, the whole story did not get in. About eight of twenty inches had to be cut.

"*We don't have the space, Jack. Whaddya, wanna write a book?*"

But most of the stuff about God and prayer made it in.

It was Easter, after all.

As our assistant city editor would say, God works in mysterious ways.

Divine Irony

Sometimes I wish that God were back
in this dark world and wide;
For though some virtues he might lack,
he had his pleasant side.
—Gamaliel Bradford,
Exit God

IF ILLNESS AND DEATH *do* come from Satan, then liver-transplant recipient Eric Danowski, a baby who had the largest eyes and the longest eyelashes you ever saw, must have frustrated the hell out of the devil.

Every time his little flame of life was about to be extinguished by one medical crisis or another, it would waver and dim and flicker, and then somehow come sputtering back. Eric was like one of those trick party candles that keep relighting themselves every time you think you've got it blown out.

"I watched four other children die after they had their transplants while Eric was in intensive care," Debbie Danowski told me in one of our Saturday night telephone conversations. "All of them were stronger and healthier than Eric," she said. "If we're just talking health, Eric is the one who should have died."

"This whole thing has brought both me and my husband closer to God," she said. "I'll tell you what—when you're in a situation like this, those doctors can do only so much and no more. The whole reality is that if the Lord doesn't have it in mind for your baby to get well, nobody is going to change that decision. Dr. Thomas Starzl, who did Eric's surgery, is the best transplant surgeon in the world. But he's not God. And if it's not the Lord's will that Eric lives, Starzl won't make a bit of difference."

It's easy to have faith when prayers have apparently been answered. I asked Debbie if she would still have that faith if Eric should die.

"If he takes a turn for the worse and something happens, I think I would still feel the same," she said. "I've finally realized you have to let the Lord do His work and accept His will. Months ago, I should have put it all in the Lord's hands, but instead I was telling Him what *I* wanted, the way *I* wanted things to be. Now, even if the Lord is to take Eric, we've just got to accept it. And I really *do* believe there would be a reason. Maybe Eric would suffer unbearably, being immunosuppressed all his life. Maybe he'd have one complication after another. But I believe we'd still feel close to God because we'd know Eric was with Him."

Debbie Danowski gave much of the credit for her faith and spiritual growth to "that little Chinese priest" who stopped at Eric's bedside every day, the priest who used to lay hands on Eric and pray while asking Debbie to do the same.

Actually, Michael Aguilar was not a priest. He hadn't been ordained yet. But he was a Catholic Eucharistic minister, empowered to take the Eucharist to the sick. He also administered Baptism to the dying.

Brother Deo Gratias was the name given him by his religious community. He is a missionary brother in Divine Word Missions of Pittsburgh. "Deo Gratias" is a Latin name meaning "Thanks be to God."

Although some people think he looks Chinese, he's Mexican, living his ministry in the United States and going home to Mexico every five years to visit his family.

"Every day before I go on my rounds I have a half hour of prayer besides our daily Mass. I use that time to pray for the children," he told me. "And when I do, I just put them in God's hands. I tell people we have to leave it all to the good Lord and accept whatever He decides for us. Of course, we have to have hope in Him, but it is still His decision, no matter how painful it might be.

"With Eric, I know great things are happening. Why? It's the prayers of his parents—your prayers—and everyone's prayers. One thing I know is that no prayer goes unheard. The good Lord may not answer our prayers the way we want, but He will answer our prayers somewhere, somehow."

Brother Deo had been ministering to the sick for four years at various hospitals and had been at Children's Hospital for nine months by the time I talked with him. "I've been trying to bring comfort to the families and to the sick. Of all the hospitals where I have been working, I think Children's Hospital is the hardest. When the parents have to bury their children, there are no words of comfort for that."

"What about Eric's case?" I asked.

"Well, I've been visiting his mom almost daily. Daily I pass her room and I see, at times, sad moments, and I offer a prayer, and once in a while

Mom receives communion. I know they are people with faith and deep trust in God. I try to bring a little comfort to them and try to be there with their pain, although many times there is nothing I can say. I just stay in the background, reciting my psalms for them. Especially the twenty-third Psalm, 'The Lord is my Shepherd, I shall not want. . . .'"

"Do you believe in healing and the laying on of hands?"

"Oh, yes, certainly. I believe in the power of healing with God's grace."

"And you would lay hands on Eric while you prayed for him?"

"Yes, I would touch him. It's always a healing of touching, yes? Touching is part of our training. We were told always to touch, just as the good Lord Jesus touched. Remember, when that woman was very sick with the issue of blood, she wanted to touch him? But she couldn't reach him so she just touched the hem of his garment, remember? And she was healed. It's the laying on of hands that heals, and a lot of priests in our church do that. Even when a man becomes a priest, it is the bishop who lays his hand on the head of the person who is to be the healer of bodies and souls, who is to carry on this ministry. It's like a transfer of power somehow. Read the Bible and see all the places where the laying on of hands is mentioned."

I did that.

Describing the consecration of offerings, Leviticus 1:4 says, "The person bringing it [the animal] shall lay his hands upon its head, and then it becomes his substitute." Leviticus 3:2 says, "The man who brings the animal shall lay his hands upon its head and kill it at the door of the tabernacle."

Describing the laying on of hands for the consecration of men for service, Numbers 8:9–10 says, "Then bring the Levites to the door of the Tabernacle as all the people watch. There the leaders of the tribes shall lay their hands upon them, and Aaron with a gesture of offering shall present them to the Lord as a gift from the entire nation of Israel." In Numbers 27:18, Moses is instructed, "Take thee Joshua the son of Nun, a man in whom is the spirit, and lay thine hand upon him." In Acts 6:6, the believers selected seven wise men filled with the Holy Spirit and presented them to the apostles, "who prayed for them and laid their hands on them in blessing." In I Timothy 4:14, Paul says, "Be sure to use the abilities God has given you through His prophets when the elders of the church laid their hands upon your head." In II Timothy 1:6, Paul says: "This being so, I want to remind you to stir into flame the strength and boldness that is in you, that entered into you when I laid my hand upon your head and blessed you."

A deaf man with a speech impediment was brought to Jesus, "and everyone begged Jesus to lay his hands on the man and heal him." (Mark 7:32)

Other instances:

- "As the sun went down that evening, all the villagers who had any sick people in their homes, no matter what their diseases were, brought them to Jesus, and the touch of his hands healed every one!" (Luke 4:40)
- "One Sabbath, as he was teaching in a synagogue, he saw a seriously handicapped woman who had been doubled up for eighteen years and was unable to straighten herself. Calling her over to him, Jesus said, 'Woman, you are healed of your sickness!' He touched her, and instantly she could stand straight." (Luke 13:10—13)
- "Paul went in and prayed for him, and laying his hands on him, healed him! Then all the other sick people of the island came and were cured." (Acts 8:8)
- A leper knelt before Jesus and said, "Sir, if you want to, you can heal me." Jesus touched the man. "I want to," Jesus said, and the man was healed. (Matthew 8:3)

And finally, Matthew 19:14

"But Jesus said, 'Let the little children come unto me, and don't prevent them. For of such is the Kingdom of Heaven.' And he put his hands on their heads and blessed them before he left."

"I do believe in touching whenever possible, but sometimes people are too sick to touch, or they have a contagious disease," said Brother Deo. "In those cases, I just touch the bed or a sheet as a sign of reaching out to them. When people are just out of surgery, you know, you see a lot of blood and all kinds of things and I just touch the railing of the bed or a part of the sheets nearby. It's a sign of reaching out.

"And always, I invite the family to touch the patient, and I say, 'Let us pray.' I always invite the people, 'Let us touch,' or if the moms are allowed to hold their babies, I will put my hand on their shoulders, you know, or maybe just on the baby's arm or whatever, and then we call on God and the Holy Spirit and Jesus. He's the healer. And if the patient gets better, it's not my prayer, but all of our prayers that God hears. And even when somebody dies, I ask that we touch one another."

Brother Deo told me that anointing of the sick, an integral part of the Catholic church in the second and third centuries, was revived by Pope Paul VI, after the Second Vatican Council, with the issuance in 1972 of the Rite of Anointing and Pastoral Care of the Sick. This decree reversed the affirmation issued by the Council of Trent in 1551 that the sacrament of anointing, or "extreme unction," be used primarily as a last rite for those who were dying.

Laying on of hands is a tradition believed to date hundreds of years before Christ, apparently having evolved from the oriental custom of massaging with water, oil, or saliva. The saliva or oil was used by the ancient healer as an agent for breaking a charm, for warding off evil, and for the introduction of divine power. Boys and girls have often been anointed as a preliminary to the ceremonies of puberty. Through time, many people have believed in the "magical" power of spittle. Early Scots had their priests at Christenings moisten the nostrils and ears of the baby with spittle, "that the nostrils may be opened to receive the odor of God, and the ears to hear His mandates." Some Yorkshire fishermen still spit into their boats for luck; some Irishmen believe "If two persons wash in the same water, it produces bad luck, unless one of them spits into the water.")

"Many times," said Brother Deo, "I get a call to go to the hospital for a dying child and ask the Lord what I am supposed to say to the parents. I say, 'Lord, you say it for me,' and as I walk over—it's about two blocks and I always walk, except at night, when I take the car—I say, 'Dear Lord, please use me. You are the healer. Just put the words in my mouth.' But many times, there is still nothing to say. Sometimes I am just present. Sometimes I just touch the sick. Sometimes the only thing I can do is just be there with the people, especially when they have only one child and that child dies. What is there to say at that moment? But still, there is the sacrament of the sick, and Our Lord often touched people, you know. So I truly believe in that, and that's why I touch.

"And you know, I have seen wonderful healings, although I'm not saying I'm responsible. It's the prayers of everyone, as in Eric's healing.

"I think of him often. I always passed by his room in intensive care at about 9:00 A.M. or so. I have my schedule. I start on the tenth floor, then the ninth floor, and I work my way to intensive care. I try to visit all the children and to see the parents or at least to say hello. And that day when Eric was very sick, I remember seeing him, and his eyes had begun swelling. And usually, that's a bad, bad thing because I've seen it with other children who were about to die. He was very, very sick. And now, praise Jesus, he's out of intensive care and in a private room on the ninth floor."

Brother Deo said Debbie Danowski's act of surrender might have had much to do with Eric's turnaround. "That is the prayer of all Christians, the act of surrender: 'Lord, not my will, but *thy* will be done,' no matter how painful it is. Whatever the good Lord wants. Maybe Eric will grow to be a wonderful person later on or maybe the good Lord will soon take him to Himself. We do not know what the future holds for him. But the act of surrender must always be there. We must turn to our loving Father and just give Him the glory even in our pain and sorrow, just like Jesus, who died young and surrendered himself to his father. He said, 'Not my will, Father, but *thy* will be done."

God has such terrible elegance—and such elegant terribleness, I thought.

"Now you've really gotten something started!" Zona said, by way of greeting when I came into work just two days after the Danowski "miracle" story ran.

I just went to my desk, sat down, and went into my keep-a-low-profile mode.

I had a pretty good idea of what he meant, but I didn't find out for sure until I read our story on the local page that afternoon, boxed and all, with a photo of a little girl named Brianne Foster.

"MOTHER SEEKS PRAYERS FOR VERY ILL DAUGHTER," the headline read.

The parents of six-year-old Brianne Foster, who suffers from lymphocytic leukemia and needs a bone marrow transplant, are asking the community to pray for their daughter as they have for Eric Danowski.

Brianne's parents, Tom and Sue Foster of Harborcreek, said, "We have been reading in the *Times* how little Eric has been responding after his family requested prayers for him and we would like to ask that Brianne be added to your prayers."

. . . Mrs. Foster is seeking prayers for Brianne after learning last Wednesday from doctors at the Cleveland Clinic that Brianne has had another relapse, for the third time, after only a few weeks of being in remission. The bone marrow will be donated by Brianne's father.

"Gee," I said to Zona, after reading the article. "I never thought that would happen."

"I did. Now we'll be getting a *ton* of these things. "And who are we to say which prayer requests we have room for and which we don't?"

Zona was getting ready to do lunch—slipping into his dashing royal blue nylon windbreaker with *Erie Daily Times* stenciled on the back and donning a navy blue Greek fisherman's hat at a particularly rakish angle.

"Another new hat, eh?"

"Don't talk to me about hats—you and your yellow suspenders with blue polka dots. Where'd you get those anyway? Lech Walesa's clothing store? Whaddya, wearin' the new Polish farmer-chic style? You and your prayer stories anyway. It used to be pneumonia, tuberculosis and severed limbs. Now it's organ transplants and bone marrow. We didn't have to cover these things years ago. We don't cover diseases like hepatitis now. We don't cover severe bladder infections. We don't even cover cancer.

Even if somebody had cancer of the dingus we wouldn't cover it. So why do we have to cover transplants? People get sick all the time. Everybody gets sick. People have gotten sick for *years*, Jack. It didn't just start in the last few years. I just don't think it's news."

By this time I was in my Follow-Zona-Out-the-Door mode.

"I just had a lady get really snotty with me over the phone," he said, walking quickly down the long hallway. "Her daughter's been in a coma for three weeks and she wants us to tell everybody how she's doing. I told her it just wasn't news. She got really upset. She wants everybody to pray for her daughter, and I'm trying to explain the situation—which I don't know what it is—and she gets really snotty with me. I almost hung up on her."

"But you have to admit, the prayers for Eric Danowski seem to have helped," I said.

He sighed heavily, grunted, and shook his head. "Seems that way. Don't get me wrong. I'm glad they did," he said. "You know that." Then he straight-armed the door and headed toward the parking lot and his green Plymouth van.

I took a step back, both physically and mentally, to watch him though the glass doors and to savor the situation, to roll it around in my mind like a mental malted milk chocolate ball.

Here we were, in 1988, little lumps of clay having managed to evolve fingers and ears and eyes, trying to apprehend God and infinity with our puny organs made of flesh. Physicists like Stephen Hawking of Cambridge stalking God on the Serengeti Plain of mathematics, pondering the beginning of the universe, if indeed there was a beginning, wondering if indeed there is, or was, a God. Physicists contemplating the remnants of stars collapsed to absolute, infinite sizelessness. Postulating how twenty billion years ago a sizeless point in space exploded, creating all the galaxies, each with a hundred billion stars. Astrophysicist J. Richard Gott of Princeton proposing that our universe is just one bubble in a froth of space-time, only one of an infinite number of universes that have percolated out of some gigantic starpot in a space-time rip. Fermilab's Edward Kolb trying to explain how the universe sprang into being from nothing, and how, even when you have nothing, something's going on. Anthony Peratt of Los Alamos speculating that the universe is filled with prodigious electrical filaments hundreds of millions of light-years long that twist and tangle and break into galaxies and star clusters. Berkeley's Marc Davis saying that if there is a God, He's pretty far removed from His creation.

And in Erie, a bunch of molecules arisen from some primordial clay in Ellwood City, Pennsylvania, have grouped themselves into a cluster nicknamed *Luigi Bigacheesie*—to somehow be placed, funny-looking hats and all, smack at the nexus of the temporal and spiritual universes at a point of space at the city desk of the *Erie Daily Times*, there to try to figure out what part, in the grand scheme of things it calls The Daily News, the plight of a dying child plays.

Who says there is no God?

I was looking forward to seeing how Zona liked being at the interface where I'd been ever since Jamestown.

I never would have believed we'd ever see prayers on the front page of the local section, yet there they were. And it was all started by the Hunters in Jamestown. The Möbius was looping again.

"So put 'em all in," I said when Zona got back from lunch. "Put all the stories about little kids and their transplants in. How many would we get? One a month? So what's the big deal with that?"

Zona shook his head. "First it would be one a month. Then one a week. The one a day. Then pretty soon we'd have to decide if prayers for an adult's broken toe are as important as prayers for a baby's. Where do we draw the line? *No published prayer requests for anything less serious than a broken arm?*"

He shook his head again. "I told you that was going to be a pain-in-the-butt conversation, and it still is."

A few weeks later, on June 2, we ran a story with the headline, "BRIANNE FOSTER COMING HOME; LEUKEMIA NOW IN RE- MISSION."

"The grandmother thanked the community for their prayers on Wednesday and said: 'They must have worked,'" our story said.

Out of the Whirlwind

We must not sit down, and look for miracles. Up, and
be doing, and the Lord will be with thee. Prayer and
pains, through faith in Jesus Christ, will do anything.
—John Eliot, *Indian
Grammar Begun:
Postscript*

PEOPLE prayed for Robbie Snyder too.

Three-year-old Robbie was with his mother, Jodi, when the tornado
struck their mobile home in the rural northwestern Pennsylvania town of
Cranesville. The twister was one of many that devastated sections of
Pennsylvania, Ohio, New York, and Canada, killing 89 people and
injuring over a thousand, on the evening of May 31, 1985.

The tornado destroyed the trailer and killed Jodi, seven months
pregnant. It left Robbie buried with her underneath the walls of their
flattened mobile home for almost four hours. When he was found, he had
a large cut on his forehead, one of his toes was almost severed, and he was
in a coma, in his own land of Oz where no one could reach him.

On the night of the tornado, Dr. James Mikula, whose own house in
Cranesville had miraculously been skipped over by the twister, slogged
through the mud to the top of the hill where the trailer court had been.
Trailers and trees were flattened into the ground. Not a single home was
left standing.

A native of the Midwest, Mikula had seen his share of tornadoes, but
never devastation like this. (Later, the National Weather Service would
cite the Cranesville twister as one of the strongest ever recorded in the
United States.)

Mikula and other volunteers looking for survivors amid the debris
could see the foot of a woman under the sides of a crushed trailer. He

crawled underneath to try to help her, but she was dead. She was on her back, with her right arm outstretched, and a finger pointing.

"I looked off to the left where she was pointing, and there was Robbie, about four feet away, lying there moaning, with his eyes half open," he recalls. "If she hadn't led my eyes that way, I wouldn't have seen him."

Mikula was then the director of program development for the Lake Erie Institute of Rehabilitation (LEIR), the largest independent head trauma center in the country, where Robbie was later taken for therapy.

Later, people would shake their heads and speculate about the coincidence, which some called Divine Providence:

"If a head-injury specialist hadn't found him first, and directed the proper treatment . . . and if his mother hadn't been pointing that way . . ."

The Friday evening the tornado struck, I was one of the reporters called in by Zona to cover the disaster. It was my job to call area hospitals to determine how many people had been killed or injured by the twister. Robbie and his twenty-four-year-old mother were among the dozens I tallied.

In the beginning, doctors had said he wouldn't—couldn't—live, and that if he did somehow manage to survive, he would never lead a productive life.

In the hospital, his physician advised the boy's family to consider donating Robbie's organs.

Robbie's father, Robert "Butch" Snyder, Jr., a shy, mustached young man of medium build, just stood there, still too stunned by the suddenness of the tragic events to react.

But Butch's mother, standing beside him, vigorously shook her head no. A graying woman in her early fifties, Ann Erven had been keeping a twenty-four-hour-a-day vigil at her grandson's bedside. Despite Robbie's injuries—he had suffered a fractured skull and severe brain damage and was bleeding from the nose, mouth, and rectum from internal injuries—she still believed it was too soon to give up hope.

One Sunday, a week after Robbie was admitted to intensive care, Ann was sitting on his bed, stroking her grandson's baby-fine hair with a hand roughened by detergents and hard work. She talked softly to him. He had the round, puckishly familiar face of a cherub, with longish blond hair and wide blue eyes; with his eyes closed, she could swear he was just a normal little three-year-old, sleeping.

Suddenly a chill came over her, starting at the base of her spine and going up to her shoulders. Later she said it was as if "a Presence" had entered the room, almost like a little breeze. With it came a feeling, a calmness, like none she had ever had before, one she couldn't shake or ignore.

"You know what?" she said, looking over to her husband. "Robbie's going to make it."

Robbie did improve. From that day on, Ann Erven never lost faith that he would come back all the way.

Weeks later, when Robbie was finally released from the hospital, Ann continued to administer large doses of love and faith. (Robbie's father, a full-time welder, was unable to care for his son himself.)

Every day, from 6:30 A.M. until 9:30 P.M., Ann and Robbie's step-grandfather, Ralph Erven, would work with their grandson. They would hold him and roll him in their arms. They would rub his legs and tickle his feet. And they would one-two-three him through the floor routines prescribed by his therapist.

Soon Robbie began to move his limbs, ever so slightly. He began to open his eyes frequently.

"It's a miracle that he's made it this far, after what he's been through," Ann would say when people asked how Robbie was doing. "I think we're going to have another miracle. Robbie's going to wake up."

I was writing an article on coma arousal for *McCall's* when I interviewed, by phone, Dr. Karl Manders at University Heights Hospital, Indianapolis, Indiana.

In Dr. Manders's program, coma patients are taken several times daily for an hour or so each time into a hyperbaric oxygen (HBO) chamber, a long, clear plastic tube.

Dr. Manders explained that even after severe head injury or stroke there are brain cells called "idling neurons" that are still alive, but thrown "off-line" by the injury. The hyperbaric oxygen chamber forces oxygen, under pressure, to the cells and increases circulation, allowing the cells to function again.

Often, in under a month, the treatment produces significant improvement.

I told the doctor about Robbie and he said he'd be happy to take a look at the child.

"Maybe this is part of God's miracle we've been praying for," Ann Erven told me.

Although Robbie's CAT scans showed severe brain damage, his youth was in his favor, Dr. Manders said, explaining that the growing brain is often "plastic" enough to compensate for damaged areas by redirecting brain impulses around them. The oxygen would speed this process.

When Robbie entered University Heights Hospital about 3 1/2 months after the tornado, tests showed no significant brain activity. Hearing and vision potential were nil.

But after five weeks of HBO treatment, the same tests showed brain activity in both hemispheres of the brain. Hearing and vision tested almost normal.

Robbie began to recognize voices and people, and he started taking medicine on command. Soon he was able to chew his food. When his father would tell him he was going to leave, tears would fill Robbie's eyes.

"Before the treatments he couldn't do anything except just lie there," says Ann. "He was just stiff, like a board."

But in the tank during the treatments, she says, Robbie sometimes would lift his hands in front of his face and look at them, like a baby discovering his fingers for the first time. It was a sign of hope.

It didn't take long for the hospital staffers who cared for Robbie to fall in love with him. Not long after he arrived, they began pulling him to his HBO and physical therapy treatments in a little red wagon instead of pushing him on the standard hospital gurney.

One visitor asked the Ervens if he and his wife could pray with them, and the families did so, in the hallway.

The couple came back an average of three times a week to visit Robbie and pray for him after that. They even offered to do the laundry that kept piling up during the long hospital stay.

Despite weeks of treatments and many positive signs, Robbie still lingered on the fringes of coma in a state that physicians call "vegetative," although he had progressed higher on the scale toward full consciousness. Reluctantly, Dr. Manders had to release Robbie from the arousal program to make room for others.

Ann Erven vowed to work at home with Robbie daily, still hoping for her miracle.

Meanwhile, Don McKinney, who was then managing editor of *McCall's*, said his magazine might like a piece on the little boy's struggle to wake up.

I knew the magazine would need photos for the story, so I asked Dr. Manders if any photos of Robbie being treated in the HBO tank had been taken. None had. Dr. Manders called the family to ask if they had photos.

"Do you believe it? They volunteered to drive all the way out here again just so we could take some photos," he told me later. "What an unbelievable family they are. You just want to knock yourself out to help people like that."

Hospital staffers told Ann and Ralph that because they had made the eight-hour drive for Dr. Manders, they'd give Robbie another HBO treatment at no charge.

One more treatment, after weeks of twice-daily treatments—it wasn't much to build hope on, but it couldn't hurt.

"Imagine our surprise . . ." said Dr. Manders. "We gave Robbie that one additional treatment—and when we took him out of the tank, he was laughing. For the first time, he was laughing. If they hadn't come back for the pictures, this wouldn't have happened."

What was he laughing about?

Robbie had wet himself in the HBO tank, as children in the tank often do. When he was brought out of the tank and placed on a table so his grandmother could clean him up, he "spritzed right in my face!" Ann says. The four or five nurses around them laughed, and Robbie joined in with a great big laugh of his own.

It was the breakthrough that doctors had been hoping for, a sign that perhaps Robbie finally was beginning the long process of "waking up."

Robbie's story was beginning to whirl me along with a momentum of its own. I felt a strange chill myself as Dr. Manders described the latest twist.

Imagine the odds against Robbie being found by a head-injury specialist, one who would later admit him to his own hospital—the same specialist who was a primary source for the earlier article I'd done for *McCall's* on coma arousal—the same article that led Robbie to Dr. Manders. Then, my request for photos from Dr. Manders just *happened* to lead Robbie back to Indianapolis for one last treatment—which resulted in such a surprising breakthrough.

There were other little things. Like while I was driving to work one morning, I was thinking I should check Robbie's progress, since I hadn't heard any recent news. Two minutes after I sat down at my desk in the city room, a color photo of Robbie with his father, from I don't know where, fell out of my phone book. Then that same afternoon, who calls me at home but Dr. Manders, to tell me that Robbie laughed for the first time.

It seemed that the Möbius was looping back on itself again.

Stacey would call it coincidence, no doubt. Carl Jung would call it synchronicity. M. Scott Peck would call it grace. Grace Tullio would call it God's confirmation. And Bob Barker would say, "*It all depends on what God you serve.*"

Soon after Robbie returned home from the photo session in Indianapolis, his grandmother was startled to hear him cry out, for the first time. It was a cry of terror, she thought. His doctors said it was possible he was remembering the tornado.

Because of these positive signs—Robbie hadn't made a sound before —University Heights Hospital agreed to admit Robbie back for another seven weeks of oxygen treatments and therapy.

*   *   *

Wind-whipped snow made driving difficult as Debbie and I drove slowly along the slippery highway to visit Robbie and his grandparents before they went back to Indianapolis. Ann and Ralph planned to make the drive in four days, on New Year's Day, no matter what the weather. It had taken us forty-five minutes to drive just fifteen miles. I couldn't help but admire their determination.

My wife was five months pregnant with Ian. We hadn't stopped to think that seeing her that way, a reminder of Jodi, might be painful for the family. Everyone, though, seemed genuinely happy for us.

I couldn't stop looking at Robbie's eyes, and I was trying not to be obvious about it. One pupil was a third again as large as the other, conspicuous evidence, despite the progress everyone had said he'd made, that his brain was still severely damaged.

"Sometimes I think he tracks with his eyes, but maybe it's just me thinking that," his grandmother said, following my gaze. "I do know one thing, though," she said, putting a hand behind his head to lift his face closer to hers, to touch her cheek to his, to pour love into him. "He's 100 percent better because of Dr. Manders's treatments."

Was it the treatments, or her faith? I wondered.

"Look how well Robbie chews solid foods now," Ann said, feeding him spaghetti. "He couldn't do that before the first round of HBO treatments."

The sauce made a red ring around Robbie's mouth. "His father likes to see his face with chocolate or spaghetti sauce on it. Says he looks real natural that way.

"Dad likes to see you that way, doesn't he? Dad likes to see that dirty face."

"We treat him like an ordinary little kid," said Ann. "I get him up every morning and bathe him and dress him, and we keep him in bed only at naptime and at nighttime, and the rest of the time I lay him on the floor or the couch, or put him in his stroller and take him with me wherever I go.

"If I'm in the kitchen cooking, I take him there with me. In the warm weather, we take him outside on the patio. When I'm making the bed or doing dishes, he's right there."

She read the question on our faces: A lot of grandparents love their children, but still. . . .

"I think it's the love for his mother," Ann said. "She was a believer, you know. He had such a great mom, and they were so close. If I had to say it's any one thing, I'd say I'm doing it for her. . . ."

"Anyway, the stroller makes it easy," she said, giving it a little push along the carpet with her foot. "He only weighs forty-five pounds. He's not heavy."

It isn't that bad, is it, buddy. It's not bad. Could be better. Could be better, huh? Could be better, huh, buddy?

Debbie was silent for most of the long ride home.

She sat with her hands clasped tightly over our own baby.

A few days later, alone in my attic office, I said a prayer for Robbie. This one was a product of my latest foray into the Bible, where I met "the daughter of Jairus," and my last cable TV viewing of *The Empire Strikes Back*, in which Yoda, the master Jedi warrior, showed Luke Skywalker how to use the Force.

I asked God to heal Robbie. Not in six months or two months. But now. I told him I knew He did things in His own time. But why not this time, just one time—in our time?

In the back of my mind floated a glowing image of Yoda, eyes closed, raising Skywalker's seventy-two-thousand-pound star fighter out of the swamp and into the air through the strength of his belief alone.

The time was 6:08 P.M. I made a mental note, and I told myself that if the phone rang the next day, and if it was Ann Erven telling me that Robbie had awakened, I would tell her the time he awoke: 6:08 P.M.

That call didn't come.

We all had to accept the fact that while Robbie seemed to be awakening slowly, it was likely to be a step-by-step process that could take weeks—or years. He faced years of therapy and hard work on his road to recovery, and his awakening could continue to be a gradual one, with no clear-cut line between "before" and "after." Sudden awakenings from coma, contrary to popular folklore, don't happen that often. That's why they make national headlines when they do. Robbie would have to heal in God's time, not ours, apparently.

As of the fall of 1988, Robbie still was fighting his way back. He giggled and laughed when his grandparents teased him, and he had begun crawling. But still he couldn't talk, although he tried to.

"It doesn't matter, said Ann. "I've got the time. And I've got the patience. And I wouldn't have that if I didn't have such a strong feeling Robbie is going to be all right.

"If we don't have faith, we don't have anything. Because while the doctors do what they can for him medically, you and I know it's going to take God to heal him."

Where did her faith come from?

"I guess I got it in the hospital room that Sunday," she told me.

Ann is a Hebrew name meaning "full of grace, mercy, and prayer."

<table>
<tr><td>CHAPTER

3I</td><td>Healers in Black</td></tr>
</table>

The purpose of the healing ministry is to invigorate the
world that lies in anguish, that has lost hope. Through
the healing manifestation, the lives of many people are
brought to the person of the Lord, who revisits His
people by bringing love back to the Church and the
Church to love.

—Father Ralph A. DiOrio,
Called to Heal

WHY doesn't God heal children, adults, societies, and relationships all
at once? It seems that for an all-powerful God, He would have to but say
the Word, and the world would be healed.

Perhaps at least a partial answer is provided in a book called *The
Archko Volume.*

In a group of holy writings found in St. Sophia Mosque at Constanti-
nople, there is a description of how a reporter named Gamaliel was sent
by the Sanhedrin to find out about the man called Jesus and to search for
the truth about his wondrous cures. The story of Gamaliel is told in *The
Archko Volume—or the Archeological Writings of the Sanhedrin and
Talmuds of the Jews,* originally published in 1887 by the Reverend W. D.
Mahan and republished in 1975 by Keats Publishing, Inc., of New
Canaan, Connecticut.

Gamaliel tells how he went to a wise man named Massalian, a former
priest and teacher who lived on the road to Bethany. This man had spent
much time with Jesus. Massalian told Gamaliel that Jesus was a young
man of "the finest thought and feeling" he had ever seen in his life and
that his answers to every question seemed to bring almost a "universal
satisfaction."

But Massalian told Gamaliel that he was tempted at times to become impatient with Jesus, saying it seemed almost a waste of time for a man who came to save the world to linger over a special case of disease. (You can almost imagine Massalian saying, like Fuller Seminary's Dr. Lewis Smedes, "In this world of incredible suffering on such a cosmic scale, it's laughable how some people can celebrate a millimeter's lengthening of a left leg as a triumph of the Lord and Creator.")

And why, Massalian asked the reporter, did the individuals who were healed have to suffer so long? Why did they have to await the healing touch of Jesus? "Why not speak one word and remove every sick patient from his sickbed at the same hour?" asked Massalian.

And on a more "cosmic" scale: "If he is to be king of the Jews and heal all nations, why not do it at once? If he would, there would be nothing more required to establish his kingship."

The reporter Gamaliel thought for a moment and said to the teacher, "Is it not equally so with God's creative power? See what time and labor it takes to bring forth a grain of corn. Why not have caused the earth to bring forth every month instead of every year?"

Christ works for his Father, Gamaliel told Massalian, adding, "The people must learn to love and obey the Father before they would reverence the Son."

*   *   *

In the early part of this century, healing services were dominated by men in tents, wearing white linen suits and asking believers to reach for faith with one hand and for their checkbooks with the other. Most Catholics had little use for that kind of "faith healing," although they might have heard of the works of Father Solanus, Padre Pio, and Brother André. And vast numbers of Catholic pilgrims had, of course, sought healing of body and mind at the Marian shrine at Lourdes, although these same pilgrims probably wouldn't have been caught dead going to a faith healer.

In the late 1960s and early 1970s, through the teachings of people such as Francis MacNutt, thousands of Catholics began to take wondrous cures more seriously. Prayer for healing became a regular part of many Catholic charismatic prayer meetings. Physical and spiritual healings were reported, and individual members of Catholic prayer groups began to acquire reputations as healers.

By the 1980s, priests such as Father Ted Carter, in charge of the healing ministry for the Erie Catholic Diocese, were saying, "Healing has become a part of the normal Christian life," and bishops such as Anthony M. Pilla, bishop of Cleveland, were acknowledging that the "healing ministry has a long history in our Catholic tradition."

Many Catholics don't know it, but laying on of hands in the Catholic church is a tradition that goes back centuries.

Father Johann Josef Gassner, for instance, an Austrian priest of the eighteenth century, attracted a great deal of attention in his time by healing the sick and curing disease he believed to be of demonic origin by the laying on of hands.

St. Jean Baptiste Marie Vianney was one of the best-known Catholic healers of the early nineteenth century. Born in France in 1786, he was a confessor with many healings reported by the penitents whose confessions he heard. Thousands of healings have been attributed to him both before and after his death in 1859.

Other well-known Catholic healers are two English bishops, St. Cuthbert and John of Beverly, who practiced the laying on of hands in the seventh century, and sixteenth- and seventeenth-century healers St. Vincent de Paul, St. Francis Xavier, St. Philip Neri, and St. Francis de Sales.

Healing priests such as Father John Lubey of Washington, D.C.; Father Edward McDonough of Boston; Father Dennis Kelleher of New York; and Father Ralph DiOrio of Leicester, Massachusetts, are carrying on the healing tradition in our time.

"God uses any instrument He wishes," says Father Lubey. "Everyone is used by God without them realizing it. When a mother comforts a little child who is in distress, or when we listen to another person's problems, God works in that and heals something in that person. God is love and healing is love."

Two of the healings Lubey most vividly recalls involve infants. In one case, a child had been born with only half a skull. One of the halves was normal, while the other was composed of a soft, jellylike material. As he placed his hand on the soft part of the child's skull, "it suddenly became firm," Lubey says. He admits he was startled by the healing.

The other incident involved a fetus that X-rays showed had an unusually large head. Doctors said the baby probably would not survive. Lubey blessed the mother and child, and when the baby was born, it was normal. X-rays taken before and after birth confirm the healing, according to Lubey.

Like other healers, Lubey emphasizes that a person need not be physically present to be healed, recalling an incident where a man asked to stand in for his father, who was in the intensive-care unit of a hospital and not expected to live. The heart condition of the father improved dramatically at about the same time the son was blessed.

"I think when the Lord heals someone physically, He's trying to get their attention to get them to work on the relationship with themselves, which is the inner healing so many need today," he says.

The Reverend Edward McDonough, of Boston, is a Roman Catholic priest and a member of the religious order of the Redemptorists. Several of Mayor Tullio's friends had recommended the mayor seek out McDonough because he has a well-known healing ministry.

McDonough describes his viewpoint on healing this way:

"St. Paul in his beautiful letter to the Ephesians teaches us about Christ and the mystery of our salvation. He tells us, "We are God's work of art, created in Christ Jesus, to live the good life, as from the beginning He had meant us to live it.

"If you meditate on Paul's imagery, you can consider yourself as a beautiful painting conceived and painted according to the infinite wisdom, love, and power of Jesus. This painting has a beauty, a purpose, and a message that comes from the heart of Christ Jesus. Praying for healing in this context is merely coming to Jesus for his help. You ask him to repair, in the canvas of your life, the damage done by your own neglects, the failures of others, and the wear and tear caused by life's sicknesses and problems. Divine healing is merely allowing the Divine Artist to restore his beautiful painting and then you can be spiritually, physically, and emotionally made whole again . . ."

"We are just instruments," says Father Dennis Kelleher, a Redemptorist from New York whose ministry is devoted entirely to healing. "I heal nothing," says the priest, whose reputation once won him a spot on television's *Ripley's Believe It or Not.* "Jesus heals whatever he wants."

"I tell people that I'm preaching myself out of business," says Kelleher. "I firmly believe that in five years we won't have big, nationally known healing ministries with priests like me and Fathers DiOrio and McDonough. There are going to be so many other priests in the healing ministry on the local level that we won't be needed."

Father Matthew Linn and his brother Dennis, also a priest, established a healing ministry in Omaha in 1978 and together have written books on the subject and traveled in thirty countries, conducting seminars and services.

Their approach is simply to teach people to pray with and for each other and to teach them to ask God for "the next loving step."

"Every Catholic can heal," says Dennis Linn. "Everyone has the gift of healing insofar as they can love."

Healer Peter Youngren echoes that, saying that today we're seeing a ministry in which the healing power of Jesus becomes available to every believer, to any person who believes—not just priest or preacher or pastor or full-time minister. "For so long clergymen have kept their people in the pews. It's still a threat to some of the clergy when lay people start to emerge and do the work of Jesus. The clergy has always been threatened when a grass-roots movement starts because that movement could be a threat to their power."

I knew the type.

The keepers of the Holy Flame. The Maintainers of the Mainframe.

The wearers of funny clothes, the issuers of commandments:
"Thou shalt not scroll . . .
"Thou shalt not spilleth coffee into the keyboard . . .
"People do tend to be jealous of their areas of knowledge," said Youngren. "I guess that's just human nature. But nowadays I think even the clergy is getting used to the new teaching that has emerged, a teaching that has brought awareness that everybody has the same access to God as everybody else. If healing is available to one person, it's available to everyone. We'll still have religious leaders in the forefront, I'm sure. But they'll be leading by example—showing us examples that others can follow—not just expecting people to sit back in their pews and just watch them work *their* franchise."

"DROP YOUR CANE, PRIEST EXHORTS ILL," read the headline in the April 29, 1985, edition of the *Cleveland Plain Dealer*.
"10,000 Crowd Public Hall to Pray for Healing Miracles," the deckhead read.
"You came here looking for a miracle," the paper quoted the Rev. Ralph DiOrio as saying. "The miracle you are looking for is the Lord Jesus Christ."
The article described how many of the ten thousand priests, nuns, ministers, and laypeople of all ages fell onto the floor or across their seats during the service, slain in the Spirit.
At one point, according to the newspaper, DiOrio called out, "There's a police officer in here who has just been totally healed!" Then a man got out of his seat and went up to the altar in the center of the auditorium to describe his ailment.
The man identified himself as a policeman. He said he had fallen off a roof and was told by doctors that he would never regain the use of his arm.
"How do you feel now?" DiOrio asked.
"I can't believe it," the policeman said before dropping to the floor to do a few push-ups.
"Hallelujah!" DiOrio exclaimed.
At one point DiOrio called for silence, then asked those with hearing problems to place their fingers in their ears. After DiOrio's prayers, several people came to the altar holding hearing aids and told the audience how their ears had opened up.
"You know what it costs to be healed," DiOrio tells his audiences. "It's an attitude, a disposition. Your soul, that's what it costs.
DiOrio is said to have changed a Down's syndrome child's facial features with the touch of his hand. (The father of that child will no

longer grant interviews about the healing, having had enough pestering by journalists, curiosity-seekers, and would-be moviemakers.)

DiOrio's assistants take great care to document his cases. Jean Hill, a former newspaperwoman who edited one of his latest books, *Signs and Wonders*, told me there wasn't one case included in that book of over twenty healings that wasn't fully researched and documented beforehand.

Like those of Father Dennis Kelleher, DiOrio's healings have been featured on network television. One thoroughly documented case was aired on NBC-TV's *That's Incredible* series on September 29, 1980. The program featured an interview with Leo Perras of Easthampton, Massachusetts, who had suffered severe back injuries in an industrial accident when he was eighteen years old. The surgery performed on his back left him paralyzed from the waist down. The muscles of his legs then atrophied, and arthritis set in.

Perras said on television that he had been in a wheelchair for twenty-one years, but when he went to one of DiOrio's services and DiOrio prayed over him, he was able to immediately leave his wheelchair and walk out of the church. The pain that had made his life miserable for so many years left as well, he said.

Also interviewed on the program was Perras's family doctor, who examined Perras soon after the healing. The physician found that Perras's legs were still atrophied, and physiologically there was no way he should have been able to walk. But walk he could—and did.

Perras's legs gradually strengthened and healed completely.

The case is similar to that of Gerard Baillie, the little boy mentioned in a previous chapter who was cured of blindness at Lourdes—the boy who was able to see after his cure even though his optic nerves were still atrophied and sight should have been impossible. In both cases, the healings were instantaneous or occurred within a short time, and both patients recovered the use of organs that should have been physiologically nonfunctional.

If divine healing is nothing more than the power of the mind, hypnotic suggestion or the placebo effect, how do such cures occur, contrary to the known laws of biology and physics?

<table>
<tr><td>CHAPTER

32</td><td># Inner Healing</td></tr>
</table>

> Even pain confers spiritual insight, a beauty of outlook,
> a philosophy of life, an understanding and a forgiveness
> of humanity—in short, a quality of peace and serenity
> . . . suffering is a cleansing fire that chars away trivial-
> ity and restlessness.
>
> —Louis E. Bisch, *Reader's
> Digest*, 1937, 1963

"WE'RE going to see who?" asked Stacey, flopping down onto the sofa, legs and arms akimbo. "Some priest named Ralph the Oreo? That's just great! I *really* want to spend *my* Sunday with some guy named after a cookie!"

A DiOrio service had been set for April 10, 1988, in Akron, Ohio. After all I'd heard and read about him, "Father Ralph" was one healer I thought I should see in person. After all, how many chances would I have to see someone like DiOrio, a man who healed in the grand style of Kathryn Kuhlman, ministering not to just hundreds in some hotel ballroom but to tens of thousands in an auditorium with people being slain in the Spirit right and left as the divine power of the Holy Ghost collected in the air above their heads and then zoomed in to zap them onto the floor and across their chairs?

But if the truth be told, I didn't want to go. My newspaper was celebrating its hundredth anniversary, and a lavish dinner dance was scheduled for the same day as the DiOrio service. I'd been at the paper for almost a fifth of those hundred years, and as much as I complained about the place sometimes, it was like a second home to me, and some of the people there were like family. I didn't want to miss the celebration.

It also went against my grain to turn down a free prime-ribs dinner.

I had embarked on a more prayerful life since Jamestown, what with the nature of the book and all, but still I wasn't exactly the kind of person who picked up the spiritual hotline once a day to reach out and touch Someone. Still, as I walked back to the city room, I mumbled a little prayer for guidance:

"Is it necessary to go for the sake of the book or not?"

No sooner had I sat down at my desk than the telephone rang. It was Ann Erven, calling to give me the latest on Robbie's condition and to tell me how disappointed she was that she couldn't attend a retreat her church had been planning. "I want to go so bad, Jack, my heart just aches for it. I really need something like this right about now because it's just hard to keep going with Robbie, to give him everything he needs. But I'm scared to leave him with anyone else—I just wish there was something like this I could take him to."

"Gee, Ann, I might be able to help you out," I said.

Another meaningful coincidence? Fate? Grace? Synchronicity?

I told Ann I had four tickets to Father DiOrio's Sunday service in Akron and asked her if she wanted them so she could take Robbie.

She didn't hesitate a second. "I'd love to go," she said. "After driving to Indianapolis for Robbie's oxygen treatments once a month, a trip to Akron is just like a drive across town for Ralph and me."

"You missed a good sermon, Jack," Ann told me the day after the service. "It was unreal," she said. "You've got to go see him if he comes anywhere near here again. Let me tell you about it."

"Let me get a beer first," I said, and went to the refrigerator.

"Well, first of all, it was at Akron University, at a big auditorium that holds seven thousand people. We got there at 10:45 A.M., and by eleven-fifteen the line was five blocks long. The auditorium itself was jam-packed, and right before Father started speaking, they announced that sixty-eight hundred people were there. There's a lot of people in this world that need healing, Jack."

"I guess so!"

"Naturally, there were a lot of priests there. When they came into the auditorium, there was one priest who led a bunch of other ones. He had a big gold robe on. And then there were other priests in black and two priests in white. Behind the priests came young people and old people carrying religious flags and banners with the Lamb of the Lord and all that stuff. Then they put a big cross on the stage and the priest in gold and the two priests in white sat there in chairs on the stage pretty much all day. It certainly was very *Catholic*, I'll say that. So when Father DiOrio comes out, the first thing he says is, "Anyone who isn't a Catholic, stand up!" So I'm sitting there thinking, 'Should I or shouldn't I?' But I did stand, and do you know in that whole crowd of sixty-eight hundred there were only about a hundred of us who weren't Catholic? Then you know what Father did? He gave this little speech, while we were standing, and then he asked all the Catholics in the auditorium to tell us non-Catholics they were sorry for all the times they had hurt us."

"Really?"

"Yes, and it was very touching, it really was. . . . So anyway, then he came down the aisle and started *hugging* people, and sort of worked in the audience for six hours, and kept you so enthralled you didn't even want to get up to go to the *bath*room! He was so *vibrant,* and he kept a smile on everybody's face all day long. He never stood still. He was never on the stage except for the beginning. He was in the bleachers and all over, in the crowd all the time. He was *constantly* in the crowd."

"Was he healing people?"

"Well, the first thing he explained to us was that *he* wasn't going to heal anybody. It's *God* Who does the healing, he said. There was one woman who followed him around in her wheelchair, when he was walking, and finally, two guys grabbed her. He just said something like, 'Lady, it's not necessary that I touch you, it doesn't work that way.' But she kept insisting. She went right after him. She wanted him to lay his hands on her and he couldn't do that—because if he laid hands on one person who demanded it, then everybody would demand the same thing, and with sixty-eight hundred people, where would it stop? Besides, he's had people try to *assassinate* him—I couldn't understand why he had two or three guys running after him all day until he finally said that they were there to protect him, that his staff had been fasting and praying for his safety all day because there had been several recent attempts on his life."

"Was he wearing a bulletproof vest?"

"Could be, because he had that black jacket on so you wouldn't be able to tell. People in the bleachers would grab for him, and he'd always move away like he didn't want to be touched. So maybe he was wearing a bulletproof vest and didn't want people to know it."

"So he didn't actually lay hands on people at all?"

"Yes, yes, he did. He would stop and place his hands on their heads. Like one lady who was on a stretcher—I think they brought her from the hospital. He walked by her, then stopped and put his hands on her head. You could see him close his eyes and pray."

"But I thought you said he wouldn't do that."

"No, I just think it had to be *his* choice, he had to feel moved by the Holy Spirit to do it, I guess. And anyway, he kept stressing that nobody needed to be touched to be healed, that it wasn't his touch that did the healing—that it was God's love, and that God's love was just filling that whole auditorium."

Ann said that at one point in the service, DiOrio asked the parents to bring their children to the altar. Ann took Robbie in his wheelchair.

"You should take your children and hold them in the air and give them to the Lord," DiOrio told the parents.

The parents raised their children to the Lord, but Robbie, strapped into his wheelchair, was too heavy for Ann to lift that way.

"But you wheeled Robbie up there anyway?" I asked.

"Oh, yes. And Father DiOrio walked up and down by Robbie several times. And he did touch Robbie. And he touched a lot of others too. I'd say there must have been a thousand people he touched who passed out."

Ann said that DiOrio would first call one group to the front, then another. "Like, first he'd call all rape victims up, and pray for them, and many of them would fall, although they were immediately surrounded by a group of nuns and we couldn't really see them too well. Then he'd call up the hearing-impaired and pray for that group, and most of them would be slain in the Spirit. I didn't see anyone fall over who wasn't touched, but I did see something strange—Father DiOrio was like a *psychic*. He could *feel* things, he said. Like, for instance, he said there was a deacon and a minister and a priest somewhere in the audience who were ready to give up their vocations. He called for them to come forward, but no one did. But he kept asking them to come forward anyway; he said he *knew* they were there, even though he'd never seen them before in his life or been told about them. And finally, after about a half hour, they came out of their seats and onto the stage and gave their testimony. The deacon, for instance, said he was gone every night for meetings and such and that his family was suffering for this. He told the rest of the audience how his children had said to him one evening, 'You and Mama are never home anymore.' The deacon also told us that every time he prayed, Satan kept coming into his mind, so he didn't think he could preach anymore. He was just a young man, probably thirty-eight or forty."

Ann said that DiOrio put his hands on the deacon's head, prayed for him, and he was slain in the Spirit, as were the minister and the priest when they were touched.

She said DiOrio also had a Word of Knowledge about three or four couples having marital problems.

"When he called for these couples to come to the stage and they didn't, he had all the married couples in the audience repeat their marriage vows," she told me. "When the couples he called for still didn't come down, he told them, 'The hardest thing is to take the first step forward to come testify, but I want you to do it.'

"Again, it took him about a half hour to get all four couples to come forward," Ann said, but finally four couples with marriage problems made their way shyly to the stage and told 6,792 people their stories of alcohol problems, mistrust, jealousy, and job worries. "And before you knew it, they were all hugging and kissing each other up on that stage and saying how much they loved each other. Father DiOrio saved four marriages that day, there's no doubt in my mind about that."

But what about physical healings?

Ann said there were many—like that of a girl with one leg shorter than the other: "He just touched her leg, and it shook, and she was healed."

She also described the healings of a man with a neck brace, two other men with leg braces, a man with arthritis, and a blind girl who regained partial sight.

Most of the healings, she said, were accompanied not by a physical touch, but by a Word of Knowledge, as in the Kuhlman services; DiOrio would call out to the audience that a man with arthritis was being healed, "and before you knew it, from somewhere in the audience that man would appear."

DiOrio did lay hands on Robbie as he passed him, but he said nothing as he did so, recalled Ann.

"But so many wonderful things happened that day, I know Robbie received at least *some* healing," she told me. She said that immediately after the service, Robbie looked at her and seemed to be trying to talk for the first time, making many sounds, as if he were trying to speak in sentences. Also, she said, he had stayed awake and alert throughout the whole six hours of the service, something that usually would have been far beyond his capabilities.

"I just feel that Robbie got healing yesterday, Jack. Not the kind of healing that will make him jump up and run, but *something* happened, I know that."

She paused and sighed.

"And maybe I got healed, too. I went looking for a miracle for Robbie, and I think I got healing for myself instead. I could feel the Presence of God in that building, and when I walked back out through those doors, that Presence was still with me. I realized that maybe Robbie's slow healing is what God wants. I mean, since the very beginning, I have never really expected Robbie to get up out of that chair and run away. Of course, I've prayed for it, but I know, too, that it takes a long time for the brain to heal. Dr. Manders told me it could take years. I think what happened to me at the service is that my hopes based on medicine and my hopes based on God just sort of came together. I've got a patience to *wait* now that I didn't have before. Jack, *I feel healed from my head to my toe.* And part of it came from looking around at that service and taking a hard look at the people next to me. I sat in a group of young boys—there were probably twenty-five of them—with spinal cord injuries. Many of them were paralyzed from the neck down. A boy in back of me just kept twitching and twisting all the time. A mother next to me was holding her little eight-month-old Down's baby. You know, when you see this, Jack, you realize you're there begging God to give you that little bit of healing—but you find everybody else needs it worse than you do. I hugged Robbie almost all the way home and I said to Ralph, 'You know, I'm thankful he's the way he is and not any worse, and he's certainly better than when I brought him home from the hospital.' "

She said it was hard to express how she felt.

"Now I want to go out and do more. I feel that the Lord's really touched me in what I've been doing with Robbie, and I want to let other people know there's hope out there. I don't mean hope for just plain healing. I mean *hope to keep going*."

"If this is all Robbie is going to be, a little boy sitting in a wheelchair for the rest of his life, I'm not down about it because I know that is what God wants him to be. Think of all the people who have come up to me and said Robbie's touched them. All the people who come up and look in his eyes, and say how wonderful it is that we didn't give up on him. All the people who tell us they've never prayed before, but that they pray for Robbie. And a lot of these are people who don't even know him. People just come up and look at him sometimes and they start praying—and even they don't know why they're doing it. A lot of people have told me they've even gone to church for the first time in their lives, just to pray for my grandson."

"You mean people start praying for Robbie and end up saving themselves in the process?"

"That's exactly what I think. I think Robbie is showing me and everyone else that there are different kinds of miracles. How can a person not even be able to talk, but still be able to create such big changes inside the souls of everybody he meets? That's a miracle to me. I'd always said I thought I was going to have a miracle with Robbie. I waited for it. But it's been under my nose the whole time, happening right in front of me."

As Ann spoke, I couldn't help but think of how her family had been told, after the tornado, that perhaps they should allow the life of the little boy to end.

"Pull the plug!" the world said.

"Robbie's dead."

But he wasn't. He was just caught up in a tornado and taken to Oz. But now he's coming back. He's learning to crawl. He laughs and smiles. He returns, through his eyes, all the love that's poured into him.

"He'll never lead a productive life," the world said.

But the world did not foresee the changes his life would produce in the lives of Ann Erven and those of us who would meet him or hear his story. Without even lifting a finger, Robbie managed to get thousands to pray for him; he prompted people from all over the country to write to him; he led many back to their churches; he gave hope to the distraught and discouraged to keep going against all odds; he wrought changes in their immortal souls.

"Think about his quality of life," the doctors said.

One doctor told Ann Robbie would be much better off dead.

But who's to judge the quality of anyone's life, and on what basis?

If the quality of life is defined in terms of happiness, then half of us should be terminated. But if it's defined in terms of value, then certainly Robbie's life has quality.

If quality of life is defined in terms of physical perfection and the lack of deformities, how many of us qualify for quality?

For the unborn, where do we draw the line—somewhere between a withered arm and spina bifida, with everyone on the wrong side of the line a candidate for termination? Do we *really* want to live in a society that kills children for failing a genetic test?

Is the only life that has quality the life that can be restored, refined, perfected, or made less ugly through medical engineering? Should all other life—Down's syndrome babies, the vegetative, the handicapped—be eliminated?

Maybe we should draw the line right after bedsores.

If a doctor could have foreseen physicist Stephen Hawking's future, a future in which Hawking would contract amyotrophic lateral sclerosis, would that doctor have recommended Hawking's future be canceled? If that doctor could have known that Hawking would be paralyzed and unable to communicate except by a barely perceptible twitch of a finger on the button of a computerized voice synthesizer, would he have told his mother, "I think it's best we let him slip away . . ."?

If so, that doctor probably would have terminated the greatest mind since Einstein's, one that, while confined to a twisted body, is seeking the grand unification theory which will explain the universe.

At what point did we decide to define quality of life as being more important than *sanctity* of life?

And when it comes to healing, maybe we better not try to define that, either. Maybe we should just give God the time to do it.

Healing and
Perseverance

God is with those who persevere.
—The Koran VIII

In the summer of 1975, Francis MacNutt spoke to an audience of about 750 people jammed into an auditorium in the science complex at Loyola University, New Orleans, Louisiana. His topic: how healing is not always immediate, how sometimes it is a process, a progression, a spiritual tropism, if you will. This is one of the most interesting teachings on healings I've come across, and so I've included here an edited excerpt from that talk. (Note: The lecture is available, on audio tapes titled "Not Something Happening in a Tent," from Christian Healing Ministries in Jacksonville, Florida.)

"MOST of the books I'd read on healing give the general impression that people are either healed or they're not healed. There hasn't been much said about halfway healing or improvements.

"When we'd have a workshop and pray for people, I'd ask, 'How many of you feel that you were healed when you were prayed for?' Not that many would raise their hands. I didn't realize there was another question that really needed to be answered, which was, 'How many of you felt some kind of an *improvement?*'

"When I added that question, the response was amazing.

"Ordinarily, about 25 percent would raise their hands when I asked how many had been healed. But when I began asking how many had received *partial* healing, another 50 percent would raise their hands.

"Two months ago, for instance, I was at St. Vincent Abbey in Latrobe, Pennsylvania, and we had a very large crowd there. The abbey was packed with people. We had a liturgy, and it was just magnificent—

all these people were praising God in this magnificent old church. I was asked to say a general prayer for healing, which I did, but then I wanted them to pray for one another. Apparently they hadn't had much experience with this type of prayer, but it was beautiful nonetheless.

"When I asked afterward how many were totally healed, about eight hands went up. But when I asked how many were improved, about five hundred hands went up. Now, that's saying something, isn't it? I finally began to discover that when we prayed, many, many people were improved even if they weren't totally healed."

(Note: Fuller Seminary's C. Peter Wagner came to the same conclusion: "I'm just a seminary professor, but a lot of people come to my office, and I pray for them. I also pray for people in my church and so forth. Between late 1986 and late 1987, I began handing out forms to people so I could keep statistics on their improvement. I got 114 forms back. Of the 114 people who returned their forms, 29 percent became completely well, 25 percent showed considerable improvement, 28 percent showed some improvement, and 18 percent showed no improvement at all." The problems for which Wagner prayed ranged from headaches to the Pierson baby with no ears. Students in prayer groups at Fuller also began asking those they prayed for to fill out forms so statistics on healing could be compiled.)

"I also began to notice that sometimes the gradual results of prayer could be seen," MacNutt said. "For instance, a woman came up with a hand gnarled with arthritis, a hand that couldn't move. Her fingers were twisted and misshapen due to the long-standing disease. I prayed with her for a little bit, and after while asked how she was doing. 'Well, the pain's *almost* gone, and I can move it a little better,' she said.

"So I said to myself, '*Well, if she's moving a little better, maybe if I pray a little longer.* . . something more will happen.' And sure enough, I prayed another ten minutes with her, and she said, 'All the pain is gone, and look, I can move it even more!'

"And if I was able to stay with a person like that for an hour, the whole hand would be flexible and moving. And if I was able to pray for another hour, the fingers would straighten and the lumps would diminish and disappear.

"I finally began to realize there is a time element—at least for me. I am the hope in the church for the ordinary clunker, the second-rate healer that can't work immediate healings. I just glorify God that if it takes me two hours to cure something doctors haven't been able to cure in fifteen years—that's tremendous.

"This is a teaching I haven't really seen. The time element is mostly missing in preaching and books on this subject. You get the all-or-nothing impression that you're immediately healed, and if you're not, why not?

"What I'm beginning to see is that what God is asking for, as in most areas of our lives, is people who are really willing to *lay down their lives* for their brothers and sisters. Healing is not just one instant, glorious, fantastic celebration. Instead, there is a lot of hard work involved, especially when you're sitting and kneeling with one another over a period of hours until you become utterly exhausted. I find that with most ordinary people, that's the way a great deal of healing takes place. I'm beginning to see that the reason more healing doesn't happen is because we simply haven't learned this. First, most of us haven't learned to pray for healing until recently, and then most who have, have not been taught that there often is this price of *time* to be paid.

"If something is rather simple, like a headache, that can indeed disappear almost instantly. But with something else, like cancer, the healing power of God is like a radiation treatment. You don't ordinarily expect when you go to the doctor to have just one radiation treatment. You expect to have to go back the next week or twice a week or whatever, and the longer that tumor—that death at work in the human body—is held in this radiation, the more it disintegrates and disappears. With prayer, it's the same. The longer this disease in our body is held in the presence of the life-giving force that is God, the weaker that disease gets and the more it disappears.

"We've had a chance to test this out. With tumors, for instance, sometimes you pray and then see the tumor go down. Upon occasion you start praying and the person goes home and then the tumor disappears overnight. But other times you may pray and the tumor goes down, but if you *stop praying*, the tumor *stops going down*. In these cases you have to keep praying until the tumor completely disappears.

"I've seen this with retarded children also, over and over. The way I've seen these cases healed—and these cases are rather difficult—is that *parents*, over a period of time, maybe five minutes a day, pray for their child. And the child gradually progresses faster than the medical prognosis would call for—so that the child who is told he will never go to school surprises everybody and eventually graduates from high school.

"About four years ago, there was a lovely girl, eight years old, who was brought over to our house by her parents. She had cancer throughout her lungs. We prayed for her briefly at home after the celebration of the Eucharist, and afterward she felt so good that we took her out to a restaurant and she ate for the first time in two weeks—and it did look at that moment like something had happened. Then when her parents took her to the doctor for an X-ray, they found the cancer had completely disappeared. And we rejoiced, and the parents told everybody how their little daughter had been healed of cancer.

"But then about four months later, the little girl's parents called me to say the cancer was back in her abdomen, which was swelling up. So they brought her over and we prayed, but this time nothing much happened. We prayed again, and nothing. She was rapidly going downhill. The last time we prayed for her was at her own home. She was too weak to leave.

"She apparently had a vision of Jesus, who told her she would be all right. Then she died in peace, to be with the Lord, which is the ultimate healing.

"The way I understood it, after reflecting on it—and I'm only surmising here—I think our prayer and the power of God the first time killed that cancer in her lungs, but there was still some cancer left in her. What we needed to do was to pray some more, to continue prayer until it was all gone. But because everyone was rejoicing that the little girl had been healed, we simply didn't continue on with the prayer that was needed. And as a result, the cancer that was left in her abdomen started growing again, and by the time we got to it, it was too late.

"We learned something from this for the next time:

"There was a little girl, four years old, in St. Louis, who had what doctors first thought was cancer of the adrenal gland. They opened her up in July 1975 to cut out part of the gland, but they found that the cancer was throughout the whole chest cavity and there was no point in cutting anything out. So they just sewed her back up and started massive chemotherapy on her. She had the type of cancer which, at her age, kills 95 percent of the children who have it. Four percent are healed by chemotherapy, and 1 percent are healed by some unknown factor.

"About two months after the chemotherapy was started, her parents brought her over to our house to pray. And as we prayed that evening and in the days that followed, accompanied by prayer groups in all parts of the city, some really beautiful things occurred. One was, she never got tired or weak, as children usually do with that kind of treatment. As a matter of fact, it was a real problem, holding her down while we prayed! She had this marvelous *life* in her.

"From time to time, her blood count would get low, and she'd be due for some type of transfusion. Then they'd bring her over to our house and pray, and the blood count would go up so she didn't need a transfusion. Things like that were happening all along.

"Her mother and father soon had the distinct impression that the girl was healed, but there was no way of proving that, and I told them to continue with the chemotherapy until such time as the doctors would confirm her healing.

"The prayers for this child began in September. In June, the doctors decided to do an exploratory operation because she was taking three chemicals—one of which was devastating to the human heart—and they wanted to stop that particular chemical, if they could, if there was enough progress. The amount of chemotherapy she'd had to this point would not have been enough to cure her.

"When they opened her up, however, there was *no* trace of cancer. In those areas where you'd have expected the cells to be destroyed, they found normal cells reproducing themselves. Instead of being wiped out, all the ganglions and tissues were whole and healthy. She was certified as healed and sewn back up.

"Now the family rejoiced, the child rejoiced, and all the doctors could say was, 'As far as we know, the chemotherapy didn't do it. There wasn't enough chemo to do it. We really don't know what did it.'

"Now, at what point that child was healed I don't know. Was it the first time the parents prayed for her? Was it somewhere around the sixth month? No one will ever know. What we *have* learned to do is to *stay with* people who are sick, to *continue* to pray with them, and not try to figure too much out, but just surround the person with love, and pray for them a certain amount of time, even if you have to do it in shifts.

"The most notable example of this I've encountered is a case I've told many people about, a real, unbelievable miracle that took place near Bogotá, Colombia. After a priests' retreat I came out following the last conference and found part of my healing team gathered around a woman with crutches. "Come on over here, something is happening!" they said. So I went over and found a young women, nineteen years old, who at age five had stepped on something sharp in a swamp. She had come from a very poor family and was barefoot when this occurred. She didn't get proper medical attention, and by the time they got her to a doctor, an infection had gone all the way to the bone, causing osteomyelitis. The best the doctors could do was to save the leg and stop the infection from going above her knee.

"But from the knee to the heel, the leg had stopped growing. It was about six inches shorter than the other leg and wouldn't even reach to the ground, which was why she was on crutches. Not only was the leg short, but it was twisted and had a deep scar down the center where doctors had attempted a graft which didn't take. There was no further hope for her, no point to any physical therapy, because doctors said she was going to be this way for the rest of her life.

"But the team had been praying quite a while for her, and when I got there, they told me that the leg had seemingly grown about an inch since they had begun praying an hour before. They asked if I would join them. So I got down on my knees and we prayed until suppertime, which was another hour or two, and as we prayed, the leg continued to grow very slowly. It grew so slowly that you couldn't actually see it as it happened, but if you compared it every ten or fifteen minutes, you could determine that it had grown maybe a sixteenth of an inch or so. Before supper it grew another inch. So we decided to stick at it and come back after supper. We prayed another two hours that night, and it grew another inch.

"We gathered in a private home the next day and prayed another four hours. The leg grew another inch. So in the course of *two days* it grew four out of the six inches.

"On the second day, something very extraordinary happened. The woman's bad foot was small and withered. It hadn't grown normally, and the toes were about half the size of the toes on a normal foot. Well, during the second day of prayer the toes grew out to normal size, with just a little tiny bit of difference. You'd have to look very carefully to see it. She had no arch on her bad foot, it was just flat, and the second day the arch came in. And the veins came in—you could see them underneath the skin. All kinds of things were taking place. We also noticed that her leg, which had been so crooked, was straightened a good 50 percent. We prayed with her for a grand total of eight hours.

"Over the course of the next eight months there was further growth, and the last we heard, there was only about a half-inch difference. The leg finally straightened *completely*. They say that happened when the bishop of the diocese prayed for her—there was a kind of crack, and everything shifted into place.

"That was a beautiful thing, when the bishop would come to pray. He was right in there with the rest of us taking his turn! From time to time, we'd spell each other, because it's hard work—we'd all take turns praying for an hour, go into the next room and have some coffee, and then go back to it. The bishop promised he'd pray for her every time he came to town, which was once a week. What a wonderful example! If bishops in this country would do that sort of thing in the homes of their parishioners, they wouldn't have to write any letters about the faith of the people! The only problem would be you'd have to figure out who to pray for, because you couldn't pray for everyone who wanted prayer.

"Two doctors and X-rays finally confirmed that the leg was solid and straight, and now that woman is walking.

"An even greater transformation occurred in the area of inner healing. This young woman had been a very unhappy person up to this point. She had very little chance of ever getting married, she was from a poor family and completely dependent on others. She had nothing, really. But now that this healing has taken place, they say she's wonderfully happy and utterly transformed spiritually.

"Something else, which is quite significant: At two points on that second day, the leg stopped growing. Granted, it was hard to tell. You'd have to pray for half an hour and then compare it to the other leg. The first time it stopped was in the morning, and as we prayed for some discernment as to the cause of the problem, it seemed to me that I should ask the woman about her relationship with her mother.

"She told us she did have some resentment against her mother. The mother was poor and had no money for medical treatment, so when her child was injured, she had to give her up to some people who could get this treatment for her. In this case, it was a convent of sisters who were anxious to help. That was about the only thing the mother could have done. Obviously, the mother was not at fault. But the way it came across to a five-year-old girl was that her mother didn't want her and she'd been rejected.

"So we had the young woman forgive her mother. We told her that her mother did what she had to do out of love for her. We got her to see it through her mother's eyes, not through the eyes of a five-year-old. And so she forgave her mother, and we prayed that she would have the forgiving love of Jesus for her mother, and love her mother as Jesus did. We asked Mary, too, to pray for her. And at that point the leg started growing again—which indicates the supreme importance of being aligned with God on the interior level so that healing may not be blocked and that the light of God may come completely through.

"The second time the leg stopped growing was in the afternoon. It turned out that when this woman was in her teens, her favorite brother almost died in a motorbike accident. She told God, "I give you my sickness and all my suffering for the rest of my life if only you'll spare my brother." And her brother *was* spared, leaving her with this feeling that she'd be going back on God if she were completely healed. She thought she'd made a promise and ought to stick to it.

"But fortunately, we had the bishop; and one of the principles of a vow is that it has to be for a higher good. The bishop told her that her vow was certainly not for a higher good.

"He said, 'in the name of Jesus Christ, I commute this vow!'

"We all started praying, and the leg started growing again.

*   *   *

"I had a healing myself from Francis when he was a priest in 1976," Lorraine Greski, a schoolteacher in Ansonia, Connecticut, told me. She said she had had a severe back problem.

"When he prayed over me, grasped my ankles as I was sitting down, I had the sensation of my legs growing, but it was really my spinal column that was moving. My back got better instantly. The thing I remember most is the love that poured out from God. I felt heat and electricity come from Francis's hands, along with an outpouring of tremendous love like I've never felt since. There was nothing quite like that first time. It was like the feeling of being in love, but magnified a thousand times. Even a trillion times. It was so strong that now I understand the passage that we can't receive the fullness of God's love here on earth—the complete joy—because it would probably completely overwhelm us."

Lorraine's healing occurred at a service MacNutt was holding in a gymnasium in Wilton, Connecticut. "He hadn't even planned on doing any healing that night, but at one point he just suddenly said, 'Well, does anybody have any back problems?' And I was one of the lucky ones called out of the audience. I think he used me as an example because I was really afraid at first. I started making all these excuses into the microphone, like saying maybe it was psychosomatic and so on, because I was thinking, 'Oh, my God, what if this doesn't work?' But he was very patient. He used me as an example of the typical Christian who doesn't believe and is hesitant; who doesn't believe God really cares."

*   *   *

> I am quite sure he thinks that I am God—
> Since he *is* God on whom each one depends
> For life and all things that His bounty sends—
> My dear old dog, most constant of all friends."
> —William Croswell Doane,
> *Cluny*

"Her eye has atrophied," the vet said. "See how much smaller it is than the other one? That's why the lid seems to be a couple sizes too large."

Pooh's left eye did appear to be smaller. I turned to ask Stacey if she could see the difference, too, but she was lost in thought, staring at a pickled kitten in a jar of formaldehyde on the verterinarian's bookshelf.

In a fit of parental savvy, I had decided to take my daughter to the vet with me to allow her to participate in the Real-Life Decision About the Fate of Our Old Dog. But her mind kept drifting away to the pickled kitten and the heartworm-infested hearts on the shelf.

"The eye has also become cone-shaped for some reason," the vet said. "I suspect there may be a tumor behind it, but the eye is so infected I can't see through it to tell what's going on back there."

The eye infection that had started months ago had gotten progressively worse. Now there was a small ulcer on Pooh's eye, which, when we noticed it, had prompted us to hurry her to the vet. The ulcer looked like a little fluid-filled blister, half the size of a pea.

Pooh was shaking and hyperventilating, although not as much as she used to during trips to the vet's in years gone by. The fact that she couldn't see or hear what was going on around her apparently dampened her fear.

"You might want to think about putting her down," the vet said.

"You mean killing her?" Stacey snapped, her head whirling around to give the vet her full attention.

"Yes."

"Why?" Stacey's lip was quivering. She had grown up with Pooh. "She's not in any pain or anything, and she doesn't act sick."

"She *is* very healthy, except for the eye and whatever is going on behind it," the vet said. "Her heart is strong, she's got a good appetite, and like you say, she's not in pain, although I can't understand why that ulcer doesn't seem to hurt her. The thing is, Stacey, her eye could rupture at any time."

"Rupture?"

"The little blister on her eye is right at the tip of the cone, where the pressure is the greatest. The pressure could burst the eye at its weak spot, and all the fluid could come out. She would be in terrible pain."

I had given Pooh to Debbie when the dog was only a few days old. The feistiest of the litter, she had jumped out of the pile of other puppies and pounced on my toe while her brothers and sisters cringed at my looming enormity. A miniature poodle, she was never the type of dog to save a three-year-old from being struck by a car by grabbing his collar as he headed for the street on his big wheel. She'd been lucky to avoid getting hit herself on many occasions.

But for seventeen years she had been a faithful friend, and even now, when one of the family was sick, she could somehow sense it, even though she was blind and deaf. She'd come lay by the bed until whoever was ill got better.

"I don't know how much more of this I can take," Debbie said after our latest trip to the vet. "I *hate* seeing her suffer so. Her eye must hurt. And *every morning* I wake up to find a huge puddle of urine on the floor because she can't control her bladder. The baby *plays* on that floor. He *eats the food* that falls on that floor. It's . . . not a healthy situation." Debbie reached under her glasses to wipe away tears, making the glasses ride up on her nose. "I love that old dog . . ."

"I do, too," I said.

"But now *this*. Her eye could rupture at any time. What happens if it ruptures while you're at work, Jack, and I'm here alone with the baby? What do I do? How do I handle the baby while I'm trying to get a dog with a ruptured eyeball into the car?"

"There's a fifty-fifty chance it could rupture while I'm at home—"

"Jack, Pooh would be in great pain—"

"But she's *not* in pain now, Mommy!" Stacey said, bending down to pick up the dog's head with one hand while peeling back her eyelids with the other, to make the unseeing eyes stare at Debbie. "Look at her!"

We looked. Stacey let Pooh's eyes close again. Even though she was holding Pooh's head in her hands, the old girl was still sleeping peacefully, the rest of her body curled up on her rug in the corner of the kitchen.

"Nana Korowicki's got bad eyes too, Mom. You gonna give *her* the needle?"

"A dog and a person are two different things, Stacey—"

"Neither one is a *thing*, Mother. And *how* are they different?"

"A person has a spirit, for one thing. And a person is much more intelligent."

"Have you ever *seen* a spirit?" Stacey countered.

"No—"

"Then how do you know a dog doesn't have one? And what about retarded babies? You wanna put them to sleep, too, 'cause they're not as intelligent as we are?"

The decision: Should we let Pooh live out her life until she died of natural causes, however painful that could be, or should we play God and hasten her death to protect her from pain that might never come?

"I don't care what you guys do, I'm gonna pray she gets better," Stacey said.

"You're going to what?" I asked.

"Pray," she mumbled, heading off to her bedroom.

You could have knocked me over with a feather. Stacey had always been such a little skeptic. It was comforting to see her defer, finally, to a higher power, to put trust in something she hadn't seen advertised in a television commercial.

Debbie and I were more than willing to meet her halfway. We slathered Pooh's eye with the antibiotic-steroid ointment the vet had given us. He'd also put her on oral antibiotics, and finally, in a few weeks' time, her eye began to clear.

Her "quality of life" seemed to be lacking, I'll admit. As she headed into her eighteenth year, she didn't seem to take much pleasure being with her humans anymore and slept most of her life away. She didn't even get along with her own daughter—they quarreled and snapped at each other over their food dishes every evening. Pooh was covered with little dog-warts and was losing her fur. She kept having these huge organic indelicacies all over the kitchen floor that drove Debbie and Stacey out of their minds. Debbie kept worrying about the baby playing on the floor, and Stacey kept stepping in the puddles in her bare feet. (We finally solved that problem by giving Pooh estrogen tablets.) Pooh kept bumping into the walls and tripping over Ian's Legos.

But after all those years of happiness and love she'd given us, I figured we owed her something. If she wanted to keep on keeping on, we'd keep on keeping on with her pills.

I think it was worth it. Every once in a while—every dinnertime, as a matter of fact—she twirled and danced on the kitchen floor like a little puppy while waiting for her food, giving out a few barks that sounded more like croaks. And when the weather finally turned nice enough to take her for walks around the block, she poked furiously around the bushes with her nose and sniffed up a storm.

If *she* didn't seem to know her quality of life was lacking, who was I to judge?

There were no guarantees that Pooh would stay well, of course; she was 126 years old in dog years, after all, and her eye hadn't healed completely. The vet later began to suspect she had cancer in two swollen lymph nodes under her jaw, but he thought he could control that disease for a while with medication. He was pretty sure we could buy her an extra year or so, anyway. "If she mostly eats and sleeps and gets happy once in a while, she's doing everything a seventeen-year-old dog should be doing," he said. "Quality of life can be a pretty relative thing."

And so the family finally decided that as long as Pooh wasn't in pain, we'd leave her future in God's hands.

It amazed me how this fragile old dog managed to keep clinging so tenaciously to her little spark of life, how she managed somehow to keep it from being sucked away into the cold, infinite nothingness, how this poor little furball managed to preserve its tiny essence before the boundless maw. I liked thinking that my little girl's prayers winging their way through the void might be helping a little.

"Gee, Dad, I just thought of something," Stacey said one evening. "We must be like God to Pooh. So if we're going to all this trouble to cure Pooh because we love *her,* maybe *our* God really does care about us!"

Winning the Truth

Truth in all its kinds is most difficult to win; and truth in
medicine is the most difficult of all.
—Peter M. Latham,
Collected Works, Book I

IN JULY 1986 a crowd had gathered at the Sheraton Hotel ballroom in
Cranberry Township, a suburb of Pittsburgh. About 250 people had
gathered for a Hunter healing service sponsored by the North Hills
Chapter of the Full Gospel Businessmen's Fellowship. Among those
listening attentively to Frances Hunter were Kathy Ebaugh and her son
Aaron, a tall, gangly fourteen-year-old eighth-grader at North Hills High
School.

Aaron's doctor believed the youth was suffering from a rare type of
tumor, and when teachers and students at Aaron's school couldn't
understand what ailed the boy, the doctor wrote school authorities this
letter:

"I believe Aaron has a benign tumor called a pheochromocytoma that
secretes hormones similar to and including adrenaline. This tumor
secretes these hormones in pulses, causing symptoms of flushing, dizziness, nausea, sweating, tremors, headaches (all the symptoms Aaron
complains of), as well as others. The episodic nature of this hormone
secretion means that at one moment, Aaron may be well, and the next,
he may have overwhelming symptoms. Aaron's physical examination is
suggestive of this tumor, and a blood test showed high amounts of one of
these hormones in his blood. Finding the tumor may be difficult, since it
may be virtually anyplace in the body. My efforts are now directed at
finding it."

Aaron was told the tumor could be the size of a pinhead, and that it might never be found, since it could hide anywhere in the body. His doctor had said that he'd even found one in the big toe of one teenager.

Aaron's symptoms had become so acute that he had to finish eighth grade in a wheelchair. And although he was able to walk into the hotel ballroom, he had to stop in the hallway every few yards and lean against the wall to get his breath. His heart, accelerated by the adrenaline, often beat at up to 180 beats a minute. The night he went to see the Hunters it was beating so fast it almost felt like one continuous beat. It scared him. He didn't want to faint as he walked down the hall, but he was afraid he would—it had happened so many times before. And as always, he felt hot. His body temperature was always above normal, running at about 100.2 degrees Fahrenheit. When it would be freezing cold outside, and everyone else would have goose bumps, Aaron would be sweating and all red in the face. He couldn't walk, he couldn't run, he couldn't go out by himself or do much of anything. His life was miserable and doctors said he could expect it to stay that way. He prayed that the Hunters could help him.

Kathy and her husband, Robert, were praying, too. They expected a miracle. And why not? Robert, a pastor at the Living Word Fellowship Church in Pittsburgh, had been born again since age nine. Kathy had begun her walk with the Lord when she was just a teenager. Even Aaron, by his own confession, had professed Jesus Christ as his savior when he was seven years old. The way some people go to the corner store to chat with the storekeeper and buy a loaf of bread, the Ebaughs went to church to meet their Lord, where they fully expected Him to dispense the spiritual food that would sustain their souls and the healing that would mend their bodies.

And then there was Robert's dream. He had seen, in his sleep, his son and his wife sitting at a table, in a room with scores of other people. It was a meeting of sorts, and Charles and Frances Hunter were there. He saw Aaron at this meeting, and in his dream, he saw him healed. "Charles and Frances Hunter are coming to Pittsburgh soon," he told his son the next morning. "When they get here, you have to go see them. You'll be healed."

The next day, Ebaugh called a friend of his and asked, "Do you know when the Hunters might be coming to town?"

"It's funny you called, because they're in town tonight, and I'm going to a banquet with them. I've got two extra tickets. Want to come along?"

Ebaugh ended up giving his ticket to his son and the other to his wife—they couldn't get a baby-sitter for the other six children, so he would stay home with them.

He waved to Aaron and Kathy from the door as they set out to see if his dream would come true, and he paced the floor and prayed until they returned.

Aaron wasn't sure he believed as his mother and father did, but he decided he might as well go anyway. It was a last resort, and after all, what did he have to lose?

Once at the hotel, Aaron and Kathy Ebaugh sat exactly where Robert had seen them, in his dream—at the first row of tables, with the podium to their right.

Frances couldn't miss Aaron's bright red hair and yellow shirt and couldn't help but notice the way the boy had kept his head down, eyes to the table, all through the praise and worship. She had run into a woman in the ladies' room who had told her she had brought her teenage son to the hotel for a healing. Could that be the boy? She thought that this kid was either rebellious or really sick.

Frances began her request for donations, but stopped in midsentence. "There is a young man here who has a disease that is crippling and is sometimes fatal," she said. She looked at Aaron, and Aaron thought she must have had a vision from God or something. He didn't know that Frances had talked to his mother and guessed that he was her son.

"Honey, are you sick?" she said. "I think I ran into your mother in the ladies' room and she told me about you."

Aaron said he felt like he was dying, and Frances said if that was the case, "you better get up here on this stage real fast."

"What's your problem, honey?" Frances asked.

"My parents just paid $6,840.17 for a shot to get me healed, but it didn't work," he said.

"Do you believe that God can heal you?"

"Yes, I do," Aaron said, his chin still tucked into his chest.

Frances prayed for him, a short prayer casting out whatever spirits of infirmity had taken up residence in his body. Then she touched him on the forehead, said, "In the name of Jesus, be healed," and he fell backward, slain in the Spirit. To him, it felt like he was lying on the carpeted ballroom floor for only three minutes or so. But according to the clock, he was on the floor for almost a half hour.

"It was like electricity running all through my body," he told me afterward. "It was like . . . it's so hard to explain . . . I remember falling back to the floor . . . I tried to stand up after she touched me, but I couldn't keep standing, I felt like I weighed a thousand pounds. And when I was lying there, I was just shaking from head to toe. I felt hot all over, not the usual kind of hot I felt from my fever. This was different. I felt like I had fingers of both hands in light sockets because it was just tingling all over my entire body. I remember laughing and laughing and laughing. . . .

"I think the tumor was in my stomach, on the right side, because I felt like something was pulled out of my stomach while I was lying there. I felt it being pulled out of my stomach . . . it felt like—it's hard to describe—

like something reached in and it was pulled right out of my stomach and I could feel it leaving.

"When I finally did stand up, I felt, like, so strong. Really strong."

"How do you feel?" Frances asked Aaron when she saw him on his feet again.

"I feel cool," Aaron said.

"What do you mean?" she asked, thinking he was using 1950s slang.

"My body temperature has always run a couple degrees higher than normal. But now I feel cool."

Not only did Aaron feel cool to the touch, but also all the redness had left his face. His mother, onstage with him, reached over and took his pulse. His heartbeat was normal. And he didn't feel at all dizzy.

While Kathy Ebaugh watched with tears in her eyes, Charles Hunter, grinning broadly, strode over to Aaron and grabbed him by the hand.

"Let's run!" Charles said, and across the stage, back and forth, back and forth, Charles and Aaron ran in front of the clapping audience, many members of whom came from Ebaugh's church. As she watched her son, she was sure that the prayers of her friends had made the healing before the Hunters all come together.

The next day Bob Ebaugh went out to paint a house to supplement his meager earnings from the ministry. Aaron, who hadn't been able to stand up out of his wheelchair for more than a few minutes at a time, stood at the house with him and painted all day.

Aaron's doctor later dismissed the healing, saying he believed that after all, Aaron had probably not had a "pheo." And there were other critics who pointed out, as in so many cases of "faith healings," that the healing resulted from an internal problem that no one could see and none but Aaron could feel. What ailed him, they said, was the bane of the 1980s—stress.

"But I know what I know," said Kathy. "I know what I saw. The change that night was immediate, and blood tests afterward showed that his blood was normal. I believe it was an extraordinary occurrence. I saw the power of God, is what happened."

Did Aaron have the illness that was originally diagnosed?

Was the illness already improving at the time of the healing?

Had the drugs he'd been taking suddenly taken effect?

Are there ever instances of spontaneous remissions in pheochromocytomas?

Was autosuggestion part of the cure?

And what about the placebo effect—the same force that made "Mr. Wright's" orange-size tumors disappear when he was given shots of sterile water?

Some doctors believe very strongly in the body's almost supernatural ability to heal itself through natural means. One of these is Dr. Robert White, a world-famous neurosurgeon who vaulted to world renown in 1963 by becoming the first physician in history to keep a primate brain alive outside its body and who performed the first successful monkey-brain transplant two years later.

For his work on spinal cord injuries and hypothermia, he has garnered most of the awards given for neuroscience and has become famous even in China and the Soviet Union. He also advised Pope Paul VI and Pope John Paul II on biomedical ethics.

I had interviewed him at length, asking him about coma arousal techniques, for a *McCall's* story on Robbie Snyder.

"I believe in miracles," Dr. White said. "I've just never seen one."

"I do find it appropriate to pray for my patients, though," he said. "Why not? I mean, the point is, we're dealing with life, and I need help, and I ask God for help and I'm not ashamed to say it. I take the Lord into the operating room with me. When you're operating on the brain, there are no signposts as to whether to go left or right, this way or that way in spite of all the texts and all the nonsense we tell you about the exactness of brain science. I have to make decisions, and if I make a mistake, the result may be tragic. Somebody may not speak again, may not move his side, or may be in a state bordering on irreversible coma. So in my own setting, my own mode, I need help. I think all physicians need help, because basically we are all doing God's work in trying to restore people to health, and it is axiomatic we call on the Lord to help us."

Knowing that White believed in prayer, I was eager to see what he thought of healing miracles; specifically, the experience my wife and I had had with the Hunters in Jamestown. I figured that if any man of science and medicine was capable of exploring the connections among the brain, the soul, and healing, it was Dr. White. I sent him a copy of "A Faith Healer Gave Us Our Child" and asked him what he thought.

He answered with a letter:

Regarding your questions . . . certainly, your wife was capable of pregnancy, since she had been delivered of a child six years before your story began. There are a number of things, of course, that can go wrong with the female reproductive system following a successful pregnancy. In this case, at least it was demonstrated that you also were capable in the area of reproduction. As you mentioned on the phone and as appeared in the article, both you and your wife had visited fertility specialists, and had used some of the gadgetry that is supposed to increase your wife's capability of conceiving. Here we have a problem, Jack, for it could be that, in view of your wife's previous and present conceptions, all of the many things that could have been done were not done in terms of fertility investigation and testing. But then, the key question remains: Why was it, after six years or so, and after visiting a "faith healer," you and your wife are now the happy recipients of another child? Is there any scientific explanation or is it a "true miracle"?

It would be my explanation that both you and your wife were so overwhelmed by this emotional adventure that, in all probability, not only were you mentally relaxed for the first time (people often get awfully tied up and stressed in this area) but it is also possible, because of the relationship anatomically between the emotional centers, the hypothalamus and the pituitary, all of this relaxation could have provided an entirely new neuro-endocrinologic fabric which broke through whatever was inhibiting your wife's ovulation and conception capability. I would have to argue that anatomically/physiologically/biochemically, it was always there—that is, the potentiality of conceiving, but, with time, your wife, and perhaps yourself were becoming so stressed that it was having a secondary effect on the necessary endocrinology in this area as far as your wife was concerned.

I could see what Dr. White was driving at, the old saw about the woman who wants her own baby but can't have one, then gives up and adopts a child and becomes pregnant a month later because her body had finally "relaxed."

But his letter left me with questions. Debbie was anything but relaxed after the healing, and not believing a healing had taken place, was still crying herself to sleep for weeks after her visit to the Hunters. I couldn't see that her neuro-endocrinologic fabric had changed much when she was still soaking the bedsheets with tears at night.

And what about the "slain in the Spirit" phenomenon? What causes that?

I knew Debbie and I could achieve pregnancy, since we had proven it with Stacey years before. But what got the machinery cranked up after so many years of disuse? Was it divine intervention, or was it a reweaving of the neuro-endocrinologic fabric?

It all depends on which God you serve.

Modern medicine has yet to answer many questions about the human body's own healing powers, and until it does, many believe it is useless to speculate whether divine intervention or the body's own mysterious restorative powers cause "miraculous" cures. These skeptics, however, have no answers as to how tissue *instantaneously* regenerates itself, as in the case of over an inch of immediate bone growth in the broken femur of Pierre de Rudder at the shrine of Our Lady of Lourdes.

In Aaron's case, his doctor claimed a misdiagnosis, which is one of the most typical responses of the medical profession to "faith healing" cures. Aaron hadn't been healed of a pheochromocytoma because he had never had one. It was a simple as that.

How many doctors are going to expose themselves and their reputations to ridicule for saying they believe in a faith healing cure? Not many, because such assertions could be very damaging to their careers.

In 1903, for instance, Dr. Alexis Carrel accompanied one of his patients, a young woman named Marie Bailly, on a trip to Lourdes. The woman's whole family had died of tuberculosis, and now the woman herself was rapidly approaching death. She was in the final stages of tubercular peritonitis. The infection was raging in her abdomen and she also had lesions on her lungs. She was too weak to move.

Before he made the trip, Dr. Carrel had been asked, "What kind of disease would you have to see cured to convince you that miracles exist?"

"I would have to see an organic disease cured," said Dr. Carrel. "I would have to see a leg growing back after amputation, a cancer disappearing, a congenital dislocation suddenly vanishing. If such things could be scientifically observed, they would mean the collapse of all the laws we now accept, and then and there it would be permissible to admit to the intervention of a supernatural process."

In Bailly's case, Dr. Carrel saw exactly that. Because Marie was too sick to be immersed in the pools at Lourdes, Lourdes water was sprinkled over her bloated abdomen. Afterward, Dr. Carrel noted that Marie's skin was less ashen. And then, before his eyes, the blanket over her distended abdomen began sinking. As Dr. Carrel and another physician watched, Marie's body returned to normal. Her heartbeat stabilized and she began to speak, and soon she was sitting up and moving around. After a few days she was totally cured.

When Dr. Carrel declared to the world that he believed his patient had received a miraculous cure, he was expelled from his position at the University of Lyon in 1905.

He was later redeemed, however. He joined the staff of Rockefeller Institute in New York, and in 1912 he won the Nobel Prize for his work on organ transplantation and the suturing of blood vessels.

*   *   *

When I was almost ten years old—Stacey's age—I thought sex was a surgical procedure done by appointment in the hospital.

The man wears this white hospital gown, see, with a little round hole in front.

And the woman wears a similar gown that also has a perfectly round, stitched opening in the front.

Assisted by doctors and nurses, the husband and wife, standing in a sterile field under bright hospital lights, quietly do what is necessary through the holes in their sanitized clothing, with the assistance and instruction of the doctors and nurses wearing masks and surgical gowns.

"As soon as the anesthetic takes effect, we can begin, nurse," the doctor says.

When I turned ten, I walked into Robertson's variety store at Eighth and Cranberry to buy the copy of *Sex and the Adolescent*, which had caught my eye on the book rack there.

Don Robertson stared at me over the tops of his glasses as I plopped the book down on the counter.

"It's for my [yawn] brother," I said.

"How old is your brother?"

I thought fast. I knew you had to be eighteen to read a book like that.

"Twenty-five," I said, adding a few years for good measure. He moved very, very slowly, looking at me over his shoulder, as he rang up the sale.

When I became a parent, I decided Stacey wouldn't have to go through any of that. Debbie agreed, and we promised each other than when our daughter asked questions about sex, we would answer them without beating around the bush.

So when Stacey asked me one night what "impotence" meant, I told her.

"Really?" she said.

Really.

"Impetus?"

No, *impotence*.

Stacey looked at the wall for a few seconds, then turned back to me.

"Dad?"

"Yes?"

She came over to the couch and sat down next to me, then put a hand on my shoulder and nodded her head sympathetically. She squeezed my hand tightly.

"That's what happened to you, isn't it?"

"*What?*"

"That's why it took you six years to have a baby and why you and Mommy had to go see the Hunters, right?"

The Broken Heart

How else but through a broken heart
May Lord Christ enter in?
                    —Oscar Wilde, *The Ballad of
                    Reading Gaol*

DID YOU HEAR about Caliguiri?" Assistant City Editor Dick Deckert asked me as I walked in the door at 7:00 A.M. on Friday, May 6.

"Did I hear *what* about Caliguiri?"

"He—"

Deckert's phone rang. He picked it up and listened to the caller for some time, then said, "Okay, just a minute. I'll transfer you to Jack Grazier."

The phone on my desk rang.

"Get some quotes on Caliguiri," Deckert said.

"Huh?"

"It's Tullio," Deckert said. "Get some quotes."

I picked up the phone. The mayor's voice was breaking as he told me, "To tell you the truth, I always thought *I'd* be the one to go first."

MAYOR'S DISEASE KILLS
PITTSBURGH'S CALIGUIRI

That was the headline for the top story on page one of the *Erie Daily Times* that day. Caliguiri had been stricken at home in bed with a heart attack and had died at 1:36 A.M. at Shadyside Hospital in Pittsburgh. He was fifty-six.

"I learned about it from a Pittsburgh TV reporter who called my house at 6:00 A.M.," the mayor told me. "The news came as a real shock. Dick and I had just talked on the phone a week ago. He told me he was retaining a little more water. But it didn't sound *serious*."

I was typing his words into my computer as the mayor talked:

"The first thing that Pittsburgh reporter asked me was, 'Does Mayor Caliguiri's death prompt you to reassess your own decision to remain in office?' I told him, 'No.' I told him that first of all, we're two different people, and second, I want to continue what I'm happy doing. Only the Lord knows when He's going to take me, and I have great faith that keeps me going. I pray each day for the Lord to give me another day, and that's all I can do. Why should I reassess? If something is going to happen to me, what difference does it make whether it happens at City Hall or at home? No, I'm not going to quit. I'm going to continue doing what I'm happiest doing and pray each day."

Tullio then went into the boilerplate quotations that were expected of him: "Mayor Caliguiri loved the city of Pittsburgh and the city loved him. . . . He had such a great future. . . . He would have had no problem with reelection. . . . He did so much for the revitalization of Pittsburgh and made that city number one in the country as far as places to live go."

The mayor told me that the last time he'd been with Caliguiri was in Coraopolis with the Hunters. "Go ahead, you can put that in the paper," he said.

I did. But thinking about the raised eyebrow floating somewhere above the Chippendale-style chair in the Times Publishing Co. front office, I simply wrote: "One of the last times Tullio was with Caliguiri was in the Pittsburgh area in December, when both mayors met to pray for remission of their disease."

The next day, Frances Hunter called me at the office. It was about 10:00 P.M., and I was in the middle of Saturday night police checks, asking area police agencies if they had any news. When the phone rang I half expected it to be Debbie Danowski with bad news about Eric.

"I was so sorry to hear about Mayor Caliguiri," Frances said. "How is Mayor Tullio taking it?"

"It hit him hard, I know that," I said. "But the politician in him is putting up a good front. I'm just worried that he's going to identify with Caliguiri and talk himself into the same thing."

"Well, I'm going to call him right after church on Sunday."

"And say what?"

"I'm going to tell Mayor Tullio that if he wants to identify with anybody, to identify with *me*. God gave me a *brand-new heart*, and I'm *alive.* I'm going to tell him how I have his telephone number stuck on the front of my Rolodex in my office and every time I sit down at that desk I pray for him again and *believe* for a supernatural healing."

I asked Frances how she felt about the mayor's chances. "Do you still think something is going to happen or already *has* happened?"

"I never know. I do what God tells me to do. I pray, and then I leave it in His hands. But I've said many times that Charles and I don't look at the ones that *don't* get healed. We've got to look at the ones that *do.* That's the only way we stay in this business."

I asked her how she felt about the healing prayers for the mayors in the hotel room. Did they "take"? What was going through her mind then?

"The funny thing is, as much as you learn about healing the sick, and as many people as we have healed, we keep learning that God is still sovereign. But still, I felt as we sat at that table that God had not called us there for nothing. I remember that as we were asking them questions and so forth, I felt that Mayor Tullio was far more open in the beginning than the other mayor, but I think that by the end of the evening Mayor Caliguiri had really opened up, too. Mayor Tullio was so open to receive a healing from God that I was really surprised when you told me he was still having problems breathing, because I just felt in my heart and soul that he was healed, but there again, we have to remember it is God Who is sovereign. I do remember that on the plane to Pittsburgh Charles and I prayed and we prayed and we just said, 'God, we are just going to thank you for doing miracles, and we thank you, Father, that you have not sent us here for nothing.' We were reading the Bible on the way up, and every so often we would just turn to each other and say, 'God, we just thank You for a *supernatural* miracle,' and we asked God to heal them both. But the funny thing is, God doesn't heal people so that it will be a testimony to other people. A lot of people will come up to us and say, 'Oh, if God would only heal my mother, it would be such a testimony to all the people of the neighborhood!' But you see, as a Christian, that mother should be a testimony to all the people in the neighborhood whether God heals her or not. The thing we have to remember under all circumstances is that *God is sovereign.* It is just *all totally God,* and there is nothing we can do to change it. I mean, God is sovereign, and He can do things whatever way he wants to, and He will do them His way. When we pray to God for healing, we aren't praying to change His mind; we are praying that His will be done, that we understand His will, and that no sickness or evil interfere with His will. We are praying to bring God into our lives. Do you understand the principle I'm trying to explain?"

"Yes, I do," I said, watching, out of the corner of my eye, the narrow form of Sunday editor Bill Rogosky veering in my direction.

"*Hey Jack.* Anything going on?" Rogosky asked nasally, stopping by my desk and putting his foot on the top of it. Then he crossed both arms over the top of his knee to stare at me. The only time you could see his upper eyelids was when he blinked.

"No, Bill, it's all quiet."

"We're not missing any triple murders out in the area, are we?"

"Not that I know of."

"You're on top of everything?"

"Everything." My eyes wandered around the room. The flowers in the huge arrangement Hamot Medical Center had given the Times Publishing Company for its hundredth anniversary had died—all except the dogwood blossoms made of yellow and green bits of cloth. I made a note to grab the artificial flowers for Debbie before someone threw them out with the dead live flowers.

"You're gonna watch the news at eleven, aren't you?"

"Yes."

"Don't forget."

"I won't."

"We don't want to find pink slips with our paychecks next week because we missed something tonight."

"I know. Don't worry. I'm on top of it."

"I hope so, Jack."

He had said the same things to every Saturday night police reporter for the past twenty years and the same things to me for the past *nineteen* straight weeks.

A quiet, laconic, thin man of average height, sometimes it's hard to tell if Rogosky—"Rogs," as we call him semi-affectionately—is laid back or laid out. But he takes the Saturday night police beat very, very seriously. He's that way about . . . The News. He even takes the annual Miss America Pageant very seriously.

Rogs just kept standing there, one foot on my desk, squinting at me while Frances continued.

"I just praise the Lord that Mayor Caliguiri prayed the Sinner's Prayer in that hotel room with us, because now we know he is in heaven," she said. "The Bible says, 'Precious in the sight of the Lord is the death of His saints.' None of us can question the sovereignty of God. You just simply can't question it. But you know what? Let's just say a little prayer for Mayor Tullio now because I really, *really* believe it's God's will to heal him. Okay?"

"Uh, okay," I said, wishing Rogs would leave, but he just kept standing there, staring at me. "We gonna run on time tonight?" I asked him, my hand over the receiver, hoping the question would motivate him to go to the composing room to check things out.

"Well I don't see why not. We don't have that many pages to run," he said, not moving a muscle.

Frances prayed: "We know, Father, that your Word says that if two or more of us agree in your name that we shall ask and it shall be done by our Father, Who is in heaven."

"We *should* be on time if they don't shut down or anything," Rogs said.

"And now, Father, Jack and I are agreeing in the name of Jesus for your supernatural touch on Mayor Tullio," Frances prayed. "And Father, we thank you and we praise you for a *brand-new heart* with no protein problem whatsoever, *in Jesus' name.* Amen, amen, and A-MEN! Hallelujah!"

Her short little prayer and the spontaneity with which she said it was beautiful. It was typical Frances Hunter: She loved people, she prayed for them, and to her, praying was as natural as breathing. I just wished I hadn't been preoccupied with Good Old Rogs.

The way Frances ended the prayer, with such a strong, punctuative "Hallelujah!," called for some sort of response on my part. But there was Rogs, staring at me like some steely eyed mongoose eyeing a snake.

I was talking to both Frances and Rogs with the receiver tucked between my ear and my left shoulder, the way reporters hold the phone so they can type with both hands. (If you look at me closely, head on, you'll note that one side of my neck is a little thicker than the other, right near the turn of the jaw under the ear. That's because the sternoclei-domastoid muscle, made famous by Tom Wolfe in *Bonfire of the Vanities*, is overdeveloped on my left side from holding the telephone receiver. Either that, or I'm getting a goiter because Debbie won't let me eat real iodized salt anymore for fear it will give me a heart attack.)

I let the receiver slip out of its notch in my body and go tumbling, then made a show of grabbing for it before it hit the floor.

"Amen!" I said loudly and decidedly, placing the receiver back between my shoulder and my ear.

Rogs intensified his mongoose stare. The Riki-Tiki-Tavy of the Sunday *Times-News*.

I cocked my head and gave Rogs a look that said, *"Don't look at me that way. I always say 'Amen!' like that when I retrieve a telephone receiver."*

He squinted his eyelidless squint a couple of seconds longer. Then he finally took his foot off the desk and slowly headed off to the composing room.

*   *   *

The sign in the blue room of the Erie Police Department had been stuck on the wall the same day that Pittsburgh mayor Richard Caliguiri died.

It read:

ONE MAYOR DOWN, ONE TO GO.

A number of Erie cops had been feuding with Tullio over his continued support of the new police operations director. The new director had been making life miserable for a number of them with shift and policy changes, and somebody, probably one lone cop with a mind like a festering boil, got out his Magic Marker and made the sign.

The other cops quickly tore it down.

"Babies," said one twenty-year veteran. "Only immature babies would stoop to something that low. It was probably some sergeant who got promoted by Tullio in the first place."

"Unfortunately, it reflects on all of us," another cop long-opposed to Tullio said. "But people should know that most of us wouldn't mind if the mayor lived forever. We just don't want him to be mayor forever, that's all."

Grace Tullio was standing at the back of the city room a few days after news of the "one to go" sign had broken in the newspaper. She was holding a "letter to the editor." She had written a response to the sign writer.

"You can't let things like that get you down, Grace," I said.

"I'm not down, but I do need to respond to it," she said, visibly shaken. She handed me her letter and asked me what I thought of it. It read:

Anyone, without exception, who writes, calls, or sends nasty anonymous messages is an out-and-out coward. It doesn't matter to the mayor or to me who it is. The action was not hidden to the Lord God, who knows all the motives of the heart and sees every action motivated by hate. He says, 'Vengeance is mine; I shall repayeth.' We really never have to defend ourselves against such an onslaught of viciousness. My husband is not and never has been a vengeful man. I cannot help but feel, though, that any officer capable of doing such a thing . . . could be psychologically sick and possibly a danger to society. . . .

"I wouldn't do it," I said.

"Do what?" Grace asked.

"Publish this letter. Why let the jerk who made that sign know he got to you? You're liable to encourage him to do more."

She just shook her head. "This was such a cowardly act, done at a time of such tragedy that I have to say something about it. But let me tell you a wonderful story—"

Deckert was waving across the room at me. Newspaper stories needing to be copyread had backed up on the rim, and he needed an extra hand. I gave him a nod to let him know I'd be right over.

Grace grabbed my elbow and began. She said that the Sunday after

Mayor Caliguiri died—two days before she and Lou were to attend his funeral—she went, as usual, to her church, the First Assembly of God. "As a rule, I go in by myself, you know, and pick out a seat and sit down. The ushers usually just say hello and let me find my own place. But this time an usher told me, 'I'll find you a seat, Mrs. Tullio.' So I just followed him down the aisle. He took me much farther toward the front than I usually sit. I sat down and I was thinking of Mayor Caliguiri, and really praying for the Lord to comfort Jeanne and the family, and I was upset about Lou because I didn't want Dick's death to have an adverse effect on him. I was praying very hard about the whole thing, and at the end of the service, the man next to me said, 'Excuse me, but you know, I feel I have to tell you something.' He told me the Lord seemed to have spoken to him and said, 'Give the woman alongside of you this message.' The man told me that at first he felt funny about it because he thought maybe his mind was just playing tricks on him. But then it came over him again, very powerfully, *"Give this woman my message: John 14:27."*

Grace shook her head. "How this man received this, through his spirit or what, I don't know, but he said, 'I had to give you that message.' So while we were standing there we looked it up together. And the verse says:

"Peace I leave with you, my peace I give to you; not as the world gives do I give to you. Let not your heart be troubled, neither let it be afraid."

"Isn't that amazing?" Grace asked, looking into my eyes. "I asked him if he knew who I was and he said he had never seen me before in my life. He didn't know me from Adam. 'I'm a visitor here,' he said. So I asked him where he was from. He told me he was an Assemblies of God minister from Clairton, Pennsylvania, and had a church in Wilkinsburg, near Pittsburgh. I told him he had been a great comfort to me and that I would take his words to Jeanne Caliguiri, because I thought the message might give her peace—knowing that our days are in God's hands and the ultimate healing comes when we reach heaven."

Grace said when she told her pastor the story he just shook his head. He told her that the man was in Erie to attend a district conference of ministers and had decided at the last moment to come a day ahead of time.

"How much God loves us, to make sure we get his Word that way," Grace said.

Coincidence. Meaningful coincidence. Synchronicity. God's grace. Confirmation. The Möbius strip. God's love.

Which was it?

It all depends on what God you serve.

"Jack!" Deckert shouted from his deak. "Will you sit down and start reading these stories?"

*   *   *

A few days later, Debbie took the kids to Pittsburgh to visit her relatives and to make videotapes of them with Nana Korowicki, their ninety-two-year-old great-grandmother, so they would remember her in later years. I stayed home to write this chapter. It was the first time in ages—maybe a year—that the house had been empty, quiet, and so lonely.

I had the bed all to myself, as well as the clock radio:

"It's 2:15 A.M. Enjoying the solitude you've been whining about, sucker? No, you say? Oh, gee. Too bad.

"Your book *stinks*, you know. Imagine the reviews. They'll cut you to bits. They'll cut you up in highfalutin ways you won't even understand: 'Slimebag Eerie reporter sucks wind, produces a facile-exercise-parable-nouveau while exploiting dying mayor.' Faith healing?!? You think anybody's going to take you seriously ever again after this book?"

Without a moment's hesitation I put the Kleenex box in front of the infernal red numbers and then tossed and turned, listening to my heartbeat echo through the mattress for what seemed like hours.

Debbie had been gone only a night. What would it be like to have a spouse gone forever? To grow old and wither, night by dark night, on the bed alone? Always to have cold sheets on the empty side of the bed?

The next morning, June 25, 1988, the phone rang at 7:00 A.M. I'd had only about three hours' sleep.

"Jack? It's the mayor. Did I wake ya?"

"No problem, Mayor. What's up?"

"Listen, Jeanne Caliguiri's in town for the Pennsylvania Conference of Mayors. I thought maybe you could come to the Quality and meet me and bring the permission slip for her to sign. I'll give it to her personally for you."

He was unbelievable. Months before, I'd told him that I didn't know if Mayor Caliguiri was going to want to be included in a book about faith healing and that I had doubts as to whether he'd sign the permission form allowing me to use what he'd said in the privacy of the Coraopolis hotel room. If he didn't want me to quote him and I did, I faced a possible invasion of privacy hassle even though he was a public official. My book editor had recommended I get him to sign a permission form just to be on the safe side.

"Don't worry, let me handle it, I'll get him to sign it," Tullio had said.

Cheez! The poor guy had *died* and the mayor was *still* trying to get him to sign the slip for me—if not him, then his widow. Talk about following through!

"Remember I told you I'd take care of it for you?" Tullio asked. "You comin' down?"

"Mayor, really . . . I think I'd feel funny giving her a form to sign, what with her husband just dying and all—"

The mayor was eating breakfast. I could hear him munching the cereal. "No, no. You just give me the paper and I'll have her sign it. No problem. Okay? I want you to say hello to her anyway."

"Thanks, Mayor. I'll be there."

What do I say to her? I wondered as I drove downtown.

"I'm sorry about Dick."

That was pretty trite, and by now she'd heard it over a thousand times. And if she was just starting to get over his death, I didn't want her to hear any more "I'm so sorry's."

How about, *"Debbie and I have been praying for you"*?

Too religious. It was true, but it sounded like Holy Roller stuff, especially after our experience with the Hunters. I didn't want her to judge me as a pesky Born Again about to tell her how happy she should be that her husband was with the Lord.

I decided to just say, *"Debbie and I have been thinking of you."* As I walked into the hotel lobby, I mentally rehearsed that greeting.

Jeanne was standing next to an older woman named Sophie Masloff.

"Oh, Jack! I'd like you to meet Pittsburgh's new mayor!" Tullio said, grabbing me by the wrist and leading me over to Masloff for the introduction. I told her I was happy to meet her, with my eyes on Jeanne Caliguiri. How strange and painful that introduction must have sounded to her.

I know it was strange for me—to be introduced to the new mayor of Pittsburgh with the former mayor's wife standing there—the former mayor having died of amyloidosis—the introduction being cheerfully administered by another mayor dying of the same disease.

"And you remember Jeanne, of course," Tullio said.

"How are you doing, Jeanne?" I blurted, taking her hand.

How are you doing?

How do you think she's doing, you idiot?

She smiled, and looked at me through lowered eyes, and I noticed for the first time what a handsome woman she was, apparently viewing her for the first time as her own person and not the Pittsburgh mayor's wife.

"You have to go on," she said. "Especially with young children to take care of. They make you do things you normally wouldn't feel like doing, which is very good." She shook her head. "But you know, I don't have your form signed yet. I cleaned off Dick's desk, but I couldn't find it. If you can get another one, I'll be glad to sign it for you."

I realized then that the mayor hadn't told her what I was doing there, and I didn't have enough nerve to tell her myself. But the mayor did it for me.

"That's no problem, Jeanne. Jack just happens to have another form right here with him, don't you, Jack?"

I wanted to drop through the floor.

"It's a very simple form, really, Jeanne, and it's a very nice write-up he's doing of your husband in his book," the mayor said.

Later, when Jeanne and I had been left alone, I apologized for bothering her with the form and explained how I had come at the mayor's bidding. She just laughed. "Believe me, I understand," she said. "He's just so *thorough*. He's so good to everybody. Even Sophie Masloff, our new mayor, told me, 'I can see why you like him so much. He's such a *dynamite* person. He takes care of every little detail.'"

Grace had told me that after Caliguiri died, Jeanne had told her and her husband, 'Please don't forget me, now that Dick is gone.' I thought of that when I saw Tullio standing there with his arm over her shoulders protectively. "Now I'm gonna go home for a while and you're gonna wait here till I come back, right?" he told Jeanne. "I'll meet you here around noon, and then you can all check out. Have Bob bring you out and then we can all go to the picnic together, okay, sweetheart?"

It was obvious no one was going to forget Jeanne Caliguiri as long as the mayor was around.

A week before he died, Mayor Caliguiri told Grace Tullio that he wasn't feeling well. "His voice sounded so weak," Grace said, "So I said to Dick, 'Well, keep looking to the Lord, because you're in His hands. And he said to me. 'I am, Grace, I am. I'm totally at peace with the Lord. I *have* put myself in His hands.'"

"If I didn't have my faith, I'd be lost," Jeanne told me as we stood there in the hotel lobby. "And you know, I believe everything has a purpose."

She told me how before he died, her husband told her that if anything happened to him, he wanted her to take five thousand dollars from their savings account and give it to the Pittsburgh Foundation for research on amyloidosis, a disease about which very little is known.

"The morning he died, I realized I had never done that. So that same day I set up the trust fund and called the newspaper to ask if they would follow that story. The paper did carry it. I thought maybe we would get another five thousand dollars or so. But do you know, we got about eighty thousand dollars in donations in just a few days? And now we've got at least three doctors interested in researching the disease. Next year, around Dick's birthday, we're sponsoring a run at which we hope to raise at least another twenty-five thousand dollars."

"You organized all this on the *same day* Dick died?" I asked.

"Yes, I *had* to," she said apologetically. "If I didn't do it then, it would not have had the impact it did. I really do believe that for everything there is a purpose, you see."

I didn't know what to say. I was in awe of such strength.

Later I realized this book had introduced me to a whole new class of women.

Frances Hunter. Glinda Manley, Debbie Danowski. Nancy Wiese. Grace Tullio. Jeanne Caliguiri. Ann Erven. Kathryn Kuhlman. Bernadette Soubirous. My own wife, Debbie, who would make her leap of faith carrying me piggyback if she had to. Even little Linda Martel. All streaming faith from the waters of baptism. All icebreaking *ships*.

"There is in every true woman's heart a spark of heavenly fire, which lies dormant in the broad daylight of prosperity; but which kindles up, and beams and blazes in the dark hour of adversity," wrote Washington Irving.

I'll say.

I had to wonder, to what extent was their spirit shaped by their gender? To what extent had they derived their strength from the same waters whence came The Fates; Fortuna; Mother Earth; Mother Nature; the Amazon and Boadicea legends; Cleopatra and Helen of Troy; Joan of Arc and Galla Placidia; Hyparchia and Hypatia; the "citizenesses" who fought with their men in the French Revolution in the barricaded streets of Paris; the Christian female martyrs?

These women I'd met kept forging ahead. *They progressed.* And with such *purpose*, all faithful to the Light and to their relentless tropism, the unstoppable movement of clay-to-flesh-to-spirit.

But how do these "soft, cherubic creatures" do it?

Perhaps it's easy for women to believe in the goodness of an infinite Creative Force because they've harnessed its essence in their own flesh to bring forth children.

Perhaps Nietzsche had an insight when he wrote in *The Gay Science*, "What woman understands by love is clear enough: It is not only devotion, it is a total gift of body and soul, without reservation, without regard for anything whatever. This unconditional nature of her love is what makes it a *faith*, and the only one she has."

Conrad was wrong when he said God is for men, religion for women.

God *is* for men. But women are for God.

"Well, good luck with your book, I hope you finish it," said Jeanne, shaking my hand and smiling.

The last time I had seen Jeanne Caliguiri in Coraopolis, she had walked away from me through a hotel lobby, arm in arm with her husband.

Now she was walking away alone, in another hotel lobby, past the new mayor of Pittsburgh. As I watched Jeanne go, I realized there was only one way I wanted to end this chapter.

Donations for research into the causes and cures of amyloidosis may be made to:

The Richard Caliguiri Research Fund
c/o the Pittsburgh Foundation
CNG Tower, 30th floor
625 Liberty Avenue
Pittsburgh, PA 15222

Never-Ending Stories

> Every man is his own doctor of divinity, in the last resort.
>
> —Robert Louis Stevenson,
> *An Inland Voyage*

WHAT CAUSES cures ranging from instant bone regeneration at Lourdes to the healing of cancer through positive thinking?

Why, as *Erie Daily Times* editor Len Kholos wondered, would an omniscient God need to be *asked* for anything? How can we think we can presume to change His mind through prayer?

I don't think we can change God's mind. But I've come to believe that through prayer we perhaps *create* God's mind within ourselves: "*I say to you further that if two of you shall agree on earth about anything at all for which they ask, it shall be done for them by my Father in heaven. For where two or three are gathered together for my sake, there am I in the midst of them.*"

I think praying is an *act of creation* that puts us in God's will because when we pray we create God's will within ourselves. And if our belief, our creative act is strong enough, it overflows into those we pray for, and it heals.

You'd have to wonder if the thousands of believers at Lourdes singing "Ave Maria" are not as much responsible as the holy water for the healings there. The Catholic teaching on Lourdes is that the Lourdes healings are supernatural graces bestowed through the intervention of Our Lady of Lourdes, the Virgin Mary. Dr. Leslie Weatherhead, a well-known British Methodist clergyman-psychologist, attributed the Lourdes cures to the spiritual atmosphere created by the faith and prayers of millions of pilgrims. I think both explanations are possible.

It's as if God is a giant tuning fork and we are smaller ones; when we draw near to God through prayer—or even a conscious decision to try to find Him—His ceaseless motion sets us vibrating to the same frequency, and when we share in this vibration, we share in its power. I think that when we are thus in tune with God, synchronistic events, meaningful coincidences, answered prayers, words of knowledge, the gifts of grace, and healings can happen.

Participatory physics holds that when some experiments involving subatomic particles are observed, the participation of the observer alters the outcome of the experiments; certain things don't happen unless they are observed happening.

I think that belief in God may be a similar creative act. Belief does not mean passive acceptance of a doctrine. Belief in God means creating Him within ourselves through an act of the will *to participate* in God, and if necessary, creating Him and re-creating Him when we falter, making the creative decision anew every day.

(If I am a mere lump of clay with no divine spark, how odd it is that I should feel compelled to share any of my perceptions with you other lumps. If we're just clay and there is no God, what possible survival mechanism could this sharing of ideas serve? So that we bits of clay can gather enough information to shape ourselves into a cup from which there will be no one to drink?)

The church talks of separation from God. How can we be separate from an infinite being? Because we have not created Him for or within ourselves, and thus for us He does not exist, that's how. The church teaches that hell is separation from God. Those for whom God does not exist are obviously separated from Him. They are in a hell created by default through a pure act of laziness.

We've all been told that God likes to hear our praises, as if He somehow needs to be told how great He is. I think what God knows and many of us don't is that in praising God, we create Him within ourselves, and that is why our praise and our prayers are necessary. Not for Him, but for us. The dialogue with our Creator, in I-Thou fashion, creates a Presence that wasn't there before, a whole that is bigger than the sum of its parts.

I'm not saying God doesn't exist independently of us. I believe He does, but paradoxically, in Möbius two-side-one-side fashion, He does not exist for those who haven't created Him through a continuing creative decision to believe.

I think that God is, paradoxically, dependent on us at the same time that He is independent. We must create Him within ourselves by our Word, spoken in love, as He created us by His Word, spoken in love. *That* is how we are made in the likeness of God, perhaps. How else could we be made in God's image? Certainly not physically—I can't believe any part of God looks like Phyllis Diller. In our capacity to think and reason? I don't think so. Some researchers believe monkeys and even ants can do that, and that dolphins can do it better than humans.

I think we're made in God's image in that we have, as He does, the power to create our own reality. We can do this either through the creative, and thus Godlike, act of love and reconciliation, or through the destructive, and thus evil, act of hate and revenge. All the spiritual healers I've talked with say that those who hate cannot heal or be healed; Bernie Siegel says that those who hate or cannot forgive often come down with cancer. To heal or to be healed, a person must cast out his hatred and forgive those who must be forgiven.

Sometimes I wonder, thinking about the Möbius, whether good and evil are two sides of the same coin. Perhaps that is why, in the book of Job, the Satan tests Job with God's permission. Maybe that's why God permitted the dark shadow to stand in Joppa Wiese's doorway.

Why is there pain, suffering, and disease? Are they indeed caused by Satan, as so many Pentecostals believe? Perhaps. Maybe suffering exists to make people reach out in prayer, to get them out of themselves and into the Body of Christ. Perhaps pain and suffering are simply accelerated forms of the divine tropism of clay-to-flesh-to-spirit. At any rate, they are obviously permitted by God for some reason or else they would not exist.

"Positive thinking will only take you to a certain point and then drop you," Charles Hunter told Richard Caliguiri. The question is, why does positive thinking take us anywhere at all? From what source does the mind draw its creative power to heal? Who gives "the doctor within" his power? We must be more than lumps of clay, for how could a mere lump of clay have any regenerative power, and for what purpose?

Curing ourselves through positive thinking or reweaving our neuro-endocrinological fabric is one thing. But how did Glinda Manley's faith cure her daughter? How could Fred Price look at Glinda and say, "By your faith will this child be healed"? How could the prayers of a dead nun cure the nitrate-burned eyes of baby Peter Smith? Why did Eric Danowksi get better at the moment a whole city prayed for him?

The word "love" comes to mind. "God is love and healing is love," as Father John Lubey says.

A man with a tumor thinks he has no hope. But then he's given a placebo and told he will be cured. His conscious mind, which has been fearful and at war with his body, relaxes into a state of peace. He can stop resenting himself for dying because he's been told he will be cured. He starts loving himself again because he's been told he can still be viable and thus worthy.

But even Dr. Bernie Siegel doesn't claim to have seen an inch and a half of new bone instantly created through a positive, self-loving attitude. Why does self-love have its limitations?

It seems to me that self-love is a step in the right direction, a step toward God, and that's why it works at all. We probably can't love God if we can't love ourselves. We can't be united with God if our soul is disunited. But self-love is only a step, not the complete journey. When we begin to love ourselves and cast out resentments, we are preparing ourselves for the indwelling of God, but we haven't yet brought Him within. Until we call out His name and create Him within ourselves in doing so, we are still separate.

There must be quite a difference, in terms of creative healing power, between calling out "Jack! Jack!" and "Lord! Lord!"

"This is what the Lord says, He who made the earth, the Lord Who formed it and established it—the Lord is His name: 'Call to Me and I will answer you and tell you great and unsearchable things you don't know.'"

"The Lord is near to all who call upon Him. . . ."

Man's prayer invites and assures God's response, I think, because when we pray to God and say "Lord! Lord!" we are inviting God to come within, where He can answer our prayers.

I think when we love ourselves, we can regenerate to some extent both physically and mentally because love is a continuing process of self-creation, and in that act of creation we are "made in God's image" and thus share in God's creative power. When we love ourselves we are moving toward authenticity; we are drawn ahead through divine tropisim; we are *progressing* from clay to flesh to spirit and have some of the unitive, healing powers of the latter.

In Jungian terms, when we love ourselves, we are engaging in a sort of creative integration, a building of wholeness, and thus we are able to tap into the collective unconscious so that all kinds of healings, synchronistic happenings, and "meaningful coincidences" occur.

In religious terms, when we love ourselves we are sharing in God's creative power and thus able to join in the religious community, the Body of Christ, in which we can benefit from God's grace and thus experience all kinds of wondrous events, including healings.

The power that opens Bibles to just the right page at just the right time may be the power of the Body of Christ, created through an I-Thou dialogue with God-as-universe, and if we have not separated ourselves from that universe, we can share in its power.

All believers can heal, Scripture says. Believers are those who love as Christ did. When we love others, the creative power within us overflows. We become the tuning fork that makes another person vibrate to our frequency—which is God's frequency—and healing of others occurs through prayer or the laying on of hands. An overwhelming feeling of God's love coming to them through prayer or the touch of others is the one thing in common felt by all those who have experienced divine healing.

Love is an act of creative integration that can alter reality. When we begin to love, we begin to create God within ourselves, and paradoxically, that God is drawing us out of ourselves and into the Body of Christ, into wholeness. Love in a person, gathering strength from the Body of Christ, creates faith; and faith, according to Scripture, can move mountains. I think that "faith healing" is simply using the creative power of God—love—to change reality.

Consider the "Mother Teresa effect," discovered in 1987 by David McClelland, a respected Harvard psychologist.

McClelland had a group of Harvard students watch a British Broadcasting Corporation documentary about Mother Teresa. Afterward, he tested their immune system by measuring the amount of immunoglobulin A (IgA) in their saliva. IgA is an antibody essential for fighting colds and flu viruses.

After each viewing, McClelland found a higher concentration of IgA in almost all the students who watched the documentary—even the students who saw the film and disliked Mother Teresa or the film itself. Some students disagreed with her views on abortion, some were depressed by the hopelessness of those she served, some thought the film was too religious. But even these students, McClelland said, responded to the strength of the love she displayed and thus received a boost to their immune systems.

(In view of the outcome of this experiment, you have to wonder what watching violent television programs and films does to our physical health.)

It may be, McClelland theorized, that meditation, holistic health, psychic healers, and even ordinary doctors help healing by creating a state of mind in which a person feels loved.

Now, he says, when he feels an illness coming on, he meditates on love and loving. He says it isn't foolproof, but it helps.

"People are finally starting to get the idea," a priest friend told me. "Love is the start of healing. But things like the relaxation response, positive thinking, and all the rest are just the beginning. They're like grasping at the cloth of Christ's robe as he passes through the crowd. How much stronger the cure could be if we embrace him—not just clutch at his garments."

It was Sunday, July 24, 1988, almost a year since he had been told he had only eighteen months to live. There was Lou Tullio, bold as life and looking hale and hearty, presiding over a crowd of about ten thousand in Erie's Perry Square.

Nobody could have missed the six-term mayor. He wore a lime-green suit and a foot-high hat topped by American flags and a stuffed American eagle carrying what apparently was supposed to be a torch but what looked like an ice cream cone. He would have worn the hat at the Democratic National Convention in Atlanta the previous week, but his doctors advised against going because of his amyloidosis.

As thousands in the crowd chanted "Duke! Duke! Duke!," Democratic presidential candidate Michael Dukakis was winding up his post-Democratic National Convention "victory lap" in Erie. Dukakis had chosen Erie as the only Pennsylvania city to be visited immediately after the convention—largely because of Tullio, who had managed to turn out another large crowd the last time Dukakis had visited Erie, just a few weeks before. "Lou has been such a good friend to us," he later told the crowd.

Tullio stepped up to the microphone briskly, smiling broadly. When supporters began to chant, "Lou! Lou! Lou!," Tullio grinned and said, "I won't stop you. Go ahead."

He introduced Dukakis three times before yielding the microphone. Cameras flashed as Tullio stood there with his arm around Dukakis; the Erie mayor had one more photo to add to his office Wall of Fame.

If he was a dying man, Tullio certainly didn't look it as he introduced, in a rolling, thundering voice, "The next president of the United States!"

How did the mayor weather all the days of preparation for the Dukakis visit—the Secret Service arrangements, accommodations for the visit, making all the contacts necessary for the Perry Square extravaganza?

"He loved it," Patricia Liebel, his administrative assistant, told me. "He loved every minute of it. He likes anything like that. He's like a kid putting on a birthday party."

Liebel said many people were surprised to see the mayor in such good form, so strong and forceful. But it didn't surprise her at all: "He seems to get inner strength when something big comes up, and always manages to meet the challenge somehow."

The mayor was holding his own. He certainly had become no worse since his trip to the Hunters, although he had his bad days; but lately, Liebel told me, he'd been having more good days than bad. "I think the only reason he has bad days, days when he gets especially tired, is because he pushes himself unbelievably," she said. "I think he'd be in great shape if he did what he was supposed to do and get a few hours of rest each day. But instead, he manages to get on a roll about something once a day and then keeps on driving."

It was typical, she said, for the mayor to begin his day at 8:00 A.M. and end it at 4:00 P.M., handling everything from staff meetings to appointments to labor negotiations to grievance hearings to hosting out-of-town visitors, having photos taken throughout the day and eating a sandwich while working. "He's just the type of person who can't slow down and would be worse off if he did," said Liebel. "He still thanks God every day he wakes up, prays he'll get through another day, and has great confidence and faith that he will."

I'd like very much to be able to write that Mayor Tullio made one more trip to the Cleveland Clinic, where tests showed his system had cleansed itself of amyloidosis. Or that Eric Danowski came through a third liver transplant with flying colors and is out of danger. Or that Robbie Snyder finally began walking and talking.

But it doesn't always work that way. Healings are not often immediate and clear-cut, nor do they always happen; and if they do, they happen in God's time, not ours. The endings to these stories haven't been written yet by God, and so they can't be by me.

If it was really God's will for me to write this book, as many have suggested, apparently He called me to write it on His terms, not on mine or those of my editor, however much we'd both like to break into the Möbius strip and chop it up into neat little units of comprehensible, finite reality, each with a beginning and an end.

What if the mayor and Eric Danowski and Robbie Snyder do eventually die like Richard Caliguiri, unhealed of their physical problems? What does that signify in terms of the authenticity of divine healing?

Not much, I'd say. Traditional medical doctors have patients who die, and yet we keep going to them because of all who live.

And in the face of so many apparent successes—ranging from the miracles of Lourdes to the healing of Dexter Manley's daughter Dalis as well as regenerated hearts and ears—can we call the cases of those who aren't cured failures? After all, if there are divine reasons why some people are cured, there must be divine reasons why some people are not—and if so, how can these be termed "failures" if they are part of God's ultimate plan? Are they failures or successes? If Jeanne Caliguiri thinks there was a purpose to her husband's death, who am I to question it?

In my own case, if my Perthe's hip somehow led to this book, was that illness a failure after my prayers for healing went unanswered for so many years, or was it a success?

On more cosmic scale: Is death the ultimate healing, as Francis MacNutt says? If so, it is indeed not an ending, but a beginning, and we are back in the Möbius strip again—"My joy, my grief, my hope, my love, did all within this circle move!" as Edmund Waller wrote.

It hurts to think of suffering children such as Eric Danowski with his wide-open, innocent eyes, his happy smile, and his suffering mother. His leg broke the other day. His bones are decalcifying because of problems with his liver.

Why?

"*Why have people to suffer pain, do you know, Roy? These pains are terrible, you know, Roy; they are very awful.*"*

"There is in God, some say, a deep but dazzling darkness," wrote Henry Vaughan in the seventeenth century.

I've attempted to probe that darkness in the twentieth, but I'm afraid my light hasn't shone very far.

"*We may not be able to understand, but it is absolutely important that we try,*" said St. Teresa.

*   *   *

Stacey was lying on her back on the bed, her legs sticking straight up in the air, making a tent of the covers. "I hate *The Book*," you know." (For the past five months, she'd taken to calling it *The Book*, as in, "Not now, honey, your father has to work on *The Book*.")

"Why?" I asked.

"Because it's made you different. You don't have much time to spend with me, for one thing."

"That will change. I'm almost finished."

"And the other thing is, it's made you *think* about things too much."

"What do you mean? Like what?"

"Well, now you've even canceled our cable TV. I bet that's because of *The Book*."

She was right. I had a hard time making the leap from the worldview of *The Book* to the worldview of cable TV. After writing about Ann Erven's inner healing at the DiOrio service, for instance, I came down to the living room and turned on the television. It was shortly after midnight. The screen showed a pretty young girl hiding in the corner of an old building. A slobbering homicidal maniac came up to her, carrying the face of a man he'd just hacked from the man's skull with a butcher knife. The ghoul put the dripping flesh on the girl's pretty face and made her wear the grisly mask.

---

*On December 28, 1988, Eric Danowski *did* come through his third liver transplant at Children's Hospital with flying colors. On January 16, 1989, he returned home. His new liver was functioning perfectly without the slightest sign of rejection. "I just can't get over how wonderful he looks," Debbie Danowski told me. "This is the first time since he was born that his skin and eyes haven't been yellow," she said. "I can only thank God that things turned out this way." While the future looks bright for Eric, his mother says she'll take that future a day at a time. "Things look good, but I just saw two children who had liver transplants two and three years ago return to the hospital for a second and third transplant. That could happen to Eric, too. I pray he won't need a fourth transplant, although I've learned that I can't control his destiny and I can't set the conditions for God. But I really feel that if I trust in the Lord, no matter what happens, I'll be able to handle it. I think the best advice for anyone in a situation like ours is this quote from the New Testament: 'Let not your heart be troubled, nor let it be afraid.'"

At that point, I decided cable TV was an open sewer running into our home—so much of its programming deals with a fascination with violence and death. I certainly didn't want to chance either of the kids clicking through the channels and coming across shows like that one.

"*The Book* is changing everything. You're a lot more religious now even though you still don't go to church and probably never will," Stacey said, kicking at the covers. "Before, you just stuffed your face a lot and said things like, 'Debbie, buy more cookies.' You used to push Pooh out the door with your foot. Now it's 'Pray for her, Stacey, pray for her.'"

"Oh, come on, it's not that bad."

"Oh, yes, it is!"

Did the book *really* change me that much? I wondered.

I concluded that I had, at the very least, regained the sense of the divine I had had as a child, when I believed God might appear to me under the hospital bed covers in the beam of a flashlight; I seemed to have developed the ability to discern the moments of grace when God's hand touched my life or my shoulder, guiding me with incidents I previously would have called coincidence; I had been shown to my own satisfaction that divine healing exists; and I had come to accept that there is an evil presence in the world that can cause self-doubt and troubled nights and manifest itself in everything from one-star slasher movies or the atrocities of Nazi Germany to the desperation of an R. Bud Dwyer, sucking a gun barrel like a lollipop.

I suppose the big change in me now is one in attitude more than anything. I'm *trying* now, and trying, I think, is divine tropisim. I feel like I'm at least moving and not dead in the water. Moving forward. *Progressing.* From clay to flesh to spirit.

I must have changed quite a bit without realizing it. For instance, when I first started the book, I'd asked a born-again friend, Nancy Benson, to read the first few chapters. She gave her response in the following letter, which left me somewhat huffy, as in, 'Who does she think she is to preach to me?":

Dear Jack,
After thought, prayer, and reflection regarding the work in progress:
You'll receive varied reviews and reactions to this literary embryo. You can ride an emotional roller coaster as you test human reaction, or you can spare yourself that if you shift your focus from earthly approval to the approval of God. The very nature of your subject calls you to prayer. The only way you can be sure you are on the right path is through prayer—the kind of prayer that includes silent time to listen to His voice in your inner being. If you write a Number One best seller and do not ultimately glorify God, you will not find inner peace, joy, security, or happiness. I exhort you to consider this Scripture:
"For it is written, *I will destroy the wisdom of the wise, and the prudence of the prudent I will reject.* . . . For the foolishness of God is wiser than men, and the

weakness of God is stronger than men. . . . But the foolish things of the world
has God chosen to put shame to the 'wise,' and the weak things of the world has
God chosen to put shame to the strong, and the base things of the world and the
despised has God chosen, and the things that are not, to bring to nothing the
things that are; lest any flesh should pride itself before him. . . . Let him who
takes pride, take pride in the Lord."

I believe with all my heart that God's word is true. I believe also that Ian was a
miracle. It is my prayer that you are molded by your book and that your
conclusion will be to decide to accept the reality of Jesus, Satan, and miracles!

Nancy

"Exhort"? Nobody even *uses* that word anymore. Who did that woman
think she was, talking to me like some Old Testament prophet? (Just for
the heck of it, I looked up the name Nancy in the *4,000 Names for Your
Baby Book*. It means "full of grace, mercy, and prayer.")

Nancy's letter, when I read it in February 1988, irritated me. Who was
she to presume to lecture me? I was affronted that she would dare to do
so, and in writing to boot. Who was she to *exhort* anybody?

But now, just six months later, I'm reading her letter again and see
only caring and her desire to share, with concern, her view of spiritual
reality. I take no offense, because certainly none was meant. I'm flattered
that someone would take the time to write a letter like that. I have to
admire her for saying exactly what she thinks. And I agree with
everything she wrote. (My God—does this mean I'm a Christian? Maybe
even *born again?* If such a momentous healing *has* happened, I must
have been anesthetized during the operation, because I certainly didn't
feel a thing, or hear any divine thunderclaps, and I don't think many of
my friends and co-workers noticed much of a change. That's probably
just as well. I'm the type of person who, if I suddenly thought of myself as
born again, would no doubt think my newfound spirituality made me the
best of all possible people—thus creating just another mask for selfishness
and the Annoying Observer.)

By the same token, I hope my "letter to the world" doesn't irritate my
readers. I don't know enough about anything to preach to you, and I
wouldn't presume to do so. But I certainly have seen things along the way
I'd like to pass on for your consideration.

Many of us in the 1980s are trying to return to our spiritual roots, if we
haven't become trapped in an amethyst crystal somewhere in the New
Age. A study conducted by the Center for Social and Religious Research
at Hartford Seminary in Connecticut showed that regular worship
attendance increased by 10 percent in the years 1974 to 1984 among the
older baby boomers, those born from 1945 to 1955. Benton Johnson,
professor of sociology at the University of Oregon, says that's because the
baby boomers, people in their late twenties to early forties, are drifting

back to organized religion. The baby boomers are searching for faith once more, says Johnson.

If that's the case, I offer this book to you and to them, not as a book of answers or proofs, but as a description of my own spiritual odyssey. Maybe it will prompt others to begin journeys of their own.

"What people really are, they don't know themselves," says Isaac Bashevis Singer. "The fact is, we are all searching."

Jung believed we are all embarked on a journey in search of ourselves, and that any person who has set out on the path to wholeness will be afflicted by a midlife crisis of faith.

The first half of life, Jung said, consists of a journey outward—career-making, nest-building, and begetting and raising children. In the second half, the journey arcs inward, turns into a circle, and the search for self begins. This, Jung discovered, is the time to come to terms with what has been ignored or hidden—the shadow standing in the doorway—guilt, misplaced values, repressed thoughts, feelings, and emotions. It is also the time to come to terms with our religious needs.

Jung believed that Western culture's love affair with rationalism, materialism, technology, and "progress" had obscured the sense of the divine which had once infused life with meaning and wonder. Modern men and women had become strangers in a strange land of their own making, isolated from nature and even from their own natures. We had all become, in a sense, Annoying Observers.

To restore wholeness and balance, he believed, we must all journey inward and reawaken ourselves to the spiritual through a direct experience of the "overpowering psychic fact of God."

You still don't believe in God or divine healing?

That's fine, because as some wise man I'd like to plagiarize said, "To believe with certainty, we must begin with doubting."

If nothing else, maybe my kids will want to read *The Book* when they get older, although sometimes I have my doubts; Ian's still fixated on his navel and I pretty much lost my credibility with Stacey on the subject of religion when she was four years old:

A favorite tropical fish, her big blue gourami, had just died, and as she watched me flush it down the toilet, she asked, "Where's he going, Daddy?"

"To heaven," I said.

Stacey looked at me quizzically and then snorted in disbelief. "You mean *you* think *heaven* is in the potty?!!"

Life is a shifting image. First we see the witch, then the beautiful lady. We're uncomfortable with the ambiguity of the two faces and try to resolve that ambiguity, but I don't think the ambiguity—the sovereignty—of infinity can be resolved. It can only be accepted, and if we are to grow spiritually, it has to be internalized. Debbie Danowski did just that when she said, "Thy will be done."

The Möbius has two sides, yet it has one. That's just the way it is.

God is sovereign. I can finally accept that. We hairless monkeys seem to think—because we dare to exist in the midst of infinity—that when we ask a question, we are entitled to an answer.

Sometimes there are no answers.

But that doesn't prove there is no God.

Granted, He is a God of terrible, unfathomable contradictions, but I do believe I can pray to Him for the healing of one small child or even a dog and have a reasonable chance of having my prayers answered, although I'm praying to the same God who let six million Jews be killed.

That Ian Christian Grazier exists and kisses the top of my head when I carry him around the block on my shoulders allows me to believe. I don't know this truth by reason, but I do know it in my heart.

*   *   *

Charles and Frances Hunter drove their rented car down the slippery street to the old movie theater, parked, and climbed over mounds of dirty snow to get to the theater.

The outer doors of the place were open, but the inner doors were locked, and they were trapped in the frigid foyer for quite a while before somebody finally let them in.

It was as cold in the theater as it was in the foyer. Frances looked for someone to turn up the heat but was told that the furnace had broken.

Still wearing their coats and boots, the Happy Hunters tried to set up their book table. In the entrance where their books were to be sold there was only one small, dim bulb overhead. They could hardly see the color of the covers and had a hard time reading any of the titles.

Shivering, with their teeth chattering, they went inside to look at the theater. What a shock! What a damp, dismal place it was!

It was so cold it was hard to get into the Spirit. During the weak praise and worship, Frances whispered to Charles, "What are we doing here?"

I was asking Debbie the same thing, never dreaming that this book would be one of the fruits of that visit. Perhaps I really was meant to write *The Power Beyond* all along.

Perhaps, if I was meant to write this book, you were meant to read it.

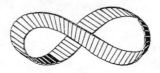

INDEX

DAVIDSON COUNTY PUBLIC LIBRARY

2 5908 00114299 6

234 G   T   315552

Grazier, Jack.
     The power beyond.

9-89

9-89